MY LIFE AND TIMES AS A POSTAL WORKER

WARREN PEARLMAN

authorHOUSE®

AuthorHouse™
1663 Liberty Drive
Bloomington, IN 47403
www.authorhouse.com
Phone: 1-800-839-8640

Published by AuthorHouse   2/29/2012

ISBN: 978-1-4685-5381-9 (sc)
ISBN: 978-1-4685-5382-6 (hc)
ISBN: 978-1-4685-5383-3 (e)

Library of Congress Control Number: 2012902786

Contents

Acknowledgments

I ENJOYED WRITING THIS book. The information and facts gathered for this book came from mostly the newspapers and going onto the internet looking for information. The mast majority of the book came from my own personal knowledge and experiences.

The newspapers I found articles in to write about are as follows. I apologize if I failed to mention anyone paper. It was not intentional.

- The American Postal Worker-paper that the American Postal Workers Union puts out. The national officers.
- Associated Press
- Atlanta Journal
- Charlotte Observer
- Daily News
- Daily Gazette-published by an independent group of Swarthmore College students
- Denver Rocky Mountain News
- Federal Times
- Florida Postal Worker—state paper that the Florida American Postal Workers Union puts out
- Fresno Bee
- Ft. Lauderdale Sun Sentinel
- Herald-Washington Bureau
- Los Angeles Times
- Miami Herald
- New York Times
- Orlando Sentinel
- Palm Beach Post
- Philadelphia Inquirer
- Seattle Post, Intelligencer
- Tampa Tribune
- USA Today

- Virginian Pilot
- Wall Street Journal
- Washington Post
- Washington Times

Some of the information I got going on the computer and looking for information. Some of which were, pay scale for clerks, list of the Postmaster general, local Postmasters, union embezzlement, and the shootings inside the post office. I received this information from:

- American Postal Workers Union's web site
- The Federal Times
- Pen! The source for all postal employees
- Postal News Archives
- Postal Reporter.com
- United States Postal Inspection Service
- United States Postal Service office of the Inspector General
- Wikipedia, the free encyclopedia

I also got information from the National Institute for Occupational Safety and Health (NIOSH), and from Corporate Alliance to End Partner Violence (CAEPV).

FORWARD

THIS BOOK IS ABOUT my life and the time I spent in the United States Postal Service. Starting from when I first starting working at the Biscayne Annex, the main post office in Miami, Florida. This was the plant, where the mail for Miami and South Florida generated from. From the Biscayne Annex, the main office, moved to the General Mail Facility in 1977, and I moved with it.

This book covers my time in the Unites States Army, when I was drafted in 1970 and where I spent 19 months and then returned to work in the Post Office in April, 1972, at the Biscayne Annex.

My book covers the time I worked at the Snapper Creek Post Office where I first was appointed a union shop steward. From the Snapper Creek Post Office I went to work at the Snapper Creek Annex then went to the Sunset Post Office and finally the Country Lakes Post office, the last post office I worked at before retiring from the United States Postal Service.

The book also covers the time when I first became a shop steward with the American Postal Workers Union, Miami Area Local in 1982. The time I covered the position as the Clerk Craft President and also the Business Agent of Homestead. The only person in the Miami Area Local to cover two positions at the same time. My story covers when I was elected as the Executive Vice-President of the Miami Area Local in 1989 for two terms with each term being three years, and then reelected in 1998 for two more terms with each term being for three years. The story tells how I failed to finish my last term of office. I was in office as the Executive Vice-President for the last time from April 1ˢᵗ 2001 until I was taken out of office on bogus charges in January, 2003.

As the union Executive Vice-President I was on a leave without pay with the United States Postal Service and therefore getting paid by the union but still on the rolls of the Postal Service.

The book covers some of my EEO settlements as a union officer. The last chance settlement cases I worked on, the cases where someone was caught stealing I had to deal with, and the way I worked with, or battled against management. The times I had the police called or me for sometimes using profanity and others times just because management didn't want me in their post office.

The book also tells a little about how I met the two loves of my life. My first wife of 19 years and my second wife from 2004 into my retirement.

But the book is not just about what I did in the Post service. I cover certain happenings of the United States Postal Service during the years I worked for the post office. The shootings that occurred inside the post offices throughout the country that has given the Postal Service the bad rap of "going postal". The shootings from others not associated with the United States Postal Service that was far worse than the postal Shootings.

The union Presidents and union Secretary/Treasures in different locals throughout the country that were charged with embezzlement. Also the embezzlement from different managers and postmasters from around the country.

The misuse of power from some of the Vice-Presidents in the United States Postal Service, from their getting paid to move less than 50 miles so they could be closer to work, to them spending lots of money, that wasn't their money, on food and drinks for entertainment. The double standard in the way top officers of the United States Postal service are treated compared to postmasters, managers, supervisors and the bargaining unit employee.

Covered in the book is some of the reports to Congress from the Inspector General and some of the investigations by the United States Postal Inspection Service, mostly outside the post office. Some of the cases involving robbery, assaults and threats, narcotics being sent through the mail, child pornography, mail bombs and anthrax.

I hope you find the book interesting and enjoyed reading it. I found it interesting finding the information I had to research to help put this all together.

CHAPTER 1

THE START OF A CAREER

MY NAME IS WARREN Pearlman. This is my story starting with the first day I started as a postal worker, December 15, 1969. This is when I first started as a postal clerk, up until June 2, 2007, the date I retired from the United States Postal Service. During my time working for the post office, the United States Postal Service changed dramatically. When I first started in the Post Office I had no idea I would stay as long as I did, 37 years, five months and 17 days.

The post office generally referred as the United States Postal Service (USPS) is the United States government organization responsible for providing postal service in the United States.

The United States Postal Service is one of the oldest government agencies of America, pre-dating even the constitution of the United States. Yet, the United States Postal Service receives no public funding and must be self-sufficient. In 1982 the United States Postal Service stopped accepting public subsidies and became a self supporting agency.

The USPS is headed by a Board of Governors appointed by the President of the United States and confirmed by the United States Senate. The Board of Governors serve as its corporate board of directors. They set policy and procedure and postal rates for services rendered. The Postmaster General is appointed by the board of governors and serves as chief operating officer and deals with the day to day activities of the USPS.

In December 1969, the Postmaster General was appointed by the President of the United States and confirmed by the United States Senate. The President of the United States at that time was Richard M. Nixon.

I started working in the post office on December 15th 1969, almost right out of high school. I had just graduated from Miami Senior High School in June, 1969, and took the postal exam a month later.

I worked at the main post office in Miami, Florida, the Biscayne Annex. The pay was $3.06 per hour, which was good money in 1969. I figured I would bring home approximately $250.00 per pay period. The pay period is every two weeks. The actually base pay was $244.80 a pay period and $6,364.80 yearly base pay. I of course worked overtime, I had no choice being a new employee. Today the starting pay is somewhere between $12.00 to $15.00 per hour, depending on the job someone might get hired for. The minimum pay in 1969 was $1.60 per hour.

I felt real lucky, and still do, to ever be hired and work for the Postal Service. When I was hired it was much easier to get a job working for the Post Office then it is now. There was no waiting list like there is today. I believe my test score was in the 70's. There was no background check and no physical to pass. There was no testing for drugs or alcohol. I only had to pick up a 70-pound sack and carry it across the room.

When I first started at the Biscayne Annex Post Office my hours of duty were 3:00 P.M. to 11:30 P.M., which is called tour three. I believe I was one of the youngest employees working at the Biscayne Annex Post Office in the outgoing section of the post office. Most of the newly hired employees were given a city scheme to learn and worked in the incoming section of the main facility. It must be understood I'm only talking about the employees hired as clerks or mail handlers. The employees hired as letter carriers were put in a station or branch post office.

The supervisors, managers, and I would have to say, most of the employees working at the Biscayne Annex were white American. The top managers were all older white men with most having a military background. I almost felt I was in the military. There were very few woman supervisors, and very few black men as supervisors. I cannot recall any black women as supervisors at this time, December 1969. This was at the Biscayne Annex, the mail facility in Miami. I don't know about the employees or supervisors or managers at the stations and branches in Miami in 1969.

When I was hired I had long hair down past my shoulders, I drank a little beer and did a lot of drugs. You name a drug and most likely I did some, or at lease tried it.

Because I had long hair and I didn't want any supervisor talking much to me, or asking me questions, I worked hard. I know I did a good job plus when I stayed busy nobody bothered me. I also felt that no supervisor questioned me because of the way I did work. I remember working on the opening belt at the post office and some other employees telling me I made them look bad by working so fast. I would just tell them I didn't want any supervisor questioning me on the way I looked or on my attendance and I felt if I stayed busy and worked fast I wouldn't get harassed. I was right.

I was calling in sick a lot, and I believed because of my long hair and being on drugs a lot of the time, and with most of the supervisors and managers being older military men they would have it in for me. Of course the supervisors had no idea I ever did drugs, or was on drugs, and most of the employees had no idea I was doing drugs so much of the time.

The sick leave policy, or lack of one, was not really enforced. Not by my supervisor anyway.

The first ninety days in the post office is a probation period. My supervisor gave me an evaluation of my work after the first thirty days and then after sixty days. On more then one occasion I was told I had to improve my attendance, and that I was lucky I was such a good worker. I would call in sick at times and had to take leave without pay because I had no sick leave. Somehow, with the grace of God, I made it through probation. I guess it didn't hurt that I had in the past gone to school with the supervisor's daughter. I was friendly to most of the other employees I worked with and seemed to get along with just about everyone.

The post office back in 1969 was hiring students to work for sixteen hours a week, or more, and called these employees NTE's, (not to exceed) what ever that meant. A lot of these employees, after the program for hiring NTE's ended, became career employees, without taking the test, and went into different crafts, clerk, mail handler, maintenance, motor vehicle and letter carrier. Some became supervisors and managers later in their career. I don't remember the post office having casual employees when I started.

My first day on the job, December 15th 1969, I worked for over eleven hours sitting on what was called a rest bar throwing letter mail. I thought I was going to go crazy and didn't know how long I was going to make it working in the post office, I hated sitting all day. Besides it being boring, the time just dragged. But I got lucky again. On my second day in the post office a supervisor came around to where I was throwing the letter mail and asked for volunteers to go work on the newspaper rack and opening belt. This was a job where you would be on your feet all day. I loved it. I knew for one thing that my ass was not going to be numb from sitting. I was young and knew I could stand all day, even being high on something. In the section I worked, besides the opening belt and the newspaper rack, there were the pouch racks. The Florida and states pouch racks is where bundles of letters and larger envelopes and small parcels were thrown into sacks or pouches. My job was to dump sacks of newspapers and bundles of magazines onto a belt and then throw the mail into sacks by using the zip code. When it was time to dispatch the mail, or the sack got full, the sack would be pulled down, closed and put on a float to take down to the first floor, I worked on the second floor, and put on a truck. Sometimes I was sent out to the platform where the trucks were being loaded and loaded trucks for a couple of hours at a time. I was always moving around which I liked and the time seemed to go by faster.

I remember joining the union when I first started in the post office but don't remember seeing any union stewards while I was at work. All I thought about was making it through another night, which on some nights was very hard for me to do.

I worked in the outgoing section of the post office and therefore, as luck would have it, was given the Florida scheme. A scheme was something most clerks were given that worked at the Biscayne Annex and throughout all the post offices in Miami. The clerks that worked in the city section were give carrier schemes. This is where the clerk had to know which carrier delivered to different addresses according to the address. The schemes were broken down by zip codes so some clerks had maybe two or three different zip codes to learn, depending on the size of the scheme they had to learn. The Florida scheme consisted of names of cities and towns throughout Florida. Since I was born in Miami, Florida I knew so much of the scheme before I even started.

I was scheduled to take my test for the Florida scheme sometime in June 1969 but decided on my own not to take the test. I knew I could pass the test, but I also knew I would be leaving at the end of June and didn't know if I would return. I was going to go into the army. I had received a draft notice from the United States Army. This was my job, working in the post office, from December 15th 1969 until June 30th 1970, working on the belt dumping sacks and throwing mail into pouches and then dispatching the sacks.

When I would go to lunch I would go with a few other guys and on the way back from lunch we would all smoke some pot. Nobody knew, or didn't care that we were high after returning from lunch.

There was no free paved parking lots at the Biscayne Annex. There was only parking for a certain number of cars and you had to pay to park. There was a parking lot for the credit union and a parking lot for the union. The One Seven Two Holding Corporation, a subsidy of the union, own the parking lot. I guess you had to have some seniority to get parking in one of these lots. Of course there were a lot more employees then there were parking spaces. I would park on the street on in a vacant dirt lot, sometimes two or three blocks away. I was lucky that my car was never broken into. This was when I had a car. Some of the time I didn't have a car and would have to catch a ride with someone or I would hitch hike. Those were the days working at the Biscayne Annex Post Office in Miami, Florida.

In the beginning of June 1970, I received a draft notice from the United States Army. I was suppose to leave for the Army on June 30th 1970. The Viet Nam conflict, it was not called a war, was still going strong. I will never forget the first sentence of the draft notice I received. "You are hereby inducted into the armed forces of the United States Army." The great government of ours had a lottery at this time of my life to see who would get drafted. Those who had a high enough number might have been safe and not drafted. My number was 125. I didn't think I would be drafted in June. The newspaper, The Miami Herald, had when the numbers were being called and going by the papers calculation I didn't think I would be getting a draft notice until around October, 1970.

At the time I was dating a real pretty lady, a stewardess from Virginia, and she helped me write a letter to the draft board to say we were getting married. My intention was to try to get out of the draft, and the Army and just stay working for the post office. Of course neither one of us had any intention of getting married at that time. I was twenty years old and just starting to live. The letter worked to a point. I still got drafted but didn't have to go into the Army until August 10th 1970. Some of the guys I know that got drafted and left in July ended up going to Viet Nam.

I still left the post office on June 30th 1970 and had six weeks to party and do whatever I wanted until August 10th 1970. And party I did. It almost killed me.

I went to Georgia to the 2nd Atlanta pop festival. I stayed up all night listening to music and doing all kinds of drugs. I had no idea if I was coming back to the post office. I was thinking that most likely I would be going to Viet Nam at some later date. My brother went to Viet Nam so I figured the Army would also send me.

At the Atlanta Pop Festival I didn't have a worry in the world. The thought of going to Canada had entered my mind a couple of times but thought better against it. I guess when I did think about going to Canada I was not thinking about anybody except me. It didn't phase me that my parents might be worried about me. They also didn't know about all the drugs I was taking. Somehow I made it back home after the Atlanta Pop Festival was over and somehow prepared myself into getting ready to enter the Army.

One good thing about leaving for the Army, even though I didn't think this way at the time, was I would not be doing any drugs for awhile. I was able to get clean and stay clean from drugs for awhile. It could've saved my life, and it most likely saved me from going to jail and losing my job. While I was in basic training in the Army a friend of mine got busted and went to jail for one year. I could've been with him the night he got busted. He was set up by a friend that both of us knew for a long time. I should've learned from this but sometimes it takes some people longer then others to learn from life.

I can honestly say being drafted into the United States Army made me grow up and was the best thing for me at this time of my life.

Chapter 2

MY IMMEDIATE FAMILY

I was born on September 13th 1949, at Jackson Memorial Hospital, in Miami, Florida. I was the last of five children born to Harry and Hilda Pearlman. My mother had three brothers and three sisters. My father had three sisters and five brothers. My father was born on May 28th 1904 in Chattanooga, Tennessee and my mother was born on November 22nd 1911 in Washington D.C. My parents were married in January, 1942. The first born to my parents was my sister born on January 8th 1943. Then my other two sisters who are fraternal twins born on July 19th 1945. My brother was next born on April 4th 1947 and then I. I was told that after my brother was born my mother had her tubes tied. When my mother got pregnant with me the doctors thought she had a tumor until I started kicking. After I was born my mother had her tubes cut and tied. I was told this on more than one occasion, but one of my sisters said this was not true. Who knows? Who cares?

By the time I was born I only had one grandparent still alive. Both of my mothers' parents had passed away. My fathers' mother was still living. I never remember her ever talking to me. What I do remember about my grandmother was that she would paint the bottom of the trees with white paint. Something I will always remember is that my grandmother passed away in 1960 and was born before Abraham Lincoln died. She was ninety-five when she passed away. To me that was, and still is amazing. I also remember hearing that my fathers' father, my grandfather, was a triplet. My mother once told me that at my grandfathers' funeral when his brother looked into the casket it was like he was looking at himself. My mother only mentioned one of my grandfathers brothers. I don't know anything about the other brother.

My first recollection of my childhood was when I was four, standing in a crib looking out the window and seeing my brother lying in the street.

A truck had just hit him as he was trying to cross the street. He ended up with a broken leg and a concussion. I cannot remember anything before this time. I'm not sure if that is a good thing or a bad thing.

My family lived in the projects across the street from Edison High School. We lived in the projects from the time I remember until I finished third grade. The year was 1958. I guess these days instead of calling the place we lived as the projects it would be called low income housing.

We then moved in with my grandmother and my uncle on S. W. 1st Street between 44th and 45th Avenue, still in Miami. I don't remember how we managed with nine people living in a three-bedroom house. I do remember my uncle was an alcoholic. I also remember my grandmother didn't like us kids watching the television while she ate breakfast, even though she ate in a different room.

My grandmother couldn't hear very well so when we would hear her walking toward the Florida room where the television was I would turn the picture off and keep the sound on. She would call us crazy kids. Sitting in front of the television and the television not being on. When she walked away I would turn the picture back on. We lived at this house for approximately six months then moved to Hialeah. In Hialeah we lived on West 56th Place, approximately two blocks from Red Road.

My oldest sister was a senior in high school at Edison and wanted to graduate from there. I remember waking up early in the morning so I could walk with her to the bus stop. I think my sister had to take two buses to get to Edison High School from Hialeah. It's sort of funny, me being the youngest and having to walk her to the bus stop. It's also sort of funning how some people, even family don't want to remember that I went out of my way to help them. Even as a young boy. My oldest sister, who wishes to be nameless, doesn't want her name mention in this book, doesn't want anything to do with her family. I guess she is too good for the rest of us.

Neither of my parents drove so we had no car in the family. After my grandmother passed away in 1960 my uncle passed away shortly there after. My family then moved back to my grandmothers' house in 1962. My oldest sister moved to Gainesville, Florida to attend the University of Florida. A couple of years later my other sisters, Marsha and Roslyn, moved out and got an apartment. When my brother graduated high school in 1965 he immediately joined the Marines. Jeff was later sent to Viet Nam. I believe he was over there for thirteen months. Jeff was one of the lucky ones. He came back alive. Jeff did get hit and had forty-two stitches put in his head. My brothers' metal helmet most likely saved his life. The doctors took eighteen pieces of metal from his helmet out of his head. I remember my parents, mostly my father, watched the news all the time to get information on what was happening in Viet Nam.

When I got my draft notice my father told me he would help me go to Canada if I wanted. I guess he was scared that I would be sent to Viet Nam. That was the only time I remember that my father showed he cared about me. Of course I didn't go to Canada and went into the service.

Before going into the Army I talked to my brother a lot about the service. My brother, Jeff, had gotten home from the service the beginning of 1969.

I don't remember all too much about my childhood. I had a lot of friends but not any really close friends. I was the only child in my family that would get into trouble. It seems trouble found its way to me. Both of my parents worked so I was left alone with my brother and my twin sisters. I don't remember my oldest sister ever being around that much, but she had gone off to college when I was starting sixth grade.

When I was in my senior year of high school I joined a fraternity. It was more like a gang. A lot of parties with drinking, some smoking pot and a few of us using drugs. On a lot of weekends a lot of us would go to my house to party and drink. We would call it Pearlmans' bar. I had a room, separate from the house, in the back of the property where the drinking was being done. My parents never bothered us and were real lucky they didn't get into trouble. I really don't think my parents knew how much was going on at our house. My father was in his 60s and my mother close to 60. The fraternity, Titans, would come up big in my life at a later time.

My oldest sister graduated the University of Florida with a master's degree in nursing. She helped write a textbook for nursing while she was at the University of Florida and was on the faculty at the University of Florida College of nursing. She met her future husband at the University of Florida when he was teaching in the Army ROTC department. They have since moved just outside Columbus, Ohio. She has three children. My father, who had to work two jobs, helped my oldest sister by helping pay for her education. When my oldest sister got married my parents were not even invited to the wedding. Of course neither were my other sisters, my brother or I. I guess we would have embarrassed her.

My sister Marsha, who has played a big part of my life, went to Miami Dade Junior College and finished up in Tampa, Florida with her husband Marcel. Marsha earned her PHR designation-Professional in Human Resources. This certification is like a CPA for the accounting field. Marcel earned his Bachelor degree in Social Work from Florida International University and his Masters degree in Social Work from the University of South Florida. Marsha became an executive with Met Life.

My other sister Roslyn, the twin to Marsha, went to Miami Dade Junior College before getting married to her husband, Sonny. Roslyn is now a housewife living in Sugar Hill, Georgia. Sonny, a really good guy, owns his own business designing heart pacers.

My brother Jeffrey graduated Florida State University with a teaching degree but has been working in the Post Office even before he graduated. Since Jeff made more money working in the post office the teaching degree was put on hold. Jeff graduated college over thirty years ago and has just recently retired from the post office. Jeff has been a big part of my life from childhood since my father was working so much, teaching me how to fight, ride a bike and how to play ball. Jeff was one of the people responsible for getting me involved with the union. Jeff was the first one in my family to get married.

I started school at Miami Dade Junior College but before I finished a semester I received my notice for employment from the Post Office, so I quit school. I wasn't much for school anyway. I just barely made it through high school. Somehow I graduated high school and got my diploma.

This is my immediate family.

Chapter 3

MY MILITARY DAYS

On August 9th 1970, the day before I was to go into the service, I still had my hair down to my shoulders so I got my brother to cut my hair. He had never cut hair before, but did a good job considering. I really wasn't concern so much about what my hair looked like anyway. I didn't want the military to see me with long hair. Even still Jeff did a lot better job cutting my hair then I would have thought possible.

On August 10th 1970 my brother, Jeff, drove me to Coral Gables, where the military induction center was located. This was where I was actually told I was now in the United States Army. It was kind of funny that some of the guys that showed up that day didn't realize that they would not be going home. I knew once I showed up I was gone.

We got on a bus, made a few stops and ended up at Miami International Airport. We took a plane to Nashville, Tennessee. This was the first time I had ever flown on a plane. From Nashville we took a bus to Fort Campbell, Kentucky for basic training.

For some reason, I don't recall why, we were at Fort Campbell for two weeks before we started our training. We did have to get our hair cut. I think they call it the 30-second hair cut. There was one guy that I remember had long hair and I was glad, seeing the barbers, I got my brother to cut my hair before going into the service. The barbers joked around about cutting our hair. You could tell the barbers really enjoyed cutting the hair of all the newly drafted and enlisted solders. The guy with the long hair was Wayne Keller, who will show up back into my life years later.

There were some funny things that happen that two weeks before we started basic training. There was a soldier we met on the base who was getting out of the service in a few days, just as we were just getting started. He had just returned from Germany and this guy had three grams of hash he was willing to sell, but we had no money. For those that don't know what hash is, it's like marijuana, but stronger.

There was this Spanish guy from Miami that talked a lot about smoking marijuana. He was one of those types of people that you just felt that it was a lot of talk. There was also this guy from a small town in Rome, Georgia, who pick up some grass from the yard outside the building, put the grass in tin foil and burned it. He then put the grass in a bag and sold it to the Spanish man and telling him it was marijuana. We then were able to buy the hash and we all got high. The Spanish man came in later and told us how good the marijuana was that he had bought. We all had a good laugh after that. If he only knew what he smoked. It was obvious he had never smoked marijuana before.

When basic training started all the fun stopped. Somehow I made it through all the training. I still don't know why they call it basic training. I remember taking hikes for ten miles at a time, marching in the hot sun all day, crawling under barb wire fence while being shot at, and other fun things to do. I didn't think there was anything basic about basic training, just a lot of marching, lining up in formation and getting yelled at by the drill sergeant.

There was one day where we got a new officer just out of officers' training school that decided to take us on a long, run, hike. I don't remember how long the hike was, or how long we ran, but do remember it being a hot day. I don't remember how many guys went to the hospital that day for heat exhaustion, or how many guys just dropped out, but know some guys did go to the hospital and others dropped out from the heat. I don't remember seeing that officer again, thank God.

While I spent my time in basic training some real big rock stars had died. Jimi Hendrix died on September 18th 1970 and Janis Joplin overdosed from heroin on October 4th 1970.

After graduation from basic training we got our orders and mine was to go to New York to work in an APO/ FPO Post Office. I knew I was lucky not going to Fort Polk, Louisiana, where a lot of guys went before going to Viet Nam. All I thought was that the military must know I was a drug user. To go to New York where drugs were more plentiful than Miami was a druggies dream. I was also able to come home to Miami before heading to New York. I just knew I had it made.

Before going into the Army I used to hang out at night at Peacock Park in Coconut Grove. I met a lot of people there, but didn't know their names. You would see people at the park all the time, get stoned with them but never really got their names. When I was able to come home before heading to New York I went to Peacock Park to get some marijuana or pot as this was what it was called. I saw this guy at the park that I had smoked pot with at different times but didn't know his name. I asked this guy if he had any pot or knew where I could get some. He told me about this guy that had some really good pot, but he hadn't seen him for a few months. He said the guy looked like me but had long hair. Of course I was the guy he was talking about. I don't think I got any pot that day.

I was stationed at Fort Wadsworth in Staten Island, New York, on the Hudson Bay. On one side of the Hudson Bay, across from Staten Island, is Manhattan. On the other side of the Hudson Bay, over the bridge, was Brooklyn. This is where the main military base was located.

Fort Hamilton was the main base where we had to go to for anything dealing with personnel. Also on the Fort Hamilton base was the military credit union. Just after I arrived in New York four masked men robbed the Fort Hamilton credit union. That was at the end of October 1970. When I was getting ready to leave New York toward the end of June 1971, the bank robbers were just getting caught.

I worked in Astoria, which is considered Long Island City, at the APO/FPO Post Office on 46 Street and Northern Blvd. I was put on the third shift at the APO/FPO Post Office. I worked from 3:30 P.M.-12:00A.M. mostly with three other soldiers, yes I was now considered a soldier. But working in the Army Post Office was almost like a regular job with less money.

The Sergeant was from Mississippi, the spec. 4 was from Texas, and the private from Alabama. I of course was also a private. We drove a bus to work and a car back to the barracks.

I was told that I was lucky not to have arrived sooner to New York than I did. Because of the employees working in New York at the post office went on strike the military had to try to work the mail, and worked 12 hours a day and more trying to get the mail out. The strike didn't last long, and the military went back to their normal shift.

When at work we only had this small section to take care of. Someone, other then a military person, would push the mail over to our section and we would work the mail. When we finished we would sit and play cards and sometimes sneak some wine into the post office. The Sergeant, who was in charge of our section on the third shift, said as long as we got up when the mail came in there would not be a problem. Of course he was not talking about us bringing in the wine, only about us sitting around playing cards.

The soldiers who worked the early morning shift, 12:00-8:30 A.M. had a different kind of person in charge. The Sergeant on the first shift, what was called tour 1 in the post office, would go looking for mail. We were told sometimes that Sergeant would be gone for an hour at a time and always came back with mail to be worked. Everyone thought he was looking for mail. The officers of our company loved him. According to the officers everyone should work like this Sargent. Approximately five months after I arrived in New York this Sergeant, who the offices praised all the time, got busted for stealing. When everyone thought this Sergeant was out looking for mail what he was really doing was looking for packages. He had address labels to put on packages. He then was sending these packages to his girlfriend's apartment. Being this was an APO/FPO Post Office there were customs labels on the packages so that the Sergeant knew what was in the packages. He was putting labels on the packages with his girlfriends' address and then the packages would be mailed to the address that was now placed on the package.

After leaving work a lot of nights we would take a detour and go to Brooklyn and get the best barbecue ribs I ever had. Of course if we had gotten caught making this detour we could have been in a lot of trouble. I would go into the store, where the ribs were being cooked, with the other private while the others waited with the car.

One night I stayed in the car with the Sergeant. The Sergeant was a big guy, about 6'2 and maybe 280 pounds. We called him juice because he could, and did drink a lot. That was before he was turned onto marijuana. I was in the back seat and rolled the window down. The Sergeant yelled at me "do you want some Niger to pull us from this car." I rolled the window up so fast it was scary. If the Sergeant had been a white man I most likely would had just laughed at him. But because the Sergeant was a black man he scared the hell out of me. That was the last time I stayed with the car. I felt safer going inside the store. The men working inside the store treated us like we were something special. The men working in the store cooking the ribs were all black men. I was told this part of Brooklyn was a bad section of town.

There was another time when I was driving the car back to the barracks and one of the other guys said that it had just started to snow. I slammed on the brakes of the car and jumped out. These guys just started laughing at me. I had never seen snow before and couldn't wait. Of course I really couldn't tell that snow was falling since it just started to fall. The next morning there was snow all over the ground. I was like a kid. I made a snowman and we had snowball fights.

The barracks I was living in was a three-story building. We were living on the third floor with the Army band on the second floor and offices on the first floor. I usually went to sleep around 3:00 A.M. in the morning and the Army band would get out under our window at 7:00 A.M. making noise, blowing their horns. It didn't take me long to get help from the guys I worked with to make snowballs. We would make the snowballs and put them on the windowsill outside. We would do this when we got back to the barracks after work, around 1:00 A.M. in the morning. By 7:00-7:30 in the morning the snowballs would be rock hard. When the Army band would stop by our window we would let the snowballs fly. Do you know what's it like to have rock hard snowballs thrown at you from three stories up? This only lasted a few days before the band got smart and moved to the parking lot, far from our window. Everyone was happy after that. The band got to practice without having snowballs thrown at them, and we were able to get more sleep without being wakened by the music.

When I was drafted into the Army I thought it was the worst thing that could have happen to me. As it turned out it was good for me. I grew up some, had some responsibilities, and saw some of the country that I wouldn't have seen had I not have gone into the service.

I'm not a religious man but really believe God was helping me when I was drafted. It got me away from the drug use, even if it was for a short time. I use to tell people I was like a cat and had nine lives. I think I went through about four or five before the service.

When I got orders from the Army to go to New York to work in the Army Post Office I felt God was testing me. I failed the test. I started doing heavy drugs again.

I met this soldier, a cook, from Connecticut, who helped me fail the test from God. I'm not really blaming this guy. I could have said no. But he didn't help me. When I was in Miami I would buy a small bag of heroin for $10. In New York I was getting a bag of heroin twice the size and for more than half the cost. The two of us, the solder from Connecticut and myself, would buy 50 bags of heroin at $3.00 a bag. We would sell 25 bags for $5.00 each and get most of our money back. We would then get high from the other 25 bags. I thought I was in heaven. Getting bags of heroin, that was bigger than what I got in Miami, for only $1.00 a bag.

There was more then one time I could have been busted. The unit I was in would conduct locker inspections. This was usually around 4:00 in the morning. I usually went to sleep around 3:00 in the morning after getting high. The officers suspected me of smoking pot, but had no idea that I was shooting heroin. The officers would come around to each bed and make you open your wall locker and footlocker. When the officers got to my bed I was always still asleep. What I was told was that the officers would come into the bay where we slept, turn on the lights and tell everyone to stand by their bed with their wall and food lockers open. The problem for me was I never heard them. I would keep a pair of works, as I called it, a needle, in my bedpost. If I had gotten caught with a pair of works I would have gone to jail. I would have gotten kicked out of the Army. Most likely I would have lost my postal job, and would not be writing this book.

One of the times when the officers came in for an inspection I had a pipe in my wall locker. I had just bought the pipe and had never used it, lucky for me. When the officer looked into my locker he didn't see the pipe, sitting on the top shelve in plain view. As the officer was closing the locker he noticed the pipe. Everyone that slept in the barracks was called over to my bed so that the officer could show them my pipe and the officer said that he better not find a hash pipe in anyone's locker again. I just sat there thinking I wished I had some hash. Before the officer left he gave me back my pipe. I gave the pipe to my buddy the cook. The main problem I had from this is some of the heavy drinkers gave me a hard time. The guy that had his bed right next to mine was a drinker and I did have some problems from him for awhile.

The soldier that had his bed and lockers right across from me was a big guy, from Kansas City, Missouri. He would drink and get nasty. He had no idea I was using drugs. He did know about the pipe the officer found in my locker, but never seen me use any kind of drug or smoke anything. One night he came in after drinking and I was high on the heroin. I guess I said something he didn't like and he jumped me. He beat the hell out of me. I had a split lip, my face was swollen and my eyes were almost completely closed. I didn't tell anyone except my buddy from Connecticut. When I was asked I told people I ran into the wall. Of course they took the hint that I wasn't going to tell them who did this to me. I'm not sure who was luckier, me or the guy from Kansas City. I was very seriously thinking of shooting this guy up with a couple bags of heroin. I know I could've done this and he would have overdosed and died. I had this all worked out with the help from my drug partner from Connecticut. I also know that most likely I would've been caught and gone to jail. I would have been kicked out of the army with a dishonorable discharge. It was good for both of us that I didn't follow my thoughts. The guy from Kansas City later apologized to me. Lucky for me I didn't get caught doing drugs and I only stayed in New York for eight months.

I got orders to go to Germany in June 1971. Again I feel God got me out of a situation. When I left New York I got rid of 25 bags of heroin I had in my possession. I was told that I couldn't quit taking heroin on my own, that I would need help going through withdrawals.

I went to Fort Dix, New Jersey before going to Germany. I was at Fort Dix for three day and had a rough time. I was having chills and my body hurt but somehow I made it. I was going through withdrawals from the heroin. I really believe that if I had stayed in New York for any more time I might not have quit the drug use on my own. But I did quit using the heroin with nobody to help me. It did make me feel good that I quit on my own. It was too bad I didn't learn from my experience because I started using the hard drugs once more.

I left New York to start my journey to Germany in July 1971. But before I left I came home to Miami in April for my brothers' wedding. My brother Jeff, was the first in my family to get married on April 29th 1971. I was the best man. After the wedding I went back to New York and Jeff and his new bride, Marsha headed to Tallahassee, Florida. Jeff had also taken the test for the Post Office in Miami and had his test scores transferred to Tallahassee, Florida. Jeff was attending Florida State University when he was hired by the Post Office.

When I arrived in Germany, I had a little over thirteen months to go before getting out of the Army. I flew into Frankfurt, Germany and went by bus through a number of cities before ending up in Kaisersiautern or K-Town as everyone called it. There were a lot of Americans in K-Town as there were a number of different military bases. I worked in the motor pool working as the dispatcher. It was an easy job, but I had to wait for the vehicles to return at the end of the day before I left work so I was one of the last to finish working each day.

The barracks in K-Town was a lot better then what I was use to in New York. In New York I lived in a big bay. There would be two beds, footlockers and wall lockers then a partition, then the same continued. There must have been twenty or more guys in the same bay. If you wanted to watch television you had to go to the day room. In K-Town there were two to three guys in each room. I was in a room with two other people. We were able to rent a television, a stereo and a small refrigerator. We set up the room to make it look like a two-room apartment. We set up two wall lockers on one side of the room and the third wall locker on the other side of the room. We then got a sheet and tied died it and hung it up like a curtain. On the other side of the curtain was the small refrigerator, the stereo and television that we rented, and a little furniture to sit on. Our room felt like a home away from home. We made the best of what we had.

When we requested to paint our room we were denied the opportunity. So we got this guy that was a really good artist, another soldier, who painted a big piece sign on the wall. Lucky for him, and us, we didn't get into trouble. The officers from our company didn't like the piece sign and wanted it covered. This is what we were hoping for. The only way to cover the piece sign was to paint over it. So we got the authority to paint our room. Since we were allowed to paint our room, everyone else in our company that wanted to paint their room was also allowed to. I felt like a hero, along with the other two guys in my room.

There was a lot to like about being in Germany. First, and foremost, it was a lot better then going to Viet Nam. The country, what I saw of it, was beautiful. There was a castle in every town. The wine was good, there was no marijuana, but plenty of hash, and real cheap. Since I had no choice about being in the Army, Germany was as good or better then a lot of other places. What I didn't like about Germany was the cold weather, almost year round, and the fog. On most mornings during the winter you could not see a foot in front of you. Since I worked as the dispatcher in the motor pool I had a car to drive to and from work. Because of the fog in the morning I quit driving and would walk to work, approximately one mile, every morning. This was approved by the officers of the company I was in as long as I got someone to cover for me. It wasn't hard to get one of the mechanics in the motor pool to drive the army jeep, instead of walking, and open the shop. After work I would drive the car back to our headquarters. In the morning one of the mechanics would drive the car back to the motor pool, open the gates and maybe dispatch a vehicle or two before I got there.

It didn't take me long before I got back to using drugs. I failed Gods' test again. The hash sold for about $1.00 a gram. There was no heroin that I could find, but the morphine more then made up for it. Between the morphine and other drug use it was obvious that I hadn't learn too much, or didn't care, and was heading back to the point I was at when I left New York.

Then one day I got help in a strange way. One of the guys I would talk to and once in awhile smoke hash with scared me into quitting everything except smoking the hash. This guy was down the hall from me one day and started yelling at me. He asked me why I was still shooting dope and when was I going to quit? I told him not to talk so loud since I thought other people might hear, but he just kept talking. I finally walked away. I was so pissed I didn't talk to him for sometime. I only thought he was trying to get me in trouble. I thought for sure that someone would hear him yelling and I would get busted. As it turned out he was a true friend. The best I could've had. I got rid of the morphine and never did it again. I started talking to this guy at a later date and he told me he was just trying to get me to quit the drugs. He told me he knew nobody was around to hear him the day he was yelling at me. Of course I didn't know that nobody was around. I guess you could say God works in mysterious ways.

One of the last things I remember about K-Town was when I was pulling guard duty. The duty I had was that of a duty runner. There were always three solders on guard duty at night. The duty officer, an officer of the division I was in, a duty runner, and a duty driver. On this night I was the duty runner. I was able to sit in the office all night and if someone had a call I would go to his room to get them. If someone important needed a ride somewhere I would go get the duty driver and he would get the car. Most of the time the duty runner would just sit in the office, watch television, or sleep in the corner of the room. The duty officer was always in the office with the duty runner and the duty driver was able to go to his room. Sometimes a friend would stop by and watch television with me and the duty officer for awhile or just shoot the bull, On night this other guy stop by and I told him nobody was allowed in the office that was not on duty. This was true, even though I let my friends in and the duty officer didn't care.

The division I was in was a big maintenance division and there was no way to know everyone. I didn't know this man but had heard about him. Other solders would say that he would wet his bed and that he smelled bad a lot of times. The man had a problem and from what I heard he should have been released from the Army.

Just the week before this man was caught in the woods with another solder and this other solder was screwing this guy in the ass. Up to this point I didn't hear anything happening to either of these solders.

After leaving the office the guy left the barracks. I remember seeing this guy walking out the gate with a big boom box. This was the last time I saw this guy alive. Around 2:00 in the morning some military police came by the office. I was sleeping in the corner of the room and wasn't seen. I heard talking and woke up to hear one of the policemen telling the duty officer that this man was stabbed fifty-one times. I sat up after hearing this. The military police officer saw me and I got thrown out of the office by the military police. The military police caught the guy that did the killing later that morning. He was another soldier in our company. He had thrown his army shirt, with his name on the shirt, in the dumpster. The shirt had blood on it from the man that he had killed. I never found out why, if there is a why, someone would kill another person, especially stabbing them so many times. I felt so guilty sending that man out of the office when it wouldn't have hurt me to let him stay. I still wonder if anything would have happen if I didn't tell the guy to leave. The other solder that was in the woods with this solder was sent stateside the very next day. I had heard the solder that did the killing was sentenced to only ten years in prison and was scheduled to take courses to finish his education.

After the soldier was killed I had heard the mother and uncle of the solder was around asking questions. All the solders of our division were told not to answer any questions about this man that was killed. Without knowing this man, but from what I had heard he should have been released from the Army long before something happened. I also think his relatives should have been told that he had a problem. I never seen anyone asking questions or I would've told them what I knew about the lady's son.

A short time later the United States Army was going to the all-volunteer army and was letting everyone who was drafted out early. I went from having six months to go before getting out of the Army to one month to go before getting out of the Army.

I went to Frankfurt, Germany to start my journey back home. Before I was aloud to leave Frankfurt and board the plane I had to get a hair cut. I couldn't believe it. I was scheduled to get out of the Army in a couple of days and I was forced to get a hair cut. Since I didn't have much of a choice I got my hair cut, boarded the plane and then flew back to Fort Dix, and was released from the service on March 11th 1972. I was taken to the Philadelphia airport and flew to Tallahassee, Florida. I visited with my brother and his wife for a few days before heading back home.

I was at the point I guess it really didn't matter that I had to cut my hair just two days before getting out of the service. My military days were over. It just left a bad feeling about what I thought of the Army. At this point I was ready to leave with no looking back. I had a good job to go back to so I didn't have to worry about looking for a job.

I was never so happy to get back to Miami and to go back to the post office. Now I know how Dorothy, from the wizard of oz, felt when she said there's no place like home. It sure felt good to me to be back home. I was glad to be getting out of the service after spending only nineteen months in the Army, but I would be lying if I said I didn't enjoy my time in the Army. It turned out to be a blessing that I was drafted when I did. I grew up a lot. I was still living and was ready to go on with my life.

To me it was amazing how you meet people from all over and then go on with your life and never hear or see these people again. When I was drafted and went to Fort Campbell Kentucky there were a number of people that were from Miami that were drafted the same time as me. I met people from Miami, other parts of Florida, Georgia, Tennessee, Virginia and throughout the states in the south. When I went to New York I didn't meet anyone from Miami. The guys I worked with were from Texas, Mississippi and Alabama. But when I went to Germany the guys I worked with and hung around with were from everywhere, throughout the United States. The other two guys in my room were from North Carolina and Colorado. The other guys I hung around with were from California, Oklahoma, Michigan, Virginia and Georgia, just to name a few of the guys.

There was one guy from Miami, Florida, that was talking about trying to get a reunion together but it never got going. I would love to talk to these old Army buddies just to see how they're doing. To see if they ever got married what kind of work they were doing, and to talk about our times in the service. It's funny that when you're in the service so many people talk about when they get out, and that you can't wait to get out. But I had so many good memories to look back on. Of course I was also very lucky not to go to Viet nam. I'm sure the memories, if I lived to talk about them, would be a lot different if I had to go the Nam.

CHAPTER 4

BACK TO CIVILIAN LIFE

I ARRIVED HOME, IN Miami, Florida, on March 15th 1972 to start my life back as a civilian. With my military days behind me I was ready to go back to the post office. Well, almost ready. I had to go to the personnel department to find out where to report and what hours I would be working. When I reported to personnel the lady working there asked me if I wanted to switch over to a letter carrier and when did I want to report back to work? Working as a letter carrier I would be working daytime hours. I didn't care to work nights, mainly because I had a hard time sleeping during the day. It seemed I was always tired. The thought crossed my mind to switch, but talked myself out of it. I was coming back to the post office as a regular full time employee. Yes, while I was in the service I went from being a part time flexible (PTF) to being a regular employee. I was told I was made a regular employee after eighteen months, which means I made it to a regular status on approximately June 15, 1971. If I had switched over to become a letter carrier I would go back to being a (PTF), part-time flexible, employee with no guarantee of working forty hours per week. As a regular employee I was guaranteed forty hours work each week. Plus working inside had its benefits. I didn't have to worry about the weather or dogs.

Since I had a choice as to when I could start working back in the post office again I took a couple of weeks before I reported to the Biscayne Annex Post Office as a full time clerk. I reported back to the post office on April 3rd 1972. I stayed working nights for several more years.

Since I had almost a few weeks before I had to go back to work I looked up a few old friends. I went to Peacock Park in Coconut Grove, I use to hang around the park a lot before the service. But things were a lot different. I was still smoking marijuana but the use of heroin and morphine had stopped.

One day this old friend of mine came by my house to get me high. When I told him I quit shooting dope he left and I never saw him again. Some friend he turned out to be. It's sort of funny, when I was using the heroin it seemed I knew so many people. People who I thought were friends. Now that I quit I didn't see hardly any of these people. Which was really a good thing since they were still using dope. I always say sooner or later you have to grow up and think about the future. If you don't you're either going to be dead or locked up.

There was this one friend of mine that was on methadone, trying to get off the heroin, and his mothers' boyfriend started a fright with him. This friend ended up stabbing his mothers' boyfriend to death and he went to prison for about seven years. His mother was the main witness against him. I know I was glad I quit using heroin.

When I finally reported back to the post office on April 3rd 1972 I was scheduled to work the same tour, with my hours of work being 3:30-12:00 midnight. I was given Tuesday-Wednesday as scheduled days off.

I was again put in the outgoing section of the Post Office and again given the Florida scheme. I passed the scheme in a short amount of time making a 100%. I was then put on the states pouch rack to work and hardly used the Florida scheme that I had just passed.

Working mostly on the states pouch rack was easy and a job I liked. I would throw small parcels and bundles of mail into the sacks and when the sack got full or there was a dispatch I would pull the sack down, weigh it and put the sack on a float to take down to the truck. Of course I didn't work alone. I worked with Joe Medeiros and John Hutton. Joe was the expediter and the union steward. He was call the hat because of this hat he would wear. John and I would do most of the work as Joe was either fighting with the supervisor or reading the paper. When it was time to get the mail dispatched Joe was always there as he was suppose to be as the expediter. Joe worked when he had to so the dispatch got out on time. We worked hard to get the mail cleaned up, but then goofed around a lot.

When we closed the sacks at dispatch time, or the sack got full, we used these metal clips. Sometimes we would throw these clips at the wall clock some distance away. One day we were throwing these clips at the clock and Joe Medeiros hit the clock just right and the glass of the clock broke. Joe went one way and John and I went in different directions. We all came back to the pouch rack, where we worked, about five minutes later and acted like we didn't know anything about the clock.

We worked across from one of the elevator on the second floor. A lot of times when another employee would go down the elevator we would open the elevator door from the outside just a little and the elevator would stop. Sometimes we would leave the employee in the elevator for a short time. Of course if they knew all they had to do was press the bypass button and the floor they needed and the elevator would move again. The ones that didn't know about the bypass button we would close the doors again and bring the employee back up before they made it to the first floor. Most of the time the employee didn't even realize we were causing the elevator to stop. All they thought was that the elevator wasn't working properly and that when the elevator started working again it brought them back up to the second floor.

At least twice a week someone would collect money and around 11:00 P.M. someone would go to the bagel factory. Just down the street was a place that made bagels for the bakeries. If we timed it right we would get there just when the bagels were being taken from the oven. I think this is the only thing I missed about the Biscayne Annex Post Office, not getting the fresh bagels right out of the oven.

Every night rubber bands would be shot to the ceiling and a lot would stick. You would see a lot of rubber bands just hanging down. We found out about five years later that the ceiling had asbestos in it and we ended up vacating the building.

The manager in charge of the outgoing section was Mr. Applebaum. Joe Medeiros was the shop steward in the outgoing section. I don't know if that's why Joe and Mr. Applebaum didn't get along, but the two of them didn't talk to each other. The only time I heard the manager talk was when he said something to the supervisor. Mr. Applebaum would walk through the section and look at the mail and wouldn't say one word to an employee.

I remember one day this other employee told me if you want to hear Mr. Applebaum talk then ask him about his daughter. Mr. Applebaum had a daughter who was on a tennis scholarship at the University of Miami. One day as Mr. Applebaum was walking through the section I asked him how his daughter was doing. You would think I was an old friend. Mr. Applebaum started telling me some of the tournaments his daughter had won. He must have talked to me that day for about ten minutes. But Mr. Applebaum, as I said before didn't like Joe Mederios When the manager, Mr. Applebaum, had to say anything to Joe Mederios he would bring the supervisor, Al Miller, with him. Mr. Applebaum would say something to the supervisor, Al Miller, and then the supervisor would have to say the same thing to Joe. Standing there John Hutton and I could hardly keep from laughing listening to these dumb shits. We could hear the manager tell the supervisor what he wanted to say to Joe and the supervisor would tell Joe the same thing. Joe would tell the supervisor to tell the manager that he heard what Mr. Applebaum had said and the supervisor would tell the manager that Joe had heard. I felt like there were little children standing there instead of adults, it was just too funny.

The supervisor, Al Miller was a royal pain in the ass. He would get mad at the shop steward, Joe Medeiros, and send John Hutton and I to the letter cases to get even with Joe. Of course Joe didn't do much work while John and I would be at the letter case, so the mail backed up. A short time later the supervisor would come get us and send us back to the pouch rack.

One day when John and I was sent to the letter cases and the mail on the pouch rack was sitting, not being worked, John asked Al Miller who's dumb idea was it to send us to the letter cases? I thought I would choke to keep from laughing. We, of course, knew that it was the supervisors' idea to send us to the letter cases, and the supervisor, Al Miller knew that we knew that it was his idea. Al Miller just walked away without answering John. Then a short time later the supervisor came back to the letter cases to get us, John and myself, and send us back to help Joe on the pouch rack.

Al Miller had a glass eye. I would always try to get John or another employee to go to the supervisor and tell him he had a fly on his eye to see if the supervisor would wipe his eye. I could never get anyone to do this and I didn't have the nerve to say anything to Al Miller about his glass eye.

The assistant Postmaster, or whatever he was called, was second in command in the management ranks, was Mr. Dupree. All the supervisors', that I worked for, acted scared of Mr. Dupree. Anyway on this one day Mr. Dupree was looking for the supervisor, Al Miller, and found him down stairs eating on the platform. We heard the supervisor got a suspension from Mr. Dupree for an unauthorized break and eating on the platform. I know I loved it. I could not stand the supervisor, Al Miller. Al Miller didn't stay in our section much longer after that. I don't know if Al Miller requested to be moved or upper management told him he would be moved. All I knew was I was glad he was gone and no longer my supervisor.

Our new supervisor was Bob Higginson. A lot of the employees in his section called him cowboy. I don't know if it was because he limped real bad or what. But I'm sure he didn't know that he was called cowboy. He was alright for a supervisor.

One day Bob Higginson asked me to watch the section while he went to lunch. I figured it wouldn't be bad to watch the section for only one hour. As soon as the supervisor left two of the mail handlers also left. The only thing was the two mail handlers were not supposed to leave. They came back about thirty minutes later. Of course I didn't say anything, but it pissed me off that these guys took off like that. The next day when the supervisor asked me again to watch the section when he went to lunch I refused. I knew right then I could never be a supervisor. I guess it was not in my blood. Another supervisor came over to me and said he saw what had happen with the two mail handlers leaving. I asked him why he didn't say anything and he said he wanted to see what I would do.

It's funny how things happen in the post office. You could be the worse employee and become a supervisor. Joe Medeiros, the shop steward, who did less then most of the other employees I worked with, became a supervisor. There was also a different manager in charged of the outgoing section. I don't believe Joe Medeiros would've became a supervisor under Mr. Applebaum, but I could be wrong. His first couple of years he was not a full time supervisor, so I covered his position as the expediter on the states pouch rack. At first it was hard working for Joe. I remember what kind of worker he was and I wasn't use to Joe telling me what to do. After a short time we worked out our differences. We were still friends and Joe was not a bad supervisor. Plus he helped me out, since I was covering his position as the expediter I was getting higher level pay from a level 5 to a level 6. It wasn't a lot more money, but even a little extra money helped. I covered the expediter job for two years.

Everyday of the week there's a color code so that management can identify when the mail came in and when the mail should be worked to get the mail out in a timely manner. I remember one evening Mr. Dupree told the manager in charged of the platform, to get all the green mail together and send it to Fort Lauderdale to be worked. There was a high volume of mail and Fort Lauderdale was going to help get the mail out. The manager in charge of the platform ordered the employees to get all the green sacks of mail, regardless of the color of the label, and send them to Fort Lauderdale. What the manager was suppose to do was to have the employees working under him get the green label mail only and send only that mail to Fort Lauderdale. The next day all the green sacks that were sent to Fort Lauderdale came back to Miami. Of course this only delayed the mail another day. So what happens to a manager that makes such a mistake? They get promoted. This manager was later promoted to Postmaster of Hialeah and later even was made Postmaster of Miami. That just goes to prove that to make it upward in management it's not what you know, it's who you know or who you service.

After Joe Medeiros became a regular supervisor his position was posted for bid and Tony Vacca got the bid. Tony was an older employee, a really nice guy and a good worker. A lot different type of worker then Joe Medeiros. Another employee, Joe Szot, also started working on the states pouch rack with me. John Hutton was then moved to the Florida pouch rack and I stayed working on the states and helped out on Florida racks when needed.

One night while working on the states pouch rack, I was working alone at this time, a lady supervisor asked me if I had seen who was the last lady to leave the ladies bathroom? I was working and wasn't really paying attention. The post office was always moving the operations around and the pouch rack where I was working was moved across from the ladies bathroom. This supervisor after asking me who was the last lady to come out of the bathroom went back into the bathroom and came back out with some letters that were all wet. Someone had tried to flush these letters down the toilet. I found out later that the letters were going to charity organizations. I found out later that the supervisor had suspected this pregnant lady. Sometime later, approximately six weeks, while working the pouch rack again, I heard all this banging. I looked around and couldn't figure out where the noise was coming from. All of the sudden the door to the postal inspectors gallery, this is the door that leads up to where the inspectors can see through two way mirrors, came flying open and a couple of inspectors came running out. Of course the noise that I heard was the postal inspectors running through the gallery, the door that lead up to the postal inspectors gallery was only a few feet from the ladies bathroom, the postal inspectors went into the isle where the clerks were casing letter mail and caught this same lady, the one who was pregnant, stealing five dollars that had come out of a charity envelope. I heard that the pregnant lady, I didn't know who she was, had just gotten back from maternity leave and while she was casing mail her ledge where she was casing mail from was loaded with charity envelopes. The postal inspectors had this lady set up and she took the bait. I'm sure the lady was fired from the post office. I never saw her again.

There was another time when Tony Vacca found a few envelopes in the hamper of mail we were working out of. A casual employee working on the opening belt downstairs would bring us the hampers of mail so we could separate the small parcels by the states. Tony took the envelopes and invoices, for various products, which were found inside the hamper of mail and gave them to our supervisor. Sometime later the postal inspectors caught this part-time employee stopping the elevator between floors and ripping open the envelopes. This casual employee got caught with a few cigarette lighters in his pocket and some cheap jewelry. There was nothing very valuable in the mail that we worked. There was also nothing very valuable that this casual employee was taking. There surely wasn't anything valuable enough to cost you to lose your job even working as a part-time casual employee.

In October 1977 the Biscayne Annex Post Office was closed and we moved into the General Mail Facility. The ceiling at the Biscayne Annex Post Office was covered with asbestos, which is known to cause cancer. I don't believe many employees knew the ceiling was covered with asbestos. I know I didn't when I would shoot rubber bands to the ceiling and small white stuff would fall down. I had heard later that the Postmaster and others in upper management knew about the asbestos and covered it up for some time.

Before we moved out of the Biscayne Annex I was assigned the primary scheme. This was the entire scheme for the city of Miami. I had to know all the zip codes for Miami. The primary scheme was broken down into two parts. Primary north and primary south. After passing the schemes and since I was an unassigned regular clerk I had to bid on a job before I was put somewhere I didn't want to work. Since management had the right to put me into a position, which would've been on tour 1, 10:30 P.M.-7:00A.M. Or hours similar to that, I bid to the outgoing flat section. I was still working on tour three with the hours of 4:30 P. M. to 1:00 A. M. plus I worked two hours of overtime almost every night. I liked working in the outgoing section of the post office so working the outgoing flats was the best job available for me at this time. It also helped that the supervisor in charged of flats was a pretty good guy. Yes there are some good supervisors in the post office. There are just not many of them. I also had Sunday-Monday as scheduled days off. This was the first time I had a week end night off, meaning either Saturday or Sunday night. I worked on the states secondary flats case, which was different states then, the regular flat case, and I also worked mail for Canada. The outgoing flats were down stairs at the Biscayne Annex, which was different for me after having worked up stairs almost the whole time I worked for the post office.

I worked with some good people and some real jerks. I became a good friend with an older man, John Johnsonbaugh. When we would go to lunch we would always play backgammon. I learn to be pretty good at different kinds of backgammon. When we moved to the General Mail Facility we got a different supervisor. The supervisor we had went to the day shift and another supervisor took over our section. This supervisor was all right but not as good as the previous supervisor. All supervisors have their favorites, and I wasn't one of the fovorites and I don't believe my friend John was either. I continued working the same job in the outgoing flats section working on the states secondary case for a couple more years.

I remember one time John Johnsonbaugh had come to me and told me he hurt his hand. He had gotten mad about something and hit his hand against something. John use to sweep the flat cases. That meant he would move a rack that had sacks hanging from it. The rack had wheels so it was easy enough to move. John would push this rack through the back of the flat cases and pull the mail for dispatches. I told John while he was pushing the rack to catch his foot and to fall down hitting his hand on the floor. He could then report an accident and be covered by the post office under OWCP. When other employees saw John fall and hit his hand nobody would have guessed that it was planned. When I saw John hit that floor I really believed, for a minute anyway, that he really had fallen and gotten hurt. John was a great actor, at lease for that day. I really believed John had broken his hand in the incident. It is amazing what one has to go through to get by at work, and in this I'm talking about the post office. John has since retired but stayed on tour 3 working nights all the time until his retirement.

CHAPTER 5

A START OF A NEW LIFE

AFTER GETTING BACK TO the post office it took a little adjusting to the fact I had to hit a time clock and work nights for forty plus hours a week, plus overtime. I worked full time in the Army, but it was different. I wasn't working nights and there was no time clock to hit. I had a Sergeant, but with me working in the office as the dispatcher I didn't see him all that much. Back in the post office there are supervisors that seem to be everywhere. Just in the outgoing section of the Biscayne Annex Post Office there were supervisors in charge of the flats, a supervisor, sometimes two supervisors in charge of the letters, and a supervisor in charge of the racks and opening belt. Then there were the managers in charge of the different areas. There were too many managers and supervisors and not enough employees.

One can only wonder how some of these people made supervisor. I guess part of the criteria to get into management was to be an ass, not just have one, and treat people like dirt. I'm talking about the supervisors and managers that were at the Biscayne Annex Post Office in the outgoing section, I didn't know about the incoming section, or the supervisors and managers at the stations and branches. The ones I'm talking about on the most part were really shit. That's the best way for me to tell you what I thought about most of them. Of course you always have a few who were out cast and were good people.

After a few weeks of being back in the post office I started meeting my sister, Marsha, for lunch. Marsha worked in the personnel department at Cordis Corporation near the garment district in Miami. Since I didn't have to report to work until 3:30 P.M. I had plenty of time to meet Marsha then come home to get ready for work. I would try to meet Marsha at least once a week.

One day as I walked into the office where Marsha worked I noticed a new girl on the front counter. She was young and pretty. As I walked past her she asked if she could help me. I just told her no, I knew where I was going. She said I couldn't just walk in without an appointment, but I just kept walking. I guess I should've told her that my sister was her boss and that I was meeting her for lunch, but I didn't. When I got to my sisters' desk this girl was beside me telling Marsha that she tried to stop me. Marsha then introduced me to this new girl, Teresa Sullivan. Teresa ended up going to lunch with us. I'm not sure who asked her that first time but most times after this first day I met Teresa she would go to lunch with Marsha and I. Some days I would go and meet just Teresa for lunch, and I started going more then once a week. Teresa was twenty years old and a pretty little girl. She was barely over five feet tall and maybe 100 pounds. I got her phone number but put off calling her for a night out. Why? I have no idea. I wanted to ask Teresa out in the worst way. I guess I was a little shy and didn't want rejection. Going out to lunch was different. It wasn't hard to talk to Teresa and I felt at ease talking to Teresa during the day.

Marsha and Roslyn, my other sister, shared an apartment and I was invited to dinner one night when I was off from work. When I got there I noticed that there were four settings at the dinner table. Marsha the matchmaker also invited Teresa. After this night I asked Teresa out on my next day off. We went to the movies and saw Fiddle on the Roof. After this I saw Teresa as often as I could. I would meet Teresa almost daily for lunch and went out at night on my days off or when I called in sick. I met her friends and her sisters Pat and Peg and her brother, Tim. I think I knew right after that first date that Teresa was the one for me. It helped that my parents liked Teresa and my match maker sister, Marsha, and Roz got along good with Teresa.

Teresa was the youngest of six children. Teresa and her family had moved down to Miami from Springfield, Ohio, when Teresa was around eight years old. Her sister Peg and her brother-in-law, Ray lived in Ft. Lauderdale. Her sister Pat lived on a big sailboat in Coconut Grove with her husband Ralph and daughter, Martina. Her brother, Tim lived nearby in Miami with his wife, Norma. Teresa didn't see or hear much from her older brother, Mike, and Greg, the youngest of the boys lived in Macon, Georgia with their father. Teresa lived with her mother as her mother and father were divorced.

I did some stupid things in my life and it seems every time something good happen to me, like meeting Teresa, then I would mess up. After our first date and I felt I had found the women for me I got high on heroin again. This time it almost killed me. I figured this was the fifth time I came close to death, and not the last time. An old friend came by the house and brought some heroin. It had been a good nine months since I quit the morphine use. I had been home from the service almost seven months and I stayed clean from drugs, except smoking marijuana, that I didn't think was wrong, except it was against the law. I was alone after my friend, brought the heroin by my house and then left. As I shot the heroin I knew right away I did too much. I would get sick every time I did too much heroin. I felt ill and got on the floor by the toilet in case I was going to be sick. The next thing I remember was waking up on the bathroom floor with a bruise on the side of my face. I must have fallen and hit my face on the toilet seat. I could just imagine that if my head had gone inside the toilet I could've died. I thought it funny after this time, but not right then. I imagine what the newspaper might say if I died and they got the story. "Man dies with head in toilet from drug overdose". This was the last time I shot anything into my body. I guess that's why they call it dope. You have to be a dope to shoot dope, or for that matter do any drugs at all. I did continue to smoke marijuana but like I said I don't consider marijuana a drug. Lucky for me I didn't lose Teresa.

Since I felt like I was getting closer to Teresa, and before things got too serious, I wanted Teresa to know about my drug use. This way if she felt the same way about me as I felt about her I would have no secrets.

Teresa and I had only been seeing each other for four months when I asked her to marry me and lucky for me she said yes. When she told her mother and that she was inviting her father to the wedding Teresa got kicked out of the house. Not only did Teresa get kicked out of her house, but also everything she owned was thrown out onto the front yard. Teresa' mother hated her father so much that she took it out on Teresa. If the stupid lady had any brains she would see the wedding was not about her and her divorced husband, but about Teresa and I. It was going to be our day. I didn't know until years later what a piece of shit Teresa had for a mother. And how much I hated this woman.

I was still living at my parents' house and since we had an extra bedroom Teresa moved into the third bedroom. My mother was old fashion and wouldn't understand if she found out that Teresa might be sleeping with me.

After a short time in my parents' house I got an apartment. It was great. The apartment was above a garage in back of this old mans' house in Hialeah. There was a swimming pool there that nobody used but us. Teresa of course moved in with me. My mother never knew that Teresa lived with me until we were married. We lived at this garage apartment for a couple of months after the wedding and then moved to a two-bedroom duplex just south of Flagler Street and 79th avenue near Midway Mall in Miami. After approximately one year in the duplex we bought a mobile home in Homestead. The Four Seasons Mobile Home Park which was right behind Harris Field in Homestead.

Before we moved out of the duplex We were suppose to get our money back for putting in a new floor in the kitchen. When we moved into the duplex the kitchen floor was all chipped up from the people that lived there before us. It seems they worked on their motorcycle in the kitchen. I was told that if I put in a new floor I would get reimbursed the money it cost me to buy the tiles. When the landlord refused to give me back my money I took a hammer and a chisel and tore up the entire floor. I also tore up my hands pretty good but it was worth the pain. I just wish I was there when someone walked on that floor. The person who first walked on that floor would have gotten stuck to the floor. I only hoped that it was the landlord that walked on the floor. I heard a couple of years later that the owner of the duplexes, he had approximately ten units, didn't know the people renting from him didn't get their money back. I heard the owner of the duplex would give the manager the money to give to the renter and the manager would keep the money. Of course the manager got kicked out of his free duplex by the owner but it didn't help me or anyone else renting get their money back.

We moved into the mobile home park in August, 1974, and stayed there until we bought our first house on the 13th of April, 1979.

I married Mary Teresa Sullivan on June 23, 1973 at the First Unitarian church in South Miami. Teresa's first name was really Mary, but all her friends and even her relatives called her Teresa. My whole family attended our wedding. My brother was my best man, my sister, Marsha, was a brides maid, and I had my cousin, Mark, was an usher. I thought my parents never looked so good. Teresa, she never went by her first name, had her sisters attend the wedding. Her sister, Pat, was also a brides maid. Teresa's father and one of her brothers also attended the wedding. Teresa also had two other brothers that didn't make it to the wedding. Her mother refused to come to the wedding. Her brother, Greg, was in the Army stationed in Germany when we got married.

I was married to Teresa for 19 years and one day. Teresa passed away on June 24, 1992, after being in a coma for the most part of eight months. An artery had busted in her head. One of her doctors told me Teresa had to be born with a malformation of her arteries for the artery to bust the way it did. The doctor told me when a lady is on heroin and has delivered a baby, the baby would be strung out on heroin. When Teresa was born her mother was so malnutrition, from not eating properly, Teresa was born deformed. But nobody could tell that Teresa had a problem. She looked normal, but the arteries in her head didn't form properly. It was amazing that Teresa lived 40 years. Teresa knew she had a problem. She didn't know what the problem was but knew she wasn't going to live long.

We had made out wills, since Teresa worked for a lawyer it didn't cost us much. After Teresa passed away I went to our safety deposit box we had at the bank. Inside the box was a note written by Teresa. It had no date, so I don't know when Teresa wrote the note. It said "remember me with smiles and laughter as I'll remember you all. But if you remember me with tears and sadness then don't remember me at all".

Teresa did give me two children. My son was born on December 27, 1974, and my daughter was born on May 18, 1978. I now have three grandchildren. My daughter has given me a granddaughter and grandson. My son had given me a granddaughter whom he named Teresa after my wife. I just wish Teresa was still here to see her grandchildren.

Our son graduated from Homestead High School on June 17, 1992 and our anniversary was June 23. Teresa passed away the morning of June 24, 1992.

CHAPTER 6

BUILDING MY FUTURE . . .

WHEN THE MAIN POSTAL facility moved from the Biscayne Annex to the General Mail Facility the managers went from bad to worse. I'm only talking about the outgoing section of the post office. Since I didn't work in the incoming section and didn't work for any supervisor in that section I can't say how they were as far as their supervision.

Maybe because I was now married I didn't want to continue working nights is the reason I felt the supervision got worse. We had this one manager who would hide behind the flat cases and try to catch employees not working. There was another manager who did not talk to the employees, at lease as far as I could tell. If these managers had a problem with the way an employee was working they would tell the supervisor. The supervisor would then have to come tell you of a problem this manager might have.

There was one night that I was working and this manager came up behind me and just stood there. I had just gotten back from lunch and was telling this girl, who had just reported to work, what had to be done. At the time we were working the states secondary case, but had postage due mail, Canada mail that if short postage the mail had to be return to sender. The girl I was working with, Rita, started working when I returned from lunch. Since this manager was standing behind me I worked faster then I normally did and talked loud enough for him to hear me. I wanted to make sure he knew I was talking about our job. After a few minutes this manager walked away and said something to our supervisor. I saw the supervisor look over to where we were working but the supervisor didn't say anything to us. A little later I walked over to the supervisor and asked what this manager had said. I knew he said something about me. The supervisor told me the manager said I was talking too much. I was so pissed off I approached this manager and asked if he heard what I was talking about. He said he did, but I was still talking too much. I told him he didn't even know my job and that he's why the union and management would never get along.

Back in those days, this was around 1978, I didn't know many of the union stewards. The shop stewards were assigned sections. Since I worked in the outgoing sections the stewards in the city, or incoming section, were not available to me. I found out later that the real good shop stewards worked in the city section. There was Aaron Ferris, Russell Perkins, Nester Blanco and Kenny Forbes just to name a few. Judy Johnson worked in outgoing but was assigned to the letter sorting machines (LSM).

I didn't even realize I wasn't in the union when I returned from the service. I was suppose to fill out a new form to rejoin the union but nobody said anything to me. I return to the post office on April 3, 1972 and rejoined the union in July 1973.

The President of the union in Miami, American Postal Workers Union (APWU) was a Stanley Gold. Because I didn't go to the union meetings or get involved with the union I didn't know how strong the union was, or how good a president Stanley Gold was.

I knew I had to watch what I said. Anytime I had a problem I would call my brother in Tallahassee. Jeff was elected President of the Tallahassee APWU in 1975. Jeff would tell me just to watch what I say and would suggest that maybe with my mouth I should become a union steward. I figured with me working nights and starting a family, my son, Keith, was just over three at this time, and my wife was close to having our second child. Plus the fact I didn't know the president in Miami, just his name. I didn't think I would get the backing I needed, especially if I was a new shop steward.

After my daughter was born, May 18th 1978, I knew I had to get off the night shift. I wanted to spend time with the children and it was hard to do this and get the sleep I needed. There was more then a few times I almost had an accident because I was falling asleep while driving home from work. I usually got home around 4:00 A.M. and if I was lucky I got five hours of sleep.

I remember one morning, after just waking up, my wife told me not to come outside since she was cleaning the steps. If you know anything about mobile homes then you know the door is about four feet off the ground. A few minutes after telling me not to come outside my wife called me. I went to the door and proceeded to walk out. I didn't know I could fly until that moment. I went flying out the door and almost hit the mobile home next door. Of course my wife was laughing and then I started laughing. I guess I was really lucky I didn't get hurt real bad, I also stayed on my feet. With both of us laughing my wife forgot what she wanted or why she called me at that moment. Teresa figured that when she called me I would have enough sense to just look out the door to see what she wanted.

I think of myself as a nice guy. I gone out of my way, at times, to help friends and people that I know. But there was an incident that normally I wouldn't have helped, but something told me to help. I had gotten off from work at approximately 2:00 A.M. and instead of getting on the turnpike I drove down 22nd Avenue, the Biscayne Annex Post Office was right off 22nd Avenue, to U.S.1. I was driving in the right hand lane when I saw two cars stopped in the lane. There was a sports car and a van behind the car. As I slowed to pass I saw this man push this young guy. Something told me to stop. I pulled back into the right hand lane and backed up to the sports car. Of course giving the car enough room to drive off. I got out of my car and when I walked up to the two guys I said hello to the young guy. He looked to be approximately 20 years old. The other guy, a man that looked to be in his 30's, asked me if I knew this other guy. I told him that I knew he was a friend of my cousins. I asked what was the problem and the older guy said that the van was tail gating him and he stopped to talk to this guy. The man said he was a Coral Gables policeman and when he pushed back the vest he was wearing I saw a gun inside a holster.

The first thing I thought was what the hell did I get myself into. But I reacted quickly and said to the man that it's obvious he was not on duty, I could smell that he had been drinking. I told this man that maybe he should call for a policeman that was on duty. I didn't know if this man was a policeman or not, but did know he had a gun. The man said he was going to let the young guy go this time but it better not happen again. The man then got into his car and drove off. I talked to the young guy a little longer before we both went on our way. The guy thanked me for stopping and said he didn't do anything wrong. He was driving his van when the sports car in front of him stopped and he was forced to stop. The man in the sports car never showed either one of us a badge, so we didn't know, or cared, if he was a policeman or not.

There was another time when I had gotten home from work, again approximately 2:00 A.M. and heard a noise outside. When I looked outside I saw someone leaving my mobile home. We had put a screen enclosure on our patio, lucky for me the screen wasn't there when I stepped out my door when my wife called me after taking the steps away from the door, and this man was walking out the screen door. I ran after him and grabbed his shirt and asked what he was doing. He said he was looking for an address and went to the wrong mobile home. He was drunk. I let him go before I realized the screen door on our patio was locked. I went back to my mobile home and saw the handle to the screen door had been broken off and this man used the handle to cut the screen. I went inside and called the police and then went to look for this man again.

The police got there pretty quick and my wife, who had gotten up from bed, told the police I went to look for this guy. Right after finding this man again, he was still walking around the mobile home park, the police pulled up. They talked to me and then him and told me that there wasn't much they could do. The police were taking this man in and keeping him over night but that's all they were going to do. The police believed this man when he told them he went to the wrong house. I guess it didn't matter that he broke the handle to my door and cut the screen. The cost wasn't much to get the screen fix, so the police were not going to file any report. I guess you got to love the lazy Homestead police. I myself think they really suck.

There was another time when I left home to go to work at approximately 3:30 P.M, I started work at 4:30 P.M. When I left home I had a full beard. After returning back home after work, at approximately 2:00 A.M. and my wife was asleep, I decided to shave off the beard. After doing so and then getting into bed my wife went to give me a hug. What I got instead of the hug was a hand print on my back. Some people just don't have a sense of humor.

There was another time when I got home after having worked eleven hours and as I was getting ready to unlock the door I thought I heard my wife call me. I knew I must have been hearing things. There was no way she would be awake and outside at 4:30 in the morning. As I was about to open the door I heard my name being called again. I look in the direction where I heard my wife and saw Teresa and the neighbors from across the street standing in the street. I couldn't figure out what they were doing and asked why they were awake and standing in the middle of the street. They all laughed at me and pointed to the mobile home next to ours. The mobile home was all burnt out and was still smoking. There were a couple of fire trucks there that I had just walked pass and didn't even notice them. Talk about being tired. It wasn't long after that I got a bid on the day shift.

My last week on the night shift I called in sick for one day. The night before calling in sick I told my supervisor that I wasn't feeling good, but I would try to finish that night. By me calling in the next day I guess the supervisor thought I was planning something. When I called in I was told I would have to bring medical documentation. I knew I was not going to the doctors for one day out sick so I came back to work without any documentation. I was marked AWOL (absent without leave) and given a letter of warning. My grievance went to step 2 where the union had the letter of warning thrown out of my files, but the AWOL stayed. I couldn't believe the steward settled my grievance without getting the AWOL removed. I just knew I could've done a better job.

I got a bid job with the hours of 7:30 A.M. to 4:00 P.M. with Saturday and Friday as my scheduled days off. This was my first carrier scheme job and there was a lot to learn. The scheme was for zip code 33143-73-83 and 33193. Back in those days when you got a bid job you had to study on your own time and didn't get paid for it. I remember making up my own scheme cards and getting a coke case so I could study and throw the scheme cards at home.

I had heard someone from another part of the country working in the post office filed some kind of grievance so that we would get paid for all the study time while trying to pass a scheme. The national union, American Postal Workers Union, made the case a class action so that everyone around the country would be effected. At the time I really didn't think much about the grievance because I didn't think the union would win the case. The case went to arbitration and we had to sign this form to be included in the grievance.

One Friday night, being off from work, Teresa and I got a baby sitter and went to dinner and a late movie. When we got back home Teresa had a stomachache. By the time we got to bed it must have been around 2:00 A.M. I woke up just a few hours later with a stomachache. I figured it might have been food poison Since Teresa went to bed with a stomachache and then me waking up just a few hours later with the same feeling. When Teresa woke up and said she felt good I knew we didn't have food poison. As the day wore on the pain in my stomach was getting worst. Teresa wanted me to go to the hospital but I didn't want to go and be told I had gas. Finally with the pain getting worst and Teresa telling me I had a fever I decided to go to the Homestead hospital.

Before we went to the hospital my wife went to the neighbors home across the street. She had retired as a nurse back in Boston. She had been driving around to find different yard sales and had just gotten home. When she came over and pushed on my stomach I thought my insides were going to come out. I finally went to the hospital. I had x-rays taken and blood work done. Both came back negative. Then a doctor came into my room and told me, even with the negative blood work and x-rays, I had appendicitis. The Homestead hospital had two operating rooms and both were in use. I was told we couldn't wait and that it would be faster for Teresa to drive me to Coral Reef Hospital which was approximately fifteen miles away. The doctor gave me all the x-rays that were taken that day and told me the people in the office at the Coral Reef Hospital would be waiting for them. Sure, like I believe the hospital would be waiting for me. When we got to Coral Reef Hospital and went into the office I was asked if I was Warren Pearlman. I couldn't believe they were really waiting for me. I also realized then how serious the condition I was in. I was rushed into an operating and was given something to put me out. When I woke up I was told by the doctor that my appendicitis had busted and that I could've died. This was my sixth time I came close to death. I felt God was there with me and for some reason wanted me to stay around a little longer.

I was out of work for six weeks. This was at Christmas time and I thought about all the overtime I was losing. Again I felt God was with me and some luck too. The national union did win the grievance on the scheme study time and I got two checks totally over thirteen hundred dollars. The money sure came in at the right time. I was also lucky I had sick leave to cover my absence. I went back to work toward the end of January 1979.

The year 1979 started off as a pretty good year for me. In April we bought our first and only house together. Teresa and I had wanted to buy a house when our second child was born.

When we finally closed and moved into the house my daughter, Beth was eleven months old and my son, Keith was three years old. I also had my ten-year reunion from high school in August. At the reunion I met someone I knew, but not from high school. I met up with Wayne Keller who was drafted into the army the same day as I was. Wayne had married

Billie Weiss who I did go to school with. Now I know what people mean when they say it's a small world.

The year, 1979, started to get bad for us toward the last few months of the year. One night toward the end September, 1979, I watched the children while my wife went roller-skating with her friends. While skating Teresa had fallen down and when she was getting up some big boy rolled over her hand. Teresa broke her left wrist breaking a lot of bones in her hand. The doctor said she was lucky the main artery in her hand didn't break cause Teresa could've bleed to death. Teresa did all right considering. She wore a cast on her hand for some time. Teresa had broken her left wrist, and of course she was left-handed. I guess one would have to say the year that started off good, 1979, took a turn for the worst when Teresa broke her wrist.

It wasn't long after Teresa had her cast taken off her hand that she hurt her back. This was now 1980. Teresa had wakened up one morning and couldn't get out of bed. Somehow Teresa had ruptured a disk in her back. Maybe it was from when she had fallen at the skating ring, we never knew for sure. Teresa, after sometime, had to have back surgery. I felt so bad for her and I couldn't help as much as I wanted to. I still had to work and with only one paycheck coming in it was a little rough. It took some time before Teresa felt better, even after the surgery.

The second time I filed a grievance it was for my work assignment. I worked scheme 43-73-83-93 with Saturday-Friday as scheduled days off. One week I was not brought in on my days off and management brought another employee over from another section. This man worked a different scheme and did not work or even know my scheme. When I came back to work after my days off the mail was still in the case and there were a lot of errors. My grievance went to step 2 and the union President was supposed to represent me. He did show up for the step 2 hearing. I asked for sixteen hours of overtime and that if there was work on my scheme where someone had to come from outside the section that I get called in first. I knew enough that there was no way I was going to get paid the money but was hoping to keep employees not knowing my scheme from working on my scheme before using me. I remembered my brother telling me that when I filed a grievance to ask for as much as I could, and maybe I would get something out of the grievance. At the step 2 the union President of Miami hardly open his mouth. I did all the talking for my grievance. I was told that management could bring another employee to work my section as long as it was not on overtime. The president of the APWU, Miami local signed off on the grievance thus ending my grievance, but I felt like I won. The manager that heard my grievance at the step 2 told me that they would try to avoid bringing another employee into my section from another scheme. Management kept their word and didn't bring any employee over to work my scheme again while I was working there. I was brought in on overtime almost on a weekly basis. I also knew that one day in the near future I would have to become a shop steward. I felt like I represented myself at the step 2 hearing. I also knew, even with the little knowledge I had, I could do a better job at representing employees.

The little I saw of the union then I did not like. If the union president couldn't do what I did then something was very wrong. I heard there were some good stewards but there were none in my area. Most of the stewards worked the incoming, or city section, or on the letter sorting machine, but on the night shift.

I thought more about trying to become a union steward but I also saw the politics, which I didn't like. Some of the past officers and shop stewards of the union would later go into management. That was another thing, besides the politics, that I didn't like about the union. Some people using the union as a stepping stone into management. It has to make you wonder what type of union steward or officer one is or was when at first they can't get elected or reelected they become a supervisor. I decided I would wait some more time before I would try to become a shop steward. Also I would, as a shop steward, want to set an example. I know I did a good job, overall, and would hope other employees noticed this even though at time I messed around. As a shop steward I felt I couldn't do this.

Someone had brought in a rubber snake into our work area. This snake really looked real. I, along with a few other employees would hide the snake under some mail another employee was working, or we would put the snake in a sack of mail that had to be worked. It was funny watching the employees when they first saw the snake. It seemed the male employees would be more scare when they saw the snake than the female employees. There was this one time the snake was put into a sack of mail and when the employees saw the snake, after he dropped the mail he was working, started to run and his shoulder caught the side case and almost knocked the case down. This was the last time the snake was bought in since someone could've really been hurt. Of course if we got caught or someone did get hurt someone would've been disciplined. I was given the snake and the snake went home with me.

I remember two different employees that ran for union office and didn't win and then turned around and became supervisors. I don't remember either of these guys being shop stewards but they could've without me knowing. One of the guys didn't last too long as a supervisor because he was accused of sexual harassment on more then one occasion. Instead of issuing some form of discipline management only demoted him back to the clerk craft. The other guy ran for union president against Stanley Gold and when he lost went into management. This man was a good talker, a real kiss ass and moved up real quick into management. I thought he might have been a decent president of the union had he been elected. I was totally wrong when I saw he only wanted a title. This man later became postmaster of Royal Oak, Michigan where there was a shooting inside the post office.

Once I got on the day shift I moved around by bidding on different jobs. I went from the 43-73-83-93 scheme to work on the 26-72-82 scheme to work in the foreign section. The last bid job I had at the General Mail Facility was back in outgoing where I worked on the letter cases. It was there when I met Gil Santana who was the Clerk Craft President of the union.

There were three full time union officers and a craft president over each craft. There were four crafts, Clerk Craft, Matenance Craft, Motor Vehicle Craft and Special Delivery Craft. There was also an Editor, Recording Secretary, a Business Agent from the different cities and a Trustee, that made up the Executive Board of the Miami Local of the American Postal Workers Union.

Both my brother and my wife encouraged me to become a union steward. When I got a bid to a station I talked to Gil Santana and asked how I could become a shop steward. I was told that once I qualified on my bid job I would be named a shop steward. After I qualified on the scheme I had to pass the window exam so I could work as a window clerk at the station and I did pass the window exam.

I was then given some union training from Gil Santana so I could become a shop steward. I didn't get much training; I believe the training I received that day was no more then four hours. I was told my best teacher would be me actually writing grievances. I would learn by my mistakes.

On April 3rd 1982 I went to the Snapper Creek Post Office to work. My hours were 7:30 A.M. to 4:00 P.M. and Sunday-Friday as scheduled days off. I also became the union steward at Snapper Creek Post Office for the American Postal Workers Union in Miami, Florida. I was proud to become a steward but realized right away the job was not as easy as I first thought and that there was a lot of work to do and a lot to learn. I liked working at the station away from the main facility. It took the employees at the Snapper Creek Post Office a little time to get use to me since they never had a union steward working at their station prior to me.

Working at Snapper Creek Post Office was like working for a totally different company compared to the General Mail Facility. The one thing I knew for sure was that I didn't want to go back to work at the General Mail Facility. I use to call the General Mail facility the crazy house and would call the post office the fantasy factory. I would tell people the post office was a factory and that you would fantasize about leaving but never would. I remember hearing someone say you don't have to be crazy to work for the post office, but it dam sure helps. I like the saying so much I continued to say it a lot. It doesn't take anyone long to know there's a lot of different, I don't want to say crazy, people working in the post office. Postal employees working in Miami are from everywhere.

I was one of the junior employees working in the clerk craft at the Snapper Creek Post Office. After I received my bid at the Snapper Creek Post Office other bids were posted and some younger employees working in the clerk craft came to work at Snapper Creek. There were a lot of carriers that were considered junior employees working already at Snapper Creek.

Shortly after I was awarded my bid management brought a couple of carriers to Snapper Creek and put them into the clerk craft. The carriers were made clerks because of injury and illness. This is when I met Rick Pujol and we became good friends. Rick was given the scheme 73-83-93 and I had scheme 76-86-96. The other carrier was Walter Houston and because of his injury he was made a modified general clerk. Walter had limitations on lifting and standing but there was enough light work for him at Snapper Creek. Rick didn't have any limitations but because of an illness he couldn't continue as a letter carrier.

My first day at Snapper Creek started normal enough. I started work as scheduled at 7:30 A.M. At Snapper Creek Post Office. There were of course supervisors. There was also a superintendent and a manager. The manager that was suppose to be at Snapper Creek was detailed to another location so there was an acting manager. The superintendent at the Snapper Creek Post Office was the one whom seemed to run the post office. The superintendent was the one I went to for leave or for a grievance or for any problems.

My second day at Snapper Creek I was called into the office by the superintendent and told that I was needed to report at 5:30 A.M. and that the window portion of my bid was going to be taken off. I sort of had a choice to except or reject these changes. The contract, local agreement, that the union and management went by said that management had the right to change an employees bid job up to one hour. The contract also said that if management wanted to change an employees bid job for more then one hour up to four hours the employee had the right to except or reject that change. The only problem is that if the employee rejected the change of more then one-hour management had the right to abolish the bid job and repost the job the way they wanted it.

With me being a shop steward I had what was called super seniority. What that meant was if management abolished my bid job I still could remain at Snapper Creek Post Office as an unassigned clerk, but with the time change management wanted. I was happy management was changing my bid job, but didn't want them to know I was happy with the change. Sometimes it was better to let management think you are not happy. I told the superintendent I didn't want the change but felt I had no choice so I would except the new starting time. My starting time was then changed from 7:30 A. M. to 5:30 A.M. My new hours were 5:30 A.M.-2:00 P.M. and the window part of the bid was taken off. It was amazing to me that management would send me for window training and then immediately take it off of the bid.

Management might have made a mistake by changing my bid to earlier hours. When I came in the next day at 5:30 A. M. a lot of the carriers came in at the same time and started to spread the mail to the carrier cases. This is the clerks' job and I was surprised that none of the clerks said anything to me, knowing I was the union steward. I found out the clerks' didn't want to spread the mail so there were no complaints or grievances. I don't know which was worst, getting management upset with me or the clerks' upset with me. Most of the letter carriers that came in early were great because most of them didn't want to come in to do the clerks' job anyway, even if it was for overtime. I was filing grievances approximately every ten days and sending the grievances to the next step. In the grievances I was asking for all the clerks that were on the overtime list to be paid for all the time the letter carriers worked. It took awhile before management finally stopped bringing the letter carriers in to spread the mail. I sort of won, I didn't get money for any clerk and I upset some of the old timers but the carriers quit doing the clerks' job. I also gain a lot of experience from all the grievances I wrote. What upset me later was to hear how the union in Indianapolis, Indiana won a big grievance and paid thousands of dollars because letter carriers were spreading the mail to the carrier cases. The union officers of my local had dropped all the grievances I had written. It was amazing to me that the union, because they didn't want to upset some clerks, would just give our jobs away.

My brother would always tell me to watch my mouth. It was different in Tallahassee because the local there was a lot smaller then in Miami. Jeff would always say to document the grievances as best you can and then present your documents as your argument. There were union officers and stewards that would argue all the time and most of the time this does not help. There's a saying; "you have to know when to jump in management's shit and when to back off". Jeff was the union president in Tallahassee for approximately seven years before I became a shop steward so I guess he knew what he was talking about. I also heard from the union officers at the regional level that Jeff did a real good job. I made it a point that when I was going to write a grievance I would put as much documentation as I could in the file. Jeff would always tell me to keep my contract with me all the time while writing grievances. He would tell me to write the articles of the contract I was using. This way if the grievances I filed were going to be loss or dropped it wouldn't be because I didn't cite the proper articles of the contract or document the case.

I felt the cases I was sending to the next step were grievances that could've been won if not at step 2 then at the region, which was the step 3 of the grievance procedure, or in arbitration.

After step 1 of the grievance procedure the grievance belongs to the union. The officers of the union that presented the grievances I sent to step 2 on the crossing crafts were the Clerk Craft President and a union steward who was to become the first Executive Vice-President. These grievances were either dropped or settled with language that meant nothing. The union officers that dropped the grievances that I appealed were doing so because of laziness. Some of the employees could've been paid some extra money because of the letter carriers performing clerk work. I believe the only way to get through to management, sometimes, is through the pocket. This means getting employees paid for managements not abiding by the contract.

I knew at this time, for sure, there had to be some changes within the union. A union steward or officer does not have to be radical but has to know what issues are more important. Keeping the employees jobs, and not give our work away I think is very important.

The grievances I filed for crossing crafts, carriers spreading the mail to the letter carrier cases, didn't get anyone money but management quit using the carriers to spread the mail. I guess I accomplished what I was trying to do and that was to save the clerk jobs. Of course when the clerks had to work a little more some were not happy with me, but that's the way it is. I had to, at a later date, file grievances at other stations to get the clerks to do their job of spreading the mail. I found out a couple of years later that there were some big cases won for crossing crafts where the employees received a lot of back pay, but not in the Miami Area Local.

CHAPTER 7

MERGERS &
COLLECTIVE BARGAINING

ON JULY 1ST 1971 five postal unions joined together to form the American Postal Workers union (APWU). This merger formed the largest union of postal employees in the world.

The merging unions, which formed the American Postal Workers Union, were the United Federation of Postal Clerks, the National Postal Union, which represented those employees who worked the window and sorted and processed the mail. These were the two largest of the unions that had merged. There was also the National Association of Post Office and General Service Maintenance Employees, the National Federation of Motor Vehicle Employees and the National Association of Special Delivery Messengers.

Early unions had no bargaining rights. The unions existed only as lobbying organizations that would have no say about working conditions. Wage increases depended on congress. From 1967-1969 postal wages were not increased at all, although congress did raise its own pay 41% during that time. In March 1970 full-time employees of the post office earned about $6,200.00 to start. Workers with twenty-one years averaged only $8,440.00.

On March 18th 1970 beginning in New York thousands of postal workers walked off the job. The strike spread quickly across the country, finally involving more than 200,000 workers in thirty major cities. Miami was not one of the cities. I had just finished my ninety days in the post office so maybe it was a good thing the postal workers in Miami didn't walk off the job. The strike did not last too long. Its impact was to fundamentally change labor-management relations in a major breakthrough for postal unions.

The Postal Reorganization act of 1970 was adopted establishing the United States Postal Service as an independent government agency. For the first time postal unions had the right to negotiate on all matters concerning wages, fringe benefits, cost-of-living adjustments and other financial gains. Salaries and benefits were to compare with private industry and the time to reach the top grade pay was to be reduced from twenty-one years to eight years. Additionally, postal management was required to bargain in good faith and to make a genuine effort to reach an agreement. Unresolved matters were to be submitted to final and binding arbitration. Finally postal workers had won most of the rights enjoyed by workers in private industry since the adoption of the National Labor Relations Act in 1935. The one glaring omission was the right for postal workers to strike. Collective bargaining had now replaced collective begging.

The strike and the merging of the unions helped create collective bargaining. Strengthened by the unity and solidarity of the different crafts it represents, the American Postal Workers Union has won through negotiated national agreements improved wages and working conditions for all postal workers. In the first contract as the American Postal Workers Union a starting postal workers salary was raised to $8,488.00.

By July, 1971 a level 5 clerk top step was making $9,657.00 a year. This was a two year contract. In 1973, when a new contract was negotiated the level 5 clerk at the top step was making $10,907.00. By 1975, the next contract, a three year contact, the level 5 clerk, top step, was making $13,483.00. In 1978 the APWU had to take the contract to arbitration. The result was that now the level 5 clerk, at the top step was making $16,501.00. In 1981 a level 5 top step clerk was now making $21,630.00 per year. In 1984, again, the APWU had to take the contract to arbitration. This was also a three year contract and the result was that now a level 5 clerk at the top step was making $24,173.00. The contract negotiated in 1987 jumped the pay for the level 5 top step clerk to $27,401.00. In 1990 the level 5 top step clerk was making $31,766.00 per year. This contract, again, had to be taken to a arbitration. This was a four year contract. Again, in 1994 the contract had to be taken to arbitration and again this was a four year contract. The level 5 clerk at the top step was now making $35,604.00. In 1998 a level 5 top step clerk was making $37,831.00. By 2006, the last contract the APWU received while I was still working, the level 5 top step clerk was making $47,996.00. Of course the pay that I mentioned above is the base salary which does not include overtime pay, or pay that a clerk might have received in a grievance settlement. My last four years working for the United States Postal Service I worked a lot of overtime and was paid a lot in grievance settlements. In 2004 I made $71,298.13. In 2005 I made $70,939.89 and in 2006, my last full year working for the United States Postal Service I made $97,102.17. I retired on June 2, 2007, but up to that date I made $50,987.80. Not bad for someone with just a high school education.

The last few contracts have been tough trying to get a raise out of the Postal service but overall since the Postal Reorganization Act the unions have done pretty good in getting the employees salary up to where it now is. A postal worker now makes a good salary.

Four months before the Postal Reorganization Act was signed into law, the United States Post Office Department Management and postal unions announced a joint agreement on a reorganization plan. When the Postal Reorganization Act became law on August 12th 1970 it created the United States Postal Service (USPS), which on January 20th 1971 participated in the first collective bargaining session with seven postal unions, including the unions that were soon to merge into the American Postal Workers Union. Six months later, on July 20th 1971, the new United States Postal Service and the unions signed a 2-year contract.

The only city that the Miami local represented prior to 1981 was Miami. After the local union elections of 1981 that soon all changed. The first city to merge with Miami was Opa Locka-Carol City. The main union representative in Opa Locka-Carol City was Donald Dowd. With the merger Donald was put on the Miami Local executive board as the Business Agent for Opa Locka-Carol City.

After Miami merged with Opa Locka-Carol City Miami then merged with Homestead. The former president of Homestead was then put on the Miami executive board as the Business Agent for Homestead. When he stepped down as Business Agent of Homestead Jordan Small replaced him as the business agent. Jordan Small, after a few years, transferred out west and later became a supervisor. Years later he came back to south Florida and was the District Manager that covers from Key West to Pompano Beach for a short time.

Sometime after the 1986 state convention for the American Postal Workers Union of Florida Hialeah merged with Miami. Donna Rivera-Harris had been President of the Hialeah Local and now was placed on the Miami executive board as the Business Agent for Hialeah. Donna would later run for the position of Secretary/Treasurer of Miami, and then President of the Miami Area Local, as it was now called.

After Hialeah merged with Miami the next city to merge with the Miami Area Local was Boca Raton. Boca Raton asked to meet with Miami to talk about merging. There was a meeting set up and different locals were invited. Besides Miami there was the West Palm Beach Area Local and the Hollywood Local. For some reason Fort Lauderdale Area Local did not come to the meeting. After some discussions with locals present the membership of the Boca Raton Local had to vote and they decided to merge with Miami. The former president of Boca Raton then was added to the executive board as the Business Agent.

The Postal Service sometime after 1989 built a new processing plant in Pembroke Pines. The processing plant was called the South Florida Mail Processing Facility. The employees that made up the South Florida mail facility came from Miami, Fort Lauderdale, Hollywood, Pompano Beach, Hialeah, Homestead and new hires. Since Hialeah and Homestead were part of the Miami Area Local and Hollywood and Pompano Beach were part of the Fort Lauderdale Local the employees from the South Florida Mail Processing Facility were given an opportunity to vote. Hollywood had been a local by itself but later merged with Fort Lauderdale.

The employees of the South Florida Mail Processing Facility had to decide whether to form their own local, Merge with Miami, or merge with Fort Lauderdale. While the vote was pending both the president of the Miami Area Local, Judy Johnson, and the president of the Fort Lauderdale Area Local, Bill Sullivan, were authorized to enter the facility for representation purposes. When the employees of the South Florida Mail Processing Facility voted they decided to join the Miami Area Local. This was not a merger, only because there was no union at the South Florida Facility prior to this vote. Still the Miami Area Local named a Business Agent for the South Florida Mail Processing Facility and that Business Agent became a member of the executive board.

Because of political differences the Business Agent of Opa Locka-Carol City, Donald Dowd made a motion to let Opa Locka go on its own and be its own local. This was brought before the Miami Area Local executive board and when the executive board honored Donald Dowd wishes he was surprised to say the lease. I believe he wanted Miami to pay him more money and didn't expect Miami to agree with him.

None the less Opa Locka became a local union, by itself, for a short time and then later merged with the Fort Lauderdale Area Local.

The Postal Service made Miami Beach an associate office with it's own Postmaster which resulted in the Miami Area Local appointing a Business Agent for a short time. The Business Agent for Miami Beach was Bernard Kearse. Later the local union decided that there wasn't a need for a Business Agent for Miami Beach. Because Miami Beach is an associate office employees there cannot bid back to Miami. The Miami Beach offices consist of five post offices.

The Postal Service has since opened a Priority Mail Processing Facility in Miami that is part of the Miami Area Local. The Miami Area Local is still representing employees in Homestead, Hialeah, Boca Raton, the South Florida Mail Processing Facility and of course Miami. The Miami Area Local still has a membership close to three thousand, which is the largest in the state.

CHAPTER 8

UNION ELECTIONS

AFTER THE MERGING OF the five unions to form the American Postal Workers union the first president, Stu Filbey, was appointed in 1971. Stu Filbey was later elected by the general membership of the American Postal Workers Union in June 1972. He was reelected in 1974 and 1976. Stu Filbey died in office in 1977.

After Stu Filbey had died in office the national executive board of the American Postal Workers Union elected Emmett Andrews as his replacement for the position of President on May 23rd 1977. Emmett Andrews was reelected in October 1978.

At the national convention for the American Postal Workers Union in August 1980 the membership voted to extend the term of office for the national executive board from two years to three years. Two months later Moe Biller defeated Emmett Andrews as the President of the American Postal Workers Union. Moe Biller was reelected as President in 1983, 1986, 1989, 1992, 1995 and 1998. Moe Biller retired after finishing his term at the end of 2000. Moe Biller later died on September 5th 2003.

Since I only became a union steward in April 1982 Moe Biller was the first National Union President I met. Along with Moe Biller being the union President the Executive Vice-President was William Burrus and Doug Holbrook was the Secretary/Treasurer and Kenny Wilson was the Clerk Craft Director.

This was the main union Officers in Washington D.C. when I became a shop steward. If I had to call Washington D.C. it was always to Kenny Wilson. When Kenny Wilson retired he was replaced by Robert Tunstall. But nobody could replace Kenny Wilson.

Not only was Kenny Wilson the National Clerk Craft Director, he was also the one who started the Turtle Club. When union stewards and officers went to a national convention Kenny always had a hospitality room after each day of the convention. He would then recruit members for the turtle club. To join the turtle club you would be asked a few different riddles and had to try to solve them. Of course this was after having a few drinks. Once you tried to solve the riddles, and most people gave the wrong answer, you became a member of the turtle club. Members were given a card with the riddles and were told to try to subscribe new members. The rules, or what was written on the card, were as follows; As a member in good standing you can subscribe new turtles as follows; 1). We assume all prospective turtles own a jack ass. On this assumption is the reason for the password. The password must be given if you are ever asked by a fellow member. "Are you a turtle?" You must then reply "you bet your sweet ass I am." If you do not give the password in full because of embarrassment or some other reason you forfeit a beverage of his or her choice. So it was wise to always remember the password. 2). To become an official turtle you must first solve the following riddles: 1. What is it a man can do standing up, a women can do sitting down and a dog can do on three legs? (answer: shake hands). 2. What is it a cow has four of and a women has only two? (answer: legs). 3. What is a four letter word ending in k that means the same as intercourse? (answer: talk). 4. What is it on a man that is round, hard, and sticks so far out of his pajamas you can hang a hat on it? (answer: his head). The card ended by saying: THE REAL PURPOSE OF EVERY TURTLE IS TO STOP THE USE OF OBSCENE LANGUAGE. Of course when trying to solve the riddles nobody got the right answer and you can imagine most of the answers.

This was Kenny Wilson the turtle club and a great union officer. He retired and lives in North Carolina.

When Doug Holbrook retired Robert Tunstall became the National Secretary/Treasurer and Cliff Guffey became the Clerk Craft Director. After Robert Tunstall retired Terry Stapleton was voted in by the National Executive Board.

William Burrus was elected President in 2001, after holding the position of Executive Vice-President from 1981. William Burrus has since been reelected President of the American Postal Workers Union in 2004. Along with William Burrus as National President Cliff Guffey has been voted in as the National Executive Vice-President in the 2001 and 2004 elections, and Terry Stapleton as the National Secretary/Treasurer. These officers were voted in by the membership in the 2004 election. Also James McCarthy has been voted in by the membership as the National Clerk

Craft Director in the 2001 and 2004 elections. These were the national officers that were elected and who I had dealings with while I was a shop steward and local officer.

The national convention was held every other year in August. As a union officer I was able to go the Las Vegas a few different times for the national convention. Also San Francisco, Chicago and Anaheim, California.

STATE ELECTIONS

After being voted in as the Clerk Craft President by the executive board of the Miami Area Local at the end of 1983 I went to my first state convention in 1984. Being on the executive board of the Miami area local I was an automatic delegate to the state convention and the national convention. The conventions were a new experience for me, especially the national conventions. The state convention starts on a Thursday and ends on Saturday. There was a banquet on Friday night where the newly elected officers were sworn into office. The state convention is held every other year, usually in May.

The Florida APWU had nine officers on the executive board when I first became a shop steward. Since the Special Delivery craft has been merged into the clerk craft the Special Delivery position has been done away with. Now there is the President, Secretary/Treasurer, Editor, Education Director, Legislative Director and a director of each craft, Clerk Craft, Maintenance and Motor Vehicle.

The state elections are a lot different then the local elections and the national elections. In both the local and national elections the ballots are mailed out to each members address for them to vote. There's also weeks of campaigning by the candidates running for office. In the state elections the voting is done at the state convention. The only people voting are the delegates at the convention. The nominations for office is done on Thursday and carried over until Friday morning. The voting is then done Friday after the closing of the nominations and the results of the election are announced Friday evening at the convention banquet.

I ran for a state office three times. I ran for the State Clerk Craft Director position in 1998 and 2000. I also ran for the State Education Director position in 2002. I was elected as the State Clerk Craft Director in 2000. Also my brother was reelected as the state Secretary/Treasurer. This was the first time that two brothers from different locals were elected to a state position.

My brother, Jeff, has been elected to a state position since 1986. Jeff was first elected to the position of State Education Director in 1986. Jeff has been elected to the position of State Secretary/Treasurer at every state convention since 1988.

In 2000, the same year I was elected to the position of State Clerk Craft Director, Martha Shunn-King, the President of the Sarasota local became the first women ever to be elected to the Florida American Postal Workers Union as the President. Martha has since been reelected as the Florida State President in 2002, 2004 and 2006.

My brother, Jeff, keeps getting elected to the position of Secretary/Treasurer of Florida and had no challenge from anyone until the 2006 state convention. At the 2006 convention the Secretary/Treasurer from the Lakeland Area Local ran against Jeff.

LOCAL ELECTIONS

The first union election for the Miami Area Local I paid much attention to was in 1981. I know there was Stanley Gold as president prior to the 1981 elections. There was also a John Wright as the Miami Local president. I'm not sure what years John Wright was president but know he defeated Stanley Gold and then Stanley was reelected again by defeating John Wright. Stanley Gold was the first President of the Miami Local.

In the 1981 election for the Miami Local there were three or four different tickets. To me this meant members were not happy with the job the president was doing. Stanley Gold had a ticket, and John Wright had a ticket and Judy Johnson had a ticket.

There were two full time union positions in 1981, General President and Secretary/ Treasurer. There were also the craft presidents, Clerk Craft, Motor Vehicle, Maintenance Craft and Special Delivery Craft. There was also a position for the Editor and Recording Secretary. These are the union offices that made up the executive board of the union for the Miami Local.

There were also officers for the One Seven Two Holding Corporation. The One Seven Two Holding Corporation was the ones that own the union parking lot that was across from the Biscayne Annex where I first started working. When the Biscayne Annex was closed the parking lot was sold. Anyway there was a set of officers that were different then that of the Miami Local.

When the election results came out Judy Johnson was the first female to be elected President of the Miami Local. Gil Santana had run for the Secretary/Treasurer position on Judy's ticket and Nester Blanco ran for the Clerk Craft President position, but both Gil Santana and Nester Blanco had loss. Marty Bomse was elected to the Secretary/Treasurer position and Cleveland Gator was elected to the Clerk Craft President position.

The newly elected officers took office on April 1st 1981. Why someone would set that date is beyond me. Maybe there's a message that I don't know about. To take a position as union officers on April fools day has to say something.

After Judy Johnson was elected there were a lot of changes within the union. There were by-law changes to the One Seven Two Holding Corporation so when the election for officers was held in June 1981 the officers of the union also became officers of the One Seven Two Holding Corporation. Also the union added a third full time officer and the position of Executive Vice-President was created. The union executive board voted Nester Blanco in as the first Executive Vice-President of the Miami Local.

When it was time for the 1983 union elections Judy Johnson decided to run on her own for reelection. The people that ran with her in the 1981 election decided to run against Judy. Gil Santana was running for General President, Nester Blanco was running for Executive Vice-President. Richard Wolf ran for the position of the Secretary/Treasurer on the same ticket as Gil and Nester. Dennis Aquila was also running for Secretary/ Treasurer and his wife Theresa was running for the Clerk Craft President position. Some of the people that lose the election in 1981 went into management. Stanley Gold took a job as an EEO (equal employment opportunity) investigator, which is a higher level position. Don Kimball who had previously been the Clerk Craft President prior to the 1981 election became a supervisor.

Lenny Wheeler, who worked full time for the union after getting fired from the post office, wanted me to run for the Clerk Craft President position. Since I only became a shop steward in April I told him I felt I needed more then nine months as a shop steward before I ran for office.

The nomination meeting for union elections in Miami was in February and the ballots were sent out right after getting them printed up. The results of the election were posted at the March meeting and the newly elected officers took office on April 1st. When the election results for the 1983 election were announced Judy Johnson was reelected General President. Nester Blanco was elected Executive Vice-President, Dennis Aquila was elected Secretary/Treasurer and Theresa Aquila was elected Clerk Craft President. These were the top four positions of the union in Miami.

Before the end of 1983 Theresa Aquila quit as the Clerk Craft President and the Executive board of the union had to vote on a replacement and I was voted in.

When Theresa Aquila quit she left a lot of grievances that had to be appealed to step 3. When my brother came down to Miami on leave, between Christmas and New Years, Jeff helped me and with the help of Judy Johnson we appealed the cases to the region. Talk about a crash course. I learn real fast, I had no choice, how to appeal the cases, how to make additions to the cases and in some cases write up corrections to some cases.

The good thing about the grievance procedural is the union gets last bite of the apple. What this means is if a case is not citing the right articles of the contract, or leaves out important information or even asked for the wrong remedy the union has ten days after the step 2 decision to write up additions and corrections. I like to think this crash course made me a better union officer. I had to immediately have step 2 hearings scheduled and had more then enough step 3's to appeal.

As the newly elected Clerk Craft President I was able to hire and fire shop stewards with the General Presidents agreement. What this means is both the craft president and the general president had to agree on the hiring or the firing of a shop steward.

First I looked through grievances from most of the shop stewards to see what they were doing or not doing. I ended up firing three shop stewards but brought one back after talking to her. It seems some of the stewards were told that they didn't have to send in their step 1 settlements. The shop steward I rehired was Carmen Rivera as she kept the settlements she had in a file instead of sending them to the union office. I also hired Walter Houston to replace me at Snapper Creek. Walter stayed as a shop steward for only a few months and quit. I then hired Rick Pujol who turned out to be one of the best shop stewards. Rick was very dependable and very non-political.

In 1984 I went to my first state convention for the union. The convention was in Daytona Beach, Florida. I was able to see my brother, who came to the convention from Tallahassee and enjoyed meeting other union stewards from around the state. After this state convention I went to every state convention the whole time I stayed as a union steward and officer. The state convention was held in a different city in Florida every other year.

When the 1986 elections for Miami came Judy Johnson again put together a ticket with Betty Tsang running for Executive Vice-President, Jim Davis running for Secretary/Treasurer, I was running for my first election as the Clerk Craft President on the same ticket. Judy and her whole ticket won the election except for me. I lost by approximately thirty votes to Bill Allen. I filed an appeal to the elections mainly because Bill Allen had applied for a management position. The bylaws of the union said that if someone had held a supervisor position or had applied for a management position they were ineligible to run for a union office. The union agreed with me and put me into the position as the Clerk Craft President.

Bill Allen then appealed to the labor board that he was removed from his position as the Clerk Craft President and somehow won his appeal. Bill was then given the position title but I continued doing the job. I was given the title of Chief Shop Steward. This continued for the term of office until the 1989 elections. During this same time period I was appointed the Homestead Business Agent. I am the only person in the Miami Area Local to hold two positions on the executive board of the union in Miami at the same time.

At the state convention in 1986 my brother, Jeff, was elected to the position of state Education Director. Jeff was the President of the Tallahassee local since being elected in 1975 but now was also a state officer. It was my brothers' job with the state to set up the schools and the classes to be held.

At the state convention in 1988 my brother ran for and was elected to the position of State Secretary/Treasurer. Betty Tsang had run for the position of state Editor and loss to the person who had been editor for a long time, Jim Sutton. Judy Johnson was more upset that Betty didn't win then Betty was. Judy felt because Miami was the largest local of the state then Miami should have someone in a state position.

The state unions had at lease two classes a year at different cities around the state teaching about the union. Different classes for new shop stewards, advance shop steward training, window training, how to defend against discipline etc. There was also training for the other crafts, Maintenance, Motor Vehicle and Special Delivery. Because Miami did our own training Miami never sent anyone to these classes. I use to go on my own, mainly to see my brother, but also to learn more. I wanted to learn as much as I could. Because Miami didn't go to these classes most of our stewards and officers from Miami were not known around the state. Judy was about the only one anyone knew and that was because she went to the national president's conferences that were held around the country and sometimes went to the president's conference for the state of Florida. This was held the day before the state school would start.

Before the 1988 state convention was over the Miami Area local walked out of the convention and dropped out of the state union. I was upset that we walked out and then was further upset that we dropped out of the state. Judy Johnson felt Miami didn't get the respect Miami deserved being the largest local from the state but I didn't think that had anything to do with Betty Tsang not getting elected. Also Jim Sutton had been the State Editor and did a good job. As it turned out Betty Tsang quit as the Miami Area Local Executive Vice-President before finishing her term.

I continued going to the state schools, again to learn and see my brother. I took some abuse from just a few people around the state but as I tried to explain, it wasn't my fault and that I didn't agree with Miami dropping out of the state. I learned a lot from these state schools and collected a lot of documentation for our stewards in Miami. I paid my own way to go to these schools, as it wasn't too expensive. I was able to stay in my brothers' room so only had to worry about transportation and eating. The Miami Area Local rejoined the state union years later.

As for Betty Tsang quitting as the Executive Vice-President she said it was because she needed to spend more time with her children. As it turned out it was good that Betty Tsang didn't get elected to the State Editor position. If she didn't have time for the Executive Vice-President job in Miami how was she going to do the job as an editor for the state? Betty Tsang recommended Manny Muro as her replacement to the executive board. Manny was a motor vehicle driver and hadn't been in the post office very long. Because Betty Tsang recommended Manny Muro the executive board voted Manny in as the Executive Vice-President.

In 1989 I ran for the position of Executive Vice-President of the Miami Area Local on Judy Johnson's ticket and was elected. This was the first time I was elected by the membership of the Miami area Local and it felt good. Judy Johnson also won for her fourth term as the General President of the Miami Area Local. Also Donna Rivera-Harris was elected as the Secretary/Treasurer. Donna had been the President of the Hialeah Local before Hialeah merged with the Miami Area Local. Betty Tsang had come back and won the election as the Clerk Craft President. Manny Muro had run for Executive Vice-President against me but lost. At this time the Miami Area Local still was not part of the State union after dropping out, but I was working to get Miami back in. Unfortunately it would take me approximately six more years before Miami rejoined the state union.

Before the end of my term as the Executive Vice-President I could see why Betty Tsang had quit the position. To do the job the way it should be done you have to work long hours and a lot of time away from the family. There were some good benefits being an officer but it still took away from your home life. As the Executive Vice-President the base pay was higher even though for most of the time I didn't get overtime pay. It didn't matter that some days I worked ten hours or more. One of the best benefits of being a union officer was that both your retirement and social security was being taken out of your pay. Thanks to the union I was able to build more then forty quarters toward social security. This way when I do retire I will be able to collect my pension and also some social security when I get old enough.

In the years from me being the Clerk Craft President and as the Executive Vice-President I was able to go to the state conventions in different cities in Florida and was able to take my wife, Teresa, and the kids with me most of the time. I was able to go to the national conventions and take Teresa with me most of the time. Teresa got upset with me because I didn't take her to San Francisco, California. I didn't think I could afford the money to take Teresa at that time. I made it up to Teresa later by taking her to Chicago and then to Los Vegas for the national conventions. For the Florida state conventions Teresa went with me to Panama City Beach, Daytona Beach, Saint Petersburg and Tampa just to name a few of the cities in Florida where the conventions were held.

After holding the position of the Executive Vice-President of the Miami Area Local for just over two years I told Judy Johnson I was not going to run again for election. My wife hated that I worked so much and didn't like the union. She hated the politics. I got my wife to agree with me not quitting in the middle of the term. I was going to finish my term of office and not quit like others did. My term was to end on March 31st 1992. I still wonder if I made a mistake by not quitting before my term ended.

On October 26th 1991 an artery busted in my wives head and she went into a coma. Teresa was taken to the Homestead hospital, them to South Miami hospital and then to Mount Sinai hospital. Teresa came out of the coma before Christmas but had to have an operation. When Teresa came out of the coma she talked as if she was in the past. I'm not really sure she knew what year we were in. Teresa had asked about her father and her brother, Tim. Both had previously passed away. Teresa had asked me when my daughter, Beth, went home. I think Teresa thought she just had our baby. The doctors wanted to wait for the operation so Teresa could get stronger. The doctors also gave me a lot of false hope. I was told that maybe, if Teresa kept getting stronger, she would be able to come home for Christmas. I guess all I heard was that Teresa might be able to come home. Before the operation Teresa slipped back into a coma. The doctors then felt they could wait no longer and had to operate. Before the operation the doctors told me Teresa would either get better, stay in the coma or could possibly die. I had to sign paper releasing the doctors in case something didn't go right. I still wonder if the doctors waited too long to operate. After the operation, which was the beginning of January 1992, Teresa stayed in the coma and never came out.

After the operation Teresa was taken from Mount Sinai hospital to Health South Rehabilitation Center and then was put in a nursing home where the upstairs was a Hospice center.

After the hospice doctors took over I went to our safe deposit box, where we kept our wills, and found a hand written note that Teresa had written before the artery had busted in her head. I had no idea when Teresa had written this note but it said "remember me with smiles and laughter, as I'll remember you all. But if you remember me with tears and sadness, then don't remember me at all". Somehow, maybe Teresa knew something was going to happen.

Teresa passed away on June 24th 1992. The doctor who wrote the death certificate said it was a malformation of the arteries. The doctor told me that the only way the arteries in her head didn't form properly was because Teresa had to be born with this condition. Teresa passed away seven days after my son, Keith, graduated from high school and one day after our wedding anniversary. We were married for nineteen years and one day. Keith was seventeen and Beth was fourteen. I was lost for some time. I was lucky I had my children. I even thought about ending my own life. I remember driving and thinking what would happen if I hit the wall of the expressway going about 100 miles per hour? Then lucky for me I'd wake up and think about my children.

When the nomination meeting came for the 1992 elections, prior to Teresa passing away, I once again ran for the Executive Vice-President position. At this time Teresa had already been in the hospital for five months. It was a rough decision for me at this time but felt it was a right decision for me. I was reelected for my second term. Judy Johnson was reelected for her fifth term and Donna Rivera-Harris was reelected for the Secretary/Treasurer position. Faye Dowd, who in past elections ran against me and had previously spoke out against Judy, was elected as the Clerk Craft President on the ticket of Judy Johnson. Betty Tsang who had run on the same ticket with Judy in the past had run against Judy for the General President position.

Before the election Betty Tsang wanted the union to protest the Gulf War. Since we felt the union could not speak in favor or against the war we did not go in protest against the war. Because of this Betty decided to go against Judy and ran for president. Betty asked me what I thought of the Gulf war before the United States went to war and I said I hope we do not go over there. But I also said if we do go I hope we go in and kick ass and get out real soon. I didn't want another Viet Nam. Betty didn't like what I said and said I was a war Mongol.

Before the 1992 term of office ended Judy Johnson had lost both of her parents. Before the election in 1995 Judy decided not to run for reelection. Donna Rivera-Harris put together a ticket with her running for president, Tom O'connor running for Executive Vive-President and Juan Albo running for Secretary/Treasurer. Faye Dowd also ran for president and put together a ticket. I should've put together a ticket but didn't and made a further mistake by running for the Clerk Craft President position. Looking back I should've ran for the Executive Vice-President position again or maybe president and should've put together a ticket. I lost the election to Sheldon Mcknight. To make matters worst I was fired as a shop steward. I had previously gotten a bid job at the Sunset Post Office so in June 1995 I went back to work full time in the post office after six years being in a full time union position.

I was asked to be a shop steward again to cover the Sunset Post office where I worked and also Olympia Heights Post Office. I did this for a short time before I was fired again as a shop steward. I guess the President, Donna Rivera Harris didn't like the way I dealt with management, but that's the way it was. The only good thing this set of new officers did was have Miami rejoined the state union. Of course they had a lot of pressure put on them to rejoin but I guess they had the final say.

I ran for the position of Clerk Craft Director for the Florida APWU in 1998 at the state convention even though I was not holding a union position for the Miami Area Local. I didn't win the election and I'm not sure if the Miami Area Local even supported me, but I tried.

When the 1998 elections were to be held, because of political charges, they were put off until almost the end of the summer of 1998. The election was suppose to be in March with the newly elected officers to take office on April 1st 1998. Gil Santana was elected General President. I ran on his ticket and was elected again to the position of Executive Vice-President and Edmund Campbell was elected Secretary/Treasurer.

I went into the union office the day after the election results and had all the locks changed on the outside doors to the union office. Gil Santana and the rest of the newly elected officers didn't take office until September 1st 1998. The previously elected full time officers didn't even run for reelection. Donna Rivera-Harris took a year leave of absence from the post office then quit altogether. Tom O'Connor became a supervisor, 204B acting supervisor, his first day after leaving the union, which shows he had this worked out before he even left office to go into management. Juan Albo also went into a 204B supervisor position as did Faye Dowd but they waited a short time before becoming supervisors.

At the state convention in 2000 I ran for the position of State Clerk Craft Director again and this time I was elected. My brother, Jeff, was reelected as the State Secretary/Treasurer for his seventh term.

In 2001 I was reelected as the Executive Vice-President. I ran on a ticket with Judy Johnson and Edmund Campbell. Omar Hechavarria was reelected as the Clerk Craft President. It was good to have Judy Johnson back as president but it didn't last long enough. Judy was the best president the Miami Area Local ever had but had a downfall. There's a saying you can forgive but don't forget. Judy would always bring back some of her political enemies to run with her and in the end it cost her and it cost me our union positions.

The last election I was in was at the 2002 state elections where I ran for the position of State Education Director and lost by twenty-five votes. I guess as they say all good things must end sooner or later. In the long run maybe it was good my union activities have ended. I enjoyed my time as a union officer, but don't miss it at all. From the time I was made a shop steward until the time I left office as the Executive Vice-President of the Miami Area Local I had put in over twenty years of my life.

After leaving office in 2002 the executive board of the Miami Area Local replaced Judy Johnson with Dorothy Jenkins, the Business Agent from the South Florida Mail Processing Plant. That didn't last too long because of the politics. Dorothy was replaced with Gil Santana. I was replaced as Executive Vice-President with Joe Brady.

The election of 2004 brought Wilhelmina "Cookie" Ford to the position of General President of the Miami Area Local, Carol Sutton as the Executive Vice-President and Edmund Campbell was reelected the Secretary/Treasurer and Omar Hechavarria was reelected as the Clerk Craft President. I think everyone except Wilhelmina "Cookie" Ford and Carol Sutton were real shocked that they had won. There were five or six candidates running for the office of General President and Executive Vice-President. With that many candidates running, the vote was split and this is what happens. I would have to say now the Miami Area Local has the worst union representation going back to as far as I can remember. This is just my opinion. A lot of the shop stewards were fired or quit and replaced by inexperience shop stewards.

With the elections for the 2007-2010 term Wilhelmina "Cookie" Ford was again running for the position of General President of the Miami Area Local. Also running for the position of General President was Edmund Campbell, Lester Mitchell, Omar Hechavarria and David Figueroa. Somehow Wilhelmina "Cookie" Ford was reelected as the General President.

Running for the position of Executive Vice-President was Carol Sutton, Jim Guyton and Al Pereda. Once again Carol Sutton was elected as the Executive Vice-President. For the position of Secretary/Treasurer was Kevin Baker, Mike Knowles, Rickie Mobley and Luis Sanchez. Kevin Baker was elected as the Secretary/Treasurer.

With twelve people running for the top three position of the Miami Area Local anything can happen. When the election results come out I was surprised once again. I'm sure management in the Miami Area was happy the way the union elections went. With the lack of experience management can do things against the employees and get away with it. Every union, not just the American Postal Workers Union, needs a strong leader to be president. The union is only as strong as the leader.

The Miami Area Local has a long upward road to climb. I know one thing, and that's the Miami Area Local has lost a lot of respect from other locals around the state, and around the country. It will take a long time, if ever, for the Miami Area Local to become as strong as it once was. All it takes is the right leadership and the right shop stewards and officers to be in office and the respect and force behind the union might return one day. Until that day comes, I do want to wish the Miami Area Local the best of luck.

CHAPTER 9

MODIFIED WORK SCHEDULES & GRIEVANCE PROCEDURE

SOMETIME IN JANUARY OR February 1990 the American Postal Workers Union, Miami Area Local started working on a pilot 4-day work week. The pilot 4-day work week was to be on a volunteer basis and took a long time to get to all the sections of the General Mail Facility, the Air Mail Facility, the Motor Vehicle garage along with the drivers and all the stations and branches. I don't believe we actually were able to get all the area's on the 4-day work week.

The pilot 4-day work week didn't happen over night. The idea came to Judy Johnson, President of the American Postal Workers Union, Miami Area Local, and she wrote the program to present to the Postmaster/ District Manager of Miami, Woodrow Conner. The union and management had been talking for way over a year to finally get things in place to get the 4-day pilot program off the ground. One of the reasons it took a long time to get the 4-day modified work week going was because the post office at the headquarters level and the national President of the American Postal Workers Union had to agree and give the Miami Area Local their blessings. Once that happen then the timekeeping people in Minnesota had to figure how to adjust employees time so that there would not be overtime pay for employees that worked 10 hours, 4 days a week.

The 4-day work week was part of a modified grievance procedure that was written by Judy Johnson and agreed to by local management. The Union Management Employee Grievance Assistance (UMEGA) program had to be agreed to by the National APWU and management at the headquarters level before the Miami Area Local could go forward. In total it took over two years to get everything in place before the modified grievance procedure and the 4-day work week could get off the ground.

By having employees working ten hour days there was to be no overtime pay for the ninth and tenth hour. This was not as simple as it sounded.

The national officers were concern that the union was losing the overtime rights that they fought so hard to get in negotiations with postal management. The pay center, where the employees pay checks came from, had to modify their system for the employees going on the 4-day work week. All this took time.

The union had to get employees sick leave records and get the overtime records and productivity records. What the union claimed was that the employees sick leave would improve and at the same time productivity would also improve.

While trying to get the employees on a 4-day work week the union also wanted management to allow supervisors and managers to also go on the 4-day work week. The union figured if supervisors and managers were also on the 4-day work week then management would work that much harder to make the program work. But for some reason management wouldn't allow their supervisors or managers to go on the 4-day work week.

Once the 4-day work week finally got started I was in charge of the stations and branches. Judy Johnson working with the timekeepers got the first two stations going. Norland Post Office in the North part of Miami and Olympia Heights Post Office in the South part of Miami.

I would go into a station or branch and get a copy of the work schedule and the seniority list of the clerks working at that post office. I would then meet with the manager to find out how many employees would be needed on a day to day basis and then go in order of seniority to get the employees that wanted to go on the 4-day work week what they wanted. Of course not everyone got the scheduled days off they wanted. The junior employees that wanted to go on the 4-day work week were not going to get Saturday or Monday as scheduled days off unless some of the senior employees didn't want Saturday or Monday as their days off which was the case at some of the stations. I believe that everyone that went onto the 4-day work week had two consecutive days off. The junior employees working at the stations and branches had Sunday as a scheduled day off along with Wednesday-Thursday or something similar to this.

The 4-day work week finally got started approximately January or February, 1990 and lasted until approximately August, 1992. The Postmaster/ District Manager that agreed to the 4-day work week,

Woodrow Conner, was gone and the Postmaster/District Manager that took over, James Walton, decided against continuing the pilot 4-day work week program.

I believe the program improved sick leave, but not enough to satisfy management. I blame management, mostly, for this. The union had asked management to notify the union if an employees attendance was unsatisfactory, before any discipline was to be issued. Most of the time this did not happen. Of course this part was rough on the union. Sometimes the union had to talk to an employee that continued to call in sick and ask them to try to improve their leave. Sometimes an employee had to be taken off the 10 hour 4-day work week and put back to their regular schedule.

This was the 4-day work week program. It could have been better but we gave it a go. It was a good enough idea since the national APWU has since negotiated a modified work week program into our collective bargaining agreement.

The modified work week also included part time hours that were requested by the employee. The union was able to get the employees, there were only a few employees, a part time schedule where the employee worked five to six hours a day and the employee didn't have to give up their regular bid job.

The modified grievance procedure was also the brain child of Judy Johnson. What this did for the Miami Area Local was to handle the entire grievance process here in Miami. Instead of sending the step 3 grievances to the region in Tampa, Florida, we presented all the step 3's. Between the Miami Area Local and local management six arbitrators were selected to hear our grievances that were appealed to arbitration. Also with this grievances procedure the Miami Area Local was able to have full time shop stewards that were paid by the Postal Service but only did union business. The stewards didn't have to worry about getting released to write up and present grievances. There were approximately twenty full time stewards in total.

Another program that Judy Johnson came up with was the utility overtime desired list and the holiday desired list. What this did was to try to do away with mandatory overtime. The employees that wanted the overtime worked the overtime. The union had two full time stewards working at the union hall. Management would call or fax over a list of how many employees were needed for overtime and where the overtime would be worked. The two full time stewards would then call employees that were on the utility overtime desired list that were qualified going by seniority.

These programs are now gone. The utility overtime desired list must have been a good enough idea because now in the new collective bargaining agreement the national APWU has agreed to let locals to try to administer overtime. The wording is, at the option of the local parties, the union may assume responsibility for the administration of scheduling overtime, choice vacation periods, and or holiday work. Local management has to agree to the union taking on this responsibility, but local management had to agree before when the Miami Area Local set up these programs.

The Miami Area Local had full time shop stewards until right after the 2004 elections and the newly elected General President discontinued the practice of having full time stewards. This only hurt the representation the employees were to receive from the union and it's shop stewards. It also helped management. Now there might be more shop stewards that have a hard time getting released to do union business. Employees can't get released to see their shop stewards. The shop stewards are not trying to get released or are not being given the time by management to investigate, write-up and present grievances, and there are a lot of stewards that haven't had the proper training. Because of the politics some of the shop stewards that were around when I was in office are no longer shop stewards. Some of the shop stewards we had in the past have retired. Some of the stewards have quit being shop stewards and some were fired.

CHAPTER 10

POSTMASTERS

Since I've been in the post office, December 15th 1969, there have been eleven men that have served as the Postmaster General. The Postmaster General that was in charge of the post office when I first started in the post office was Winton M. Blount. He was appointed by the President of the United States with the approval from the United States Congress on January 22nd 1969. The President at that time was Richard Nixon.

After the strike of 1970 and the postal reorganization act of 1970 established the United States Postal Service as a independent government agency the Board of Governors appointed the Postmaster General. Again Winton M. Blount was appointed but this time he was appointed by the Board of Governors. He was appointed on July 1st 1971. After Winton Blount the following were appointed by the Board of Governors as the Postmaster General.

Postmaster General	Date appointed
• E.T. Klassen	January 1st 1972
• Benjamin F. Bailar	February 16th 1975
• William F. Bolger	March 15th 1978
• Paul N. Carlin	January 1st 1985
• Albert V. Casey	January 7th 1986
• Preston R. Tisch	August 16th 1986
• Anthony M. Frank	March 1st 1988
• Marvin T. Runyon	July 6th 1992
• William J. Henderson	May 16th 1998
• John E. Potter	June 1st 2001

Locally in Miami since I started in the Post Office there have been twelve Postmasters or officer in charge. The officer in charge was just what it says, someone in charge of the post office until a postmaster is named. Sometimes this was the same person.

I would have to say the best Postmaster that has been in Miami while I was a union steward or union officer was Woodrow Conner. The American Postal Workers Union, Miami Area Local was able to get a lot of good things for our membership while Woodrow Conner was the postmaster. One of the best things the union was able to negotiate with Woodrow Conner as the Postmaster was the ten four work schedule, the modified grievance procedure, which included full-time shop stewards. The union was able to get management to have our employees work ten hours a day, four days a week. We were also able to get some employees on part time without the employee giving up their bid. Woodrow Conner was the only Postmaster that when he retired the union went to his retirement party.

Besides Woodrow Conner there was Jesus Galvez as a Postmaster that the union was able to work with pretty good. It wasn't always easy to get in touch with Jesus Galvez but he had an open door policy. If Jesus Galvez was in his office and I would go by without an appointment I was able to talk to him and get things accomplished.

The Postmasters and or Officer in Charge of Miami since I've been in the post office were:

•	Eugene M. Dunlap	Postmaster	August 31st 1959
•	E. Herbert Daws	officer-in-charge	May 26th 1972
•	E. Herbert Daws	Postmaster	February 17th 1973
•	Allie Cayard	Officer-in-charge	August 24th 1979
•	Charles Duttweiler	Postmaster	December 15th 1979
•	Reinardo Salgado	Postmaster	July 24th 1982
•	Woodrow Conner	Postmaster	April 13th 1985
•	James C. Walton	Postmaster	January 12th 1991
•	Leo B. Tudela	Officer-in-charge	
•	Rolando D. Jimenez	Officer-in-charge	October 30th 1992
•	Rolando D. Jimenez	Postmaster	November 14th 1992
•	Raul Rojas	Postmaster	January 8th 1994
•	Paul W. Sands	Officer-in-charge	November 1st 1996
•	Jesus Galvez	Officer-in-charge	February 14th 1998

- Jesus Galvez   Postmaster   January 16th 1999
- Tom Pawlowski   Officer-in-charge   July 24th 2006
- Jesus Galvez   Postmaster   December 7th 2006

These were the men in charge of the Miami Post office. Prior to Rolando Jimenez the Postmaster was in charge of the Miami district which covered from Pompano Beach south to Key West. When the post office made changes, reorganization, and brought in a District Manager. The Postmaster was then in charge of only the Miami stations and branches. The District Manager was now in charge of the Miami District which was from Pompano Beach south to Key West. The Postmaster had to report to the District Manager.

CHAPTER 11

POLITICS UNETHICAL & COSTLY

FROM THE TIME I became a union steward until the time I finished as a full time officer I put in over twenty years. In all that time I could never understand the politics that only cost the union a lot of time and money. Instead of more representation for our members the union was fighting against each other all the time.

When I ran for different union offices and put out my fliers I would tell the membership my qualifications and I would sign the information I was putting out. Then you had the politicians that would put out attacks against the union or a political opponent and not sign the fliers they were putting out. It's easy to put out garbage and not sign it. If what someone is putting out was true then why not stand behind it and sign a name to the political attacks? Of course the reason the flyers were not sign was because the flyers contained slanderous remarks about another union officer, mostly about Judy Johnson because she was the president of the union. Most, if not all was untrue.

The first costly error that I remember was when a few shop stewards put out a flyer called "meet your postal leaders." The flyer reported about some of the supervisors' sexual preferences. I had heard that most, if not all, the information that was printed was true, but really nobodies business. The President of the Miami Local at the time was Stanley Gold and since the union never put out any kind of disclaimer to let everyone know that the union had no knowledge of the flyer the union, both local and national, was sued. The national union was supposed to investigate and if they did they never followed through or put any findings out or put any kind of notice that the union had no responsibility or knowledge of the flyer "meet your postal leaders."

Nester Blanco and Gil Santana were charged with putting the flyer out and both were issued a letter of removal from the post office on May

19th 1980. The Miami Local union was sued and ended up paying one hundred twenty-five thousand dollars plus attorney bills. The National union paid out even more. The union secretary, who typed the flyer at the union hall, was subpoenaed to testify against Nester Blanco and Gil Santana. Nester Blanco had his case go to MSPB (merit system protection board) and Gil Santana had his case go to arbitration. Both won their case with back pay. So the only loser was the union both the local and the national.

After the results of the 1981 union elections were announced and Judy Johnson had won for the position of General President the One seven two holding corporation bought the building they were leasing from the Knights of Columbus. This of course was before Judy Johnson took office. As a result when Judy Johnson did take office there was no money in the bank accounts, or very little.

The One Seven Two Holding Corporation is part of the union but a separate entity. Approximately ten years before the American Postal Workers union was formed in Miami a group of employees put up money and formed a corporation, the One Seven Two Holding Corporation. They bought the parking lot across the street from the Biscayne Annex Post Office and rented out parking spaces. When the Biscayne Annex Post Office was closed the parking lot was sold. I assume the employees that put up the money for the parking lot were paid back. Before the union building was bought from the Knights of Columbus there was approximately $300.000.00 in the bank.

Within a month of Judy Johnson being elected the other tickets that had ran against Judy's ticket started a recall petition to remove Judy from office. The recall petition was not done properly and was thrown out and had to be completely redone. The recall petition was never put back together. It would seem that some people had a hard time believing that a woman had won the highest position within the union when in the past the union was run by all older men.

After Judy Johnson had time to look at the books and saw four officers, the Clerk Craft President, Maintenance Craft President, Special Delivery Craft President and Recording Secretary, were double dipping she brought the four officers up on charges. The double dipping meant both the post office and the union were paying the officers for the same time. The union upheld the charges locally and the four officers had to take the charges to the national convention.

One of the officers charged, the Maintenance Craft President, was also the president of the one seven two holding corporation. First he tried to kick the union out of the building then when that didn't work raised the rent the union had to pay to stay in the building.

The 1982 national convention was in Miami so it was easy for the four officers to bring their charges to the convention. Because of the politics, Judy Johnson had spoken out against the national president, the convention voted to throw out the charges and reinstate the four officers that were charged. The four officers finished out their term that lasted approximately seven more months. Of the four officers the only one that was ever elected again was the Maintenance craft President.

Sometime between the time Nester Blanco was elected to the position of Executive Vice-President in 1983 and the end of the term, March 31st 1986, Nester Blanco was fired from the Postal Service. Nester Blanco was in a fistfight with a shop steward in the shop steward area at the General Mail Facility. From witness accounts Nester Blanco did all the hitting and the shop steward was just covering up. Nester Blanco had his case go to the Merit System Protection Board and lost. Since he was fired from the post office he could no longer hold office in the union. The executive board of the Miami Area Local voted to replace Nester Blanco with Betty Tsang.

It was around this time that the Miami Area Local sold the union building and bought three acres of land to have a new union building built, and at the same time got the Postmaster/District Manager/ Woodrow Conner, to lease the union the land next to the Miami Postal credit Union for $1.00 per year so that the union could build a daycare for the children of our members. The problem we had was trying to do too much all at one time.

While we waited for the new union building to be built we had to rent an office and we had a lot of work to do to try to save money.

The three acres of land was all trees that had to be cleared. Since we wanted to save money, there wasn't too much money to begin with, we decided to clear the land ourselves. We rented a machine to feed the trees into once we cut them down. As we started cutting the trees and realizing that trying to put the cut trees into this machine was going to take forever I suggested we burn the cut trees. We had a great fire that day and lucky for us we kept the fire under control and the fire department didn't show up.

The land that we got for the daycare had to be cleared of trees. Unlike the land the union bought for the union headquarters we could not set any fire to the trees since the land was on postal property and next to the credit union. We also had to get the land filled in with a lot of dirt. The land next to the credit union was so low that when it rained the land would flood.

We asked all the shop stewards if they would volunteer and were able to get a few, just a few, shop stewards to help. It's sort of funny in that everyone wanted this new building and everyone knew how tight we were for money but it was even harder to get volunteers.

Once the building started going up we were able to get a few of the shop stewards, the same few, along with myself and Judy Johnson to helped inside the building of the new union headquarters putting up drywall and whatever else we could do to cut cost. Judy Johnson practically lived at the building working all the time to get the building finished.

I'm guessing that the new union building was finished approximately 1990. Since this time the union has been in and out of debt, sometimes almost losing it all, but somehow Judy Johnson got us through it all. I say Judy Johnson because she was the General President and also she had some connections but the union executive board and the membership had to vote on a lot of things that were done to keep the union above water.

In the year 2006 the union building and property was worth over $5 million dollars. Unfortunately when the building and property was sold the present union officers took all the credit for pulling the local union out of debt. Judy Johnson, myself and others, received no credit or thanks for making what turned out to be a good investment. I wasn't really looking for any credit in helping clear the land, helping lay tile and putting up drywall, but it would've been nice if someone said thanks.

It seemed that after every election of union officers in the Miami Local someone would file charges about the way the election was ran. The only real thing the election appeal did was to take away from representation. While the charges were being answered someone was not getting the representation they deserved. One of the elections was ran by the National Labor Relations Board so there was no appeals since the appeal would've had to go to the National Labor Relations Board.

After the 1992 term ended, March 31st 1995, and Judy Johnson didn't run for office there were charges filed against the 1995 elections. Judy had supported Faye Dowd for president for the term of 1995-1998. I had heard much later that the appeal that Faye Dowd did was won but instead of a possible new election Faye Dowd was paid money that was owed to her from the past and she dropped the appeal. Faye Dowd later went into management. Had the appeal not been dropped Judy Johnson would've been reinstated as President and I would've been reinstated as the Executive Vice-President until an election could've been ran again.

The elected officers of the union in 1995 wanted to sell the building to get the union out of debt but at the general membership meeting they were voted down. It wasn't too long after the selling of the building was voted down someone tried to burn the building down.

In June 1996 right after a union meeting a fire broke out in the restaurant downstairs in the union building. This is where the union meetings were held. Somehow nobody was charged with setting the fire even though gas cans were found in the ceiling of the restaurant. To this day I still believe the three full-time officers of the APWU of the Miami Area Local had something to do with the fire. The restaurant was burnt out completely but didn't spread to any other part of the building. If whoever set the fire wanted to burn the whole building down, they did a lousy job. What it did do was cost the union a lot of money. The union lost the income from the restaurant for a long time.

When Judy Johnson started asking too many questions about the fire she was brought up on some bogus charges. The charges had to do with monies the union received for a second picnic. Instead of having another picnic the union bought aprons for our members. The charges that were brought were that Judy misappropriated monies. The claim was that Judy Johnson authorized the paying of bills instead of having another picnic. Since the three full time officers didn't want their name on the charges they got the Maintenance Craft President to file the charges. All this cost the union money and a lot of time. Of course union funds were used to pay for the case but Judy had to spend her own money to defend herself.

Instead of bringing the charges up at the local level the charges were sent to the national. What should have happen was to have the charges sent back to the local to be heard first. If the charges were upheld Judy could've appealed to the national executive board. If the charges were still upheld then the appeal would have to go to the national convention. If the charges were dismissed the local would've had to live with the outcome. Because of the politics the national sent down a regional officer to hear the charges. The charges were upheld and the national executive board agreed with the decision. Judy then tried to charge the national and wait for the national convention in 2000 to have her charges heard by the membership at the national convention.

All this time, since June, 1996, the space where there was a restaurant was still empty.

In the 1998 elections Judy Johnson still couldn't run for president because of the pending charges. Gil Santana ran in the place of Judy Johnson and won. Because Gil Santana appointed Judy as a shop Steward different members that had run for election against Gil brought up more charges. Again all this did was to cost the union more money and time. All the charges were dismissed.

The three officers that were involved with the charges with Judy had all left the union. Donna Rivera-Harris had taken leave approximately three months before the elections of 1998. After the elections she took a one-year leave of absence from the post office and then resigned altogether from the post office. Tom O'connor went into management his first day from leaving office. Juan Albo went back to work as a clerk and approximately four months later went into management. He has since been promoted to manager of the Snapper Creek Post Office.

Knowing the three people that were involved with the charges of Judy Johnson had gone into management or had left the post office one would think the APWU National officers would drop the charges. Because of the politics from the past and some of the national officers who don't know a thing about union solidarity, due process or fair representation even when they talk about it all the time, the charges continued.

As I said Judy Johnson couldn't run for the General President position but could run for the holding corporation. Judy Johnson was elected president of the one seven two holding corporation and the part of the building that was burnt down in 1996 was finally rebuilt and again there was a restaurant at the union building.

On the last day of the national convention in August 2000 there was a settlement and the charges were dropped and Judy was allowed to run for office again. When the 2001 election came Gil Santana stepped aside as President and Judy Johnson was reelected again for President.

Before the end of this term Judy Johnson was once again brought up on some more bogus charges. The charges were dealing with the One Seven Two Holding Corporation and not the APWU. Because I would've moved up to the position of President with the Miami Area Local, with

Judy Johnson out I was also brought up on charges. I was the Secretary/ Treasurer of the One Seven Two Holding Corporation. This was the first time I had been brought up on any kind of charges. The charges were brought up in October 2002. We did have a local hearing and the charges were upheld. The charges were appealed to the national but nobody from the national ever came into Miami to talk to Judy Johnson or myself. We lost our appeal to the national in July 2003. It was obvious Judy and I didn't do as charged or we wouldn't have a job and possible could've gone to jail. Judy Johnson has since retired from the Postal Service, taking an early out. I retired on June 2, 2007 with 37 years, 5 months and 17 days. I am ending up number 21 on the seniority list in Miami.

I was told that the National Labor Relations Board, and even the F.B.I. came into investigate the charges and examine the financial books. I don't know if this was true. I do know the APWU, Miami Area Local hired an outside accounting firm to check the financial books. I know I didn't do anything wrong as a union steward or officer. I also believe I was one of the best at representing the employees of the Miami Area Local.

After Judy Johnson was taken out of office Dorothy Jenkins was put in as the General President for a short time. Some bogus charges were later brought up on Dorothy Jenkins and she was replaced by Gil Santana as the General President. Joe Brady was put in the position of Executive Vice-President as my replacement. Gil Santana and Joe Brady were in their position until the next election, March 2004. Gil Santana and Joe Brady were not elected into office by the membership. They were put into office by the local executive board. They have both since retired from the Postal Service.

A new General President and Executive Vice-President were elected in 2004 but nothing has changed except the representation had gotten worse. A member from the South Florida Mail Processing Facility brought up charges against the union President and the union for denial of free speech. Another set of charges that cost the union money. This member, a former shop steward, had previous brought up charges against Judy Johnson and Gil Santana. It doesn't matter who is in office when you have members like this who is costing the union unnecessary expense all the time. It appears to me that he doesn't care about the union. But this might be the one time this former shop stewards had a reason for the charges. When you try to speak at the union meeting and told you're out of order and are being interrupted when trying to speak this union member felt he had no choice but to bring up charges.

There was also appeals to the 2004 election. There was a reelection for the Motor Vehicle Craft and then a reelection for the position of Executive Vice-President. The Motor Vehicle Craft had a change of officers but the Executive Vice-President position remained the same.

Some people cannot handle power. You see it all the time in management when some employees become acting supervisors. You see this when a supervisor becomes a manager. But when the union president lets the power go to their head it gets ugly. The person elected as president of the Miami Area Local in the 2004 elections had really let the power go to her head. She had fired the Clerk Craft President as a shop steward and taken away his responsibility to present the step 2 grievances for the clerk craft. This is the job as an elected craft president. This is a by-law change that the president is doing without changing the by-laws of the local.

The Clerk Craft President of the Miami Area Local had filed charges against the president of the Miami Area Local. The Craft President was put back, by the national APWU as a steward and given back his responsibilities as the Clerk Craft President. When the Clerk Craft President had decided to run for the General President position in the 2007 elections he had been fired as a shop steward again.

Kevin Baker, who ran for the position of Executive Vice-President for the Miami Area Local in the 2004 elections filed a charge that the union president campaigned against him in the reelection for the executive vice-president position when the president sent out flyers to all the stations speaking for Carol Sutton, who is the current executive Vice-president. Kevin Baker lost the reelection for the Executive Vice-President position. One reason could be that in Miami a lot of members don't bother to vote.

Also I filed charges since the Miami Area Local has owed me money since I officially left office in July 2003. Of course the charges were never turned over to the trial board by the Secretary/Treasurer of the Miami Area Local. When I tried to bring up this issue at the union meeting on May 17th 2005 I was told I could not speak at a union meeting. Of course I never heard anything about my charges and I decided not to waist my time appealing the charges to the national Executive Board. I decided not to be like others and keep filing charges against the union so I've gone my own way and lost some money that was due me when I did leave the office of Executive Vice-President of the Miami Area Local, American Postal Workers Union.

The national was suppose to send in a national officer and an attorney to see if they can settle any of the charges brought up against the Miami Area Local. When Jim Burke and the attorney came into Miami I'm sure I was not a thought on their mind. Not only did I not get a call but have not heard from the National Secretary/Treasurer, Terry Stapleton who acted like he wanted to settle the problem. I can only guess that Bill Burrus, The National President, told him to back off Miami and let the local worry about another law suit.

You learn as a union representative about due process when defending an employee and then the national doesn't understand what they teach about due process. I'm glad I was out of the union as a shop steward and officer. I had a lot of good times, and would be lying if I said I don't miss it at all. I will not drop out of the union, even as bad as it is these days.

I always wondered how strong the union could really be if the politics were not there. I'm not talking about people running for office. I'm talking about the union stewards and officers that were either fired as stewards or not elected and no longer remained shop stewards. After every election in Miami the stewards that ran against the newly elected president were fired as shop stewards. Some of these were good shop stewards, but because of the politics they were replaced, most of the time by new shop stewards with no experience writing or presenting grievances. But that's the politics.

CHAPTER 12

TEACHING & SETTLEMENTS

OVER THE YEARS OF being a shop steward and officer of the Miami Area Local of the American Postal Workers union I tried to learn from every other union officer and steward that I had dealings with. What I mean from this is that when I took classes on representation or looked at different grievances from other union officers or just talked to other union officers.

When the APWU of Florida had seminars, twice a year, I would attend and take different classes. I would pick up as much documentation as I could so I could learn and turn around and teach others from what I picked up at these classes. I would try to pick up little things from everyone and put together my own style. I would call this tricks of the trade. I would tell the shop stewards representation is like a game and he who played the best won. The only problem I had was that the basic shop steward class was for only two days and felt it should be longer. Of course when the state APWU put together these seminars it was only for three days.

Over the years I really enjoyed teaching the new shop stewards. I taught classes for the new shop stewards for the Miami Area Local and also at the state seminars the Florida APWU would put on twice a year.

I didn't teach at every state seminar but at as many as I could. I would ask the state President and State Education Director all the time to let me teach the new shop stewards and did what I could. I always provided a lot of documentation to the shop stewards so that they could read through all the material I handed out. The shop stewards that read through the documentation would have it easier dealing with management. Knowing what articles of the collective bargaining agreement to site and different arguments to use.

When I did teach there was always two union people teaching the basic shop steward class. I taught classes for the new shop stewards, basic shop steward class, with Jack Baldwin, President of the Keys Area Local, on two or three occasions. I also taught with Sam Wood, who was the State Clerk Craft Director and President of the Southwest Area Local, and Bob Bloomer, National Business Agent and former president of the Clearwater Local.

I remember the first time I taught the basic shop steward class at a state seminar it was with Jack Baldwin and after the class different shop stewards and presidents from different locals were telling us that this was one of the best classes put on for new shop stewards that they had. It really made me feel good, and I know Jack Baldwin was feeling good that different shop stewards thought we did a good job.

Jack Baldwin being the President of a small local, Keys Area Local, and I was the Executive Vice-President from a large local, Miami Area Local, taught from our experience dealing with management and the difference between a small local and a large local. Jack Baldwin was not only the President of his local but also had to work performing his job as a postal worker and had to get released from his work as a postal worker to perform union work and represent his members. I, on the other hand, was a full time officer which meant I didn't have to worry about getting released from management. I was on leave without pay from the Postal Service to perform my job as a full time union officer. It made my job much easier from that stand point. Of course my pay came from the American Postal Workers Union, Miami Area Local.

I would tell the new stewards and others that would listen that it was amazing what a steward could get a pen to do if you thought about it. I would tell the stewards that if they were able to reach a settlement with management then the stewards should try as best as they could to write the settlement. I was once told by a national business agent for the APWU that we don't teach our stewards the tricks I would use. Of course I didn't listen and let the stewards decide on their own how they were going to write grievances and settlements. I was told and still believe that the best way to learn, if a person wants to learn, is to learn from yourself. I would tell the shop stewards that hopefully they picked up some of what was taught in the class, that they would pick up some from their local president but the best teacher was experience of writing their own grievances and dealing with different supervisors or managers. I would tell the stewards that I thought it was much easier, in some areas, coming from a large local. The stewards from Miami, as a whole, didn't have too much of a problem getting released from their regular work as a postal worker to represent employees and to write grievances. I would tell the stewards that I would get away with things that would never work in a small local. But then again, I was a full time officer and that in itself made it easier.

I would tell the shop stewards to not let management intimidate them but that they, the shop steward, should try to intimidate management. I would love to present a grievance to a new supervisor, or one that was not too smart, and keep my dark sunglasses on so that the supervisor couldn't see my eyes. I had long hair and sometimes a beard and the supervisor would not know how to take me. It was again, maybe, much easier in Miami then in other smaller locals.

In Miami there were so many different supervisors and managers I had to deal with. I would present almost all the step 2 grievances in the labor relations office when I first started as an officer and later at the stations and braches in Miami. I also would go into Homestead and did a number of the step 1 and step 2 grievances. I would also go to Boca Raton and present step 2 grievances.

I made an effort to never let a grievance go untimely. I would say there was no way a union steward should let a grievance go untimely. Sometimes an employee would want to file a grievance that was already past fourteen (14) days, which is the time limit for filing a step 1 grievance. If I felt like it was a good enough grievance I would go to a supervisor and present them an extension request. On the request for extension there was a place to put the dates from and to. I would put a date in for extension on when I wanted to meet with the supervisor and leave the date off where it had from. I would get the supervisor to sign the extension request and then go back and put a date in where it had from and just made a grievance timely. Not one supervisor ever realized what I had done. I was told before that what I did was unethical but I felt it was not my fault the grievance was untimely and I was trying to help the employees I represented. I thought of it as what ever works to help the members I represented.

The first grievances I wrote I know were not very good. I had to learn real fast and from listening to other union stewards and officers, and reading the contract and writing a lot of grievances I think overall I did a good job at representing employees and at teaching the new shop stewards. I believe I helped make some good shop stewards. It was an honor to be asked to come into different locals to teach a class for their shop stewards.

I went to Clearwater, when Clearwater had their own local and taught a class. I would put on a two day class and even then that was not enough for a new shop steward to learn all that they needed to know to really get started as a shop steward. I would start off as a basic class and provide enough documentation so that the shop steward could advance further. The president of the Clearwater Local at the time was Dean Albrecht. I also went to Gainesville for a two day class for the shop stewards of the Gainesville Area Local. I was asked to teach the class by John Moore, who was president of the Gainesville Area Local at that time and Wayne Wetherington who was also an officer of the Gainesville Area Local.

I went to Ft. Pierce, Ft Myers and Bradenton to teach classes for the shop stewards of these locals. In Ft. Pierce and in Bradenton, Manatee Area Local, there were new officers. Ft Pierce has since merged with the West Palm Beach Area Local. The president of Manatee Area Local, Debi Smith and Vickie Thiele, another officer from the Manatee Area Local, had to take over when their past president retired due to health problems. They had to learn real fast on how to run a local and deal with management. I like to think I helped them out a little in getting started.

In Ft. Myers there are a lot of experience union stewards past and present. The president, Sam Wood, invited me to teach and between the two of us put on a good class. Ft. Myers is part of the Southwest Florida Area Local which represents employees in a lot of different cities and not just Ft. Myers.

In Miami I did most of the basic shop steward classes for a number of years. Again, I like to think I helped some of the shop stewards get started.

After the shop stewards attended one of the classes I taught and provided them with a lot of documentation it was then up to the shop steward to put into action what they were given at the class. How much or how fast they wanted to learn by reading the documentation and then writing up grievances and dealing with management was the stewards choice. There's no way a new shop steward is going to remember or learn enough from taking a class. The basic shop steward class was at the most two days and to me a new shop steward needs more then that.

Sometimes I would have another union steward with me when presenting a grievance to a supervisor or manager. Sometimes we would go into a grievance with a plan for one of us to be the good guy and the other the bad guy. This was what the postal inspectors would do. One of the inspectors would ask if you wanted a drink and the other would start in on the employee. To me this is what I called the tricks of the trade.

There was one time when I was with Rick Pujol, the shop steward at the Snapper Creek Post Office. We had a lot of grievances on the same subject where management had worked employees out of their bid assignment. Management sent two employees from tour 1 that worked at the General Mail Facility to work at Snapper Creek Post office on the day shift, tour 2. The two employees had revised schedules to work days that was signed by a shop steward, so this made our grievances a little harder to win. Our argument was that the revised schedule was for a time change and not for the employees to leave their work location. The employees that had bid jobs at the Snapper Creek Post Office that were on the overtime desired list were denied an opportunity to work on their days off as long as these other two employees were there from the General Mail Facility.

Between Rick Pujol and myself we had filed grievances for each employee that worked at Snapper Creek with a bid job and were on the overtime desired list and didn't get the opportunity to work on their scheduled days off, and these two employees from the General Mail Facility worked on these days in question. We had also files grievances for all the employees in one grievance, an organization grievance.

When we went into the grievance we had a plan, Rick had all the files and when we went into the managers office Rick slammed the files on the table. I told him he didn't have to do that since this manager was a nice guy and would try to resolve the issue we had. We went back and forth with Rick raising his voice and me trying to be the nice guy and talking normal with this manager. In the end we got the manager to agree to pay all the employees that had bids at the Snapper Creek Post Office that were on the overtime desired list and to send the two employees that had bids at the General Mail Facility back to their bid assignment. I think we must have settled on an amount of approximately $7500.00. When we were getting ready to leave the manager told us that we had a good Abbott and Costillo act going. I told the manager I never thought of it like that, all we thought about was the good guy, bad guy act and it worked.

There was another time when I went to one of the postal stores to represent an employee and I had David Vega, another union steward with me. This employee we came to represent had been issued a seven day suspension for having, what management considered bad attendance. When we went there we had no plan as far as one of us being the good guy and the other being the bad guy. When we started to present the grievance, after meeting with the employee and getting some information, David Vega asked me if he could say anything. I told him to speak up at will. David was very good at presenting a grievance, he knew what I called how to talk the talk. When David Vega started to present our argument to the supervisor I pretty much sat back and let David do his thing. I would speak up a little but it was pretty much David Vega talking the talk. We ended up resolving the grievance where the seven day suspension was removed from the employees file, and the letter of warning the employee already had, he never called the union or filed a grievance, was also to be removed from the employees file within four months. I wouldn't have believed we could've gotten such a good settlement if I wasn't there, but like I said David Vega knew how to talk the talk. I would tell David he would be a lot better steward if he could write a grievance and not just present his argument but I don't think I got through to him. If David couldn't win the grievance at the first step, most of the time, someone had to help him write up the step 2 grievance.

I use to tell the stewards that you work with your ability. Some stewards were better at writing a grievance and some at presenting the grievance. I know I was better at writing the grievances and presenting the grievance at the step one and step two. I didn't like to represent an employee in arbitration. I could write up the appeal to arbitration and have all the documentation I needed in the file for arbitration but didn't want to be the one to put the case on before an arbitrator. I was a witness in many arbitrations and did present a few arbitrations myself, but like I said if possible I stayed away from presenting the case in arbitration.

George Pagliery was another shop steward that, overall, did a real good job. Another steward that didn't write the best grievances but got some of the best settlements at step 1 and did a good job presenting a case in arbitration.

There was this one time when George called me on the cell phone and said he got a verbal settlement at step 1 from a supervisor at the Snapper Creek Post Office but couldn't get by there to get the settlement signed. George didn't want to wait on getting the settlement put into writing and also didn't want to wait to give the supervisor time to think about the settlement. Since I was close by I told him I would go by there. George gave me the names of the employees that were to be paid in the settlement that dealt with bargaining unit work. The employees were to share fifty hours of overtime. There were seven names George Pagliery had given me but on the way over to the Snapper Creek Post Office I realized that four of the clerks were not union members. When I got to the Snapper Creek Post Office and wrote the settlement I forgot the four names of the employees that were not in the union and asked the supervisor for fifty-one hours of overtime since three went into fifty-one even. The supervisor asked what happen to the other names that her and George had discussed. I told her these were the only employees that had called the union office and asked for a shop steward and were the only people to give a witness statement for the grievance so these were the only employees the union was asking to be paid. If I had told the other employees why they didn't get any money the union would've had a labor charge filed against us. Only one of the four employees questioned the settlement and I told him what I told the supervisor, and that was the three that got paid were the only ones to give us statements. This employee that had questioned me later joined the union. I had taken a chance that the union wouldn't get a labor charge for what I had done in the settlement. George Pagliery didn't have a problem with what I did. When I would meet with different shop stewards I would tell them to be careful doing what I had done. I would write settlements and get money for non-members every once in awhile so I could defend myself if a labor charge was filed and also to try to get that non-member to join the union, Sometimes it worked, but most of the time it didn't make a difference. I would try to encourage employees to write statements when management violated the contract. Sometimes I got employees paid money even when they were not on the overtime desired list for giving me a statement when management preformed bargaining unit work, or when management used employees from a different craft to do our work.

My job was to defend the employees and police the contract and I took this job seriously. I would write up settlements that would be the best for the employee. If an employee was issued discipline and I was able to get management to agree on a settlement I would write the settlement. In the settlement I would write it in such a way that after a period of time the employee would have a clean record. An example would be if an employee was issued a letter for a suspension for attendance. I would try to get the supervisor to agree to either hold the suspension in abeyance, meaning to keep the grievance at step 1, or for a paper suspension, meaning the employee would lose no money, for a period of time of no more then six months. If the employee was able to be careful with their attendance for the period of time I could get their record clean. I would write the grievance, for example, saying the letter of suspension will be held in abeyance for six months from date of the letter. The employee is to understand they must maintain satisfactory attendance and after the six months the employees record would be clean of all adverse action. The way this was written the employee was to understand that they were to maintain satisfactory attendance, it doesn't say that they would have satisfactory attendance, only that they understood their requirement. Also the settlement says the employees entire record would be clean of all discipline. I'm not even sure the supervisor understood what it meant when I wrote all adverse action. I would write settlements like this a lot and only one person said anything to me. That was the Postmaster of Homestead, Sharon White. I told her it wasn't meant to sound like it was, but I had to rewrite the settlement to get the Postmaster to sign it. In reality it was up to the employee to get their attendance in better shape, I just tried to keep them from getting discipline.

The hardest cases were the ones dealing with the postal inspectors when an employee was being questioned about money orders or large shortages, while working on the window, where the employee was possible stealing. Most of the time when the postal inspector decided to question an employee the postal inspector already had the documentation needed to have the employee walked out of the post office. In these type of cases it was suggested to the employee not to say too much to the postal inspector and to find a good lawyer. When an employee is caught stealing the best I did was to get the employee to resign from the post office with a clean record.

When I presented the grievances at step 2 or step 3 a lot of times I didn't even know the employees I had to represent. The Miami Area Local has approximately three thousand members. I had a file to read and had to represent from what was in the file. Sometimes the case would be sent back to step 1 for more documentation, and sometimes I would make phone calls to a shop steward or the employee to get more information. Sometimes you just can't do anything to help the employee win their case.

There was this one case where an employee that worked the night shift, tour 1, was busted for attempting to bring cocaine into the country from Panama. This employee had put the cocaine up inside her vagina and when customs asked to search her she asked to go to the hospital. She was lucky one of the bags didn't bust open.

When I received the case at step 3 this employee was already in jail and therefore had no chance of winning any case or getting back to work in the post office. The manager I was presenting the case to was Mike Yagodnik. Mike, I'm sure, had more cases then I did and had not read the case yet. I told Mike Yagodnik that this lady was a big lady and that while the employee was waiting in line to go though customs someone came up from behind her and put the cocaine up inside her and she didn't even know it was there. It was hard for me to keep a straight face but I managed it for a short time. When Mike Yagodnik asked me if I was serious I gave in and told him what really happened and I had no choice but to withdraw the case. I couldn't believe Mike Yagodnik didn't burst out laughing when I told him this story. Maybe that shows how some of the managers were I had to deal with.

My three biggest cases were in an arbitration and equal employment opportunity (EEO) hearings. The EEO hearings I handled myself and the arbitration I did all the paper work including the write-up and putting together all the documentation but a lawyer presented the case.

One of the EEO hearings was for Walter Houston, a modified general clerk. Walter had been a carrier that got hurt on the job and was offered a modified clerk position at the Snapper Creek Post Office. When I say he was offered a position he was basically told he had to take this offer for a job or be removed from the postal service. If that happen he would have to deal with OWCP to get paid. Of course he accepted the position at the Snapper Creek Post Office.

Since Walter was hurt on the job and now was put into the clerk craft he had restrictions on his job. He was not suppose to lift any weight over fifteen pounds, and he had restrictions on standing.

The problem that Walter faced was that he wanted to work overtime, and he had the problem with the manager of the Snapper Creek Post Office, Dennis Press. Dennis Press would not give Walter Houston any overtime. I told Walter he had to get a letter from his doctor saying that he could work more then eight hours in a day within his restrictions. There was plenty of work at the Snapper Creek Post Office within the restrictions Walter had. Once Walter received the letter from his doctor then he would have to ask for the overtime. Walter put his name on the overtime desired list informing management he was interested in working overtime when needed within his restrictions. Of course it was not that easy. Dennis Press would not give Walter any overtime even though there was work available so Walter Houston had to file grievances.

I presented a letter by the Postmaster/District Manager Woodrow Conner, that stated that employees on limited duty could be required to work overtime within their restrictions. This didn't make a difference to the manager. I would write up the grievances for Walter Houston and send them to the next step after being denied at step 1. This continued for a long time. Finally a supervisor authorized Walter to work overtime for two days that the manager was not at work. I don't think Dennis Press knew about this, and then when Walter was denied overtime again by the manager Walter filed an EEO for handicap discrimination.

When the case went to an EEO hearing I presented the case and lost. I then filed an appeal to the EEO commission and the case was overturned and I won the case and Walter Houston was due some money.

The case was sent to labor relations and the labor representative for management, Luis Cadavid was assigned the task of dealing with me. When Luis Cadavid asked me what I thought Walter Houston should get I told Luis $25,000.00. I was offered $7,000.00 after taxes. I told Luis I had to call Walter Houston and if Walter accepted that amount we would settle. When I called Walter Houston I was told he would accept $10,000.00 after taxes. This amount was refused by Luis Cadavid, so the case had to be sent back to EEO for someone to figure out how much Walter Houston should get. After figuring out how much time Walter could've worked overtime but was denied by the manager Walter Houston was awarded a settlement of $20,000.00. I really felt good after really working a lot on this case. As for Dennis Press he was promoted to Postmaster of Boca Raton sometime later. Walter Houston was later moved to the Quail Heights Post Office and has since retired from the Postal Service.

My other EEO hearing was for another modified clerk. Jim Loper was an employee working in the Homestead Post Office. Jim worked in the office behind a desk. The EEO was because management would not let Jim Loper work after he had broken his foot, off the job, and couldn't wear a shoe. Jim filed an EEO because there was a letter carrier who hurt their foot and was working on the work room floor without a shoe. Jim didn't even have to go onto the workroom floor since he had a job in the office. In total Jim Loper was out of work for six weeks.

The EEO hearing was to start at 9:00 A.M. but the judge who was hearing the case was late. When the judge walked in, at approximately 9:15 A.M., he had a cast on his foot. He had broken his foot in some sort of accident. I loved it since my case for Jim Loper was that he was denied work because of a broken foot. I could almost fill a smile on my face, and it was hard not to show that smile. If I had too I already had another argument when I saw the judge walk in with a cast on his foot.

After putting on my case with the two witnesses, Jim Loper and the letter carrier who was aloud to work, we went to lunch. When we returned from lunch the judge suggested that I get with the management official, Mike Yagodnik, and try to settle the case without the judge making a decision. After Mike Yagodnik got upset for the judge making the suggestion of settlement we went outside the room and I was offered to split the time which meant Jim Loper would be paid for three weeks of work. I would have loved to continue mainly because I wanted to questioned the postmaster of Homestead to find out their reason for not letting Jim Loper work. But I left the decision up to Jim Loper. Jim Loper had a choice to take the offer of a split or go forward with the hearing. Jim decided to accept the offer and he got paid for three weeks of work.

Jim Loper became a shop steward at the Homestead Post Office, and was a real good steward. The only problem was, because of his health problems, he missed a lot of work. I, as an officer of the union, needed someone to be a shop steward that was going to be at work on a regular basis. So I replaced Jim Loper with someone else. Jim Loper, because of his health problems, later passed away, just a couple of years later.

This other case was for Art Ward. Art was an clerk working at the Airmail Facility working incoming express mail. He was working one night when he saw a box that was torn a little at the top and he noticed inside that there were telephones inside. Since the box wasn't torn too much he let it go. The package was put in a wire cage and sent to the General Mail Facility with other express mail for Miami. After being off for two days Art Ward returned to work and saw a phone placed on a table in his work area. Art told me he didn't think too much about the phone until later when he saw the postal inspector that he knew. Then he remembered the package that was open a little and he remembered seeing phones inside the box. Art had said when he saw the postal inspector that he knew the inspector was with two other men. Most likely they were also postal inspectors. Art decided to wait for a little time to pass before he picked up the phone and was taking it to the inspectors office. Art got as far as the stairs that lead up to the inspectors office. The postal inspector was walking down the stairs at that time and asked Art where he was going with the phone. He told Art that he had been looking for the phone for two days. Art Ward showed the postal inspector where he had found the phone and went back to work.

Towards the end of the day, Art was on the modified work schedule, working 10 hours a day, Art was approached by the same postal inspector and another inspector. Art was told he had to come up to their office to answer some questions. Art went to the inspectors office and never requested a shop steward. That was his first mistake, but not his last. The union is always putting out information telling employees to never talk to the postal inspectors without a union steward or officer being present. There was also a shop steward working at the Air Mail Facility, where Art was working, at this same time. The only problem was the shop steward didn't know that Art was taken to the postal inspectors office.

Art Ward went to the postal inspectors office and again told the same inspector where he found the phone. The other inspector, who was in charge, pulled out a pair of handcuffs and told Art Ward that they didn't believe his story and that it better change. Art was then put into the back seat of the postal inspectors car and taken to the General Mail Facility where he was finger printed and had pictures taken of him. Art was then taken back to the postal inspectors office at the Airmail Facility where he was asked to write a statement. With Art Ward being so scared he couldn't write a statement and gave the postal inspector permission to write the statement for him. This was Arts' second mistake. Of course what was written on the statement was not what happened. The postal inspector wrote that Art Ward had taken the phone out of the box and hid it under some express bags with the intention of going back later and taking the phone, but decided to turned the phone into the inspectors instead. Then Art made his third mistake, he signed the statement. Art Ward was placed on 16.7 emergency suspension and charged with delaying express mail with the intention of stealing the mail.

When Art Ward called me and told me what had happen I told him to get some rope and a knife. I told him to put the rope around his neck and to stand on a chair and as he was jumping off the chair to stab himself with the knife. There was silence from Art Ward. I guess after I told him this he didn't know what to say. I asked what he wanted me to do since he just signed a confession. Art then told me he didn't do anything wrong. I told him that he did do a lot wrong. He went into an office with postal inspectors without a shop steward and then he let these two postal inspectors coerce him into signing a confession. I asked him if he was willing to take a lie detector test? Art then told me he was scheduled to take a lie detector test the next day with the postal inspectors. I told Art Ward if he wanted me to represent him then he was not to meet again with the postal inspectors alone and he was not to take a lie detector test for them. Lucky for Art Ward, he didn't make another mistake and listened to me.

I called the postal inspector and told him who I was and that I was representing Art Ward and that Art would not be there for their lie detector test. The postal inspector told me that another postal inspector was coming in from Memphis, Tennessee to give this lie detector test to Art Ward and that if Art wasn't going to show up then Art would have to call. I, again, told the postal inspector that Art Ward was not going to show up and Art Ward was not going to call them and that the postal inspector should be thanking me for calling ahead of time so that money wasn't spent to bring this other postal inspector in for nothing.

I then called the Metro Dade Police department and got the name of the man who gave lie detector test for the police department. I called this man and found out that he had been giving lie detector test for ten years and was a DEA, drug enforcement agent, prior to that. I figured that I would take Art Ward to take this lie detector test and if Art failed the test nobody would know, except us, that he took the test. When Art Ward took the test and passed I knew I had to win this case. The man that gave the lie detector test told me that the only thing Art Ward was guilty of was to let these two want-a-be policemen coerce him into signing a confession. I don't think this man, a former policeman and drug enforcement agent thought too much of the postal inspectors.

This is where my investigation really started. At the Airmail Facility where Art Ward worked there were two buildings. The main building where the postal inspectors had their office, also the managers office and most of the work. The building where Art Ward worked was a lot smaller and of course a lot less mail brought into that building. I showed that if Art Ward really wanted to steal the phone he had more then one opportunity. When you walk out of the smaller building there was a dumpster just approximately twenty feet from the door. Art could've put the phone in the dumpster and then after work could've either driven his car around and retrieved the phone or could've gotten an empty bag and put the phone in the bag and walk out with it. Or when Art walked into the main building there was a belt where the mail came down that you have to walk around. If Art Ward really wanted to take the phone he could've gone to the right after walking around the belt and gone to his locker. From the postal inspectors stairs you cannot see Art Wards locker. This didn't happen. Art Ward went around the belt and then walked to the left right past the managers office and right up to the stairs leading to the postal inspectors office. I even had a shop steward, who could draw really good make me a poster with the belt and the locker area along with the managers office and the stairwell leading up to the postal inspectors office.

When the manager of the Airmail Facility called Art Ward and told him to report for a pre-discipline hearing the union was not notified. In the contract that management and the union go by it states that the union must be notified when an employee is called in for a pre-discipline hearing. I told Art to go into this hearing and to make sure he has paper and something to write with. I told Art I would not be there unless the manager notified me and that if asked Art Ward didn't tell me about his hearing. I told Art to try as best as he could to write down everything the manager says in the hearing and when it's over to try to get the manager to sign what Art wrote down.

The manager of the Airmail Facility was Steve Bloom. Steve worked well with the union and was a good guy. I also think Steve Bloom knew to call the union and for whatever reason didn't. Art Ward did as I told him to and wrote down everything that he could and also got Steve Bloom to sign the notes that Art took. This again surprised me. I didn't think a manager would sign an employees notes like that. But the manager, Steve Bloom, did sign the notes that Art Ward had written.

When I wrote the grievance my main argument was that the discipline was procedurally defective because the union was never notified by the manager and Art Ward was given a pre-discipline hearing without union representation. I also brought up the fact that Art Ward passed a lie detector test. I was told that the lie detector test is inadmissible in an arbitration case unless I could get management at step 2 or step 3 of the grievance procedure. So I had to try to get management to mention the lie detector test in writing. At the step 3 hearing I mention the lie detector test as much as I could. When management gave me their step 3 decision they had mention the lie detector test. Their decision was short and to the point. All it said was "after reviewing the lie detector test the case is denied at step 3". For me it was good enough. I didn't think the manager at step 3 had the authority to resolve the case. I wrote up my appeal to arbitration and to me this was my best brief that I appealed to arbitration. I felt, with a decent arbitrator that was fair, I could win this case. I know it was well documented and I had a professional witness in the man that gave the lie detector test.

Art Ward, with the help of his father, decided to get a lawyer. I had written the grievance and appealed the case to arbitration. I also had the man who gave the lie detector test on standby since he said he would testify when the case went to arbitration. I met with the lawyer, who was a criminal attorney, a couple of times to go over the union contract, the lawyer knew the law but not the contract the union went by.

When the case was scheduled for arbitration and the arbitrator came into the room the first thing he said was that since he had already read the case and he had a flight to catch the case shouldn't take too long. It appeared to the union, Judy Johnson was the union officer in the room at this time, that this arbitrator had already made up his mind and we didn't want to take a chance on this arbitrator so Judy Johnson pulled the case and asked the arbitrator to step aside. After some argument the arbitrator agreed and the case was rescheduled.

By the time Art Ward had his case come up for arbitration again he had been out of work for over one year, approximately fifteen months. Art had been out of work for approximately six months the first time the case came to arbitration. This time the arbitrator wasn't in any hurry, the case took two days, and when the arbitration was finished the arbitrator gave management and the lawyer thirty days to write a brief so that the arbitrator could make the decision. After the thirty days Art wards lawyer didn't write the brief so with managements okay the lawyer was given another thirty days. When the lawyer still failed to write the brief the arbitrator made his decision on what he heard in the arbitration.

I told Art Ward that his lawyer may have cost him his job since the arbitrator had a written brief from management and nothing from his lawyer. The arbitrator had to make his decision from what he heard in the arbitration and of course managements brief.

But Art Ward did win his case with full back pay. The arbitrator took away the time between the first arbitration and the time he gave the lawyer to write the brief that wasn't written. In total Art Ward was awarded a years back pay.

I told Art Ward he should call his lawyer and tell him that he, Art Ward, was going to call the Bar Association to report what the lawyer failed to do. If Art was to call and proved the lawyer failed to properly represent Art the lawyer could've been in some big trouble. Since the lawyer failed to write the brief the lawyer gave Art Ward back the money he charged for handling the case. Of course I felt the lawyer used my investigation and all my arguments to win the case.

There was a case I had where the employee came to work after reading in the paper about a shooting at an insurance company in Jacksonville, Florida. When this employee was talking to a supervisor he said "with supervisors like you I could see that happening here". The supervisor asked this employee if he was making a threat? The employee told the supervisor to take it anyway he wanted too. The supervisor felt that this employee had just made a threat toward him and put the employee on 16.7, emergency suspension. I won my argument at step 2 that the employee didn't make a threat but a statement that he could see this happening. The employee at no time said that he was going to do something in a threatening manner. The employee received back pay plus some overtime pay that he missed out on.

There was another case I had at step 2 dealing with a Motor Vehicle employee. This was a case that I knew was a sure loser. The employee was charged with possession and sales of drugs. The buyer of the drugs was a postal inspector. I believe it was marijuana, but cannot remember for sure. The employee was placed on 16.6 of the collective bargaining agreement. This meant he was placed on indefinite suspension due to a crime situation that could cause jail time.

There wasn't much I could do with the case except to have management at step 2 hold the case in abeyance pending judication. This meant the case would go no further then step 2 pending the outcome of this employees court hearing. This also meant when the employee was found guilty in court the union would just drop the case since the employee would be charged with a felony and possibly be in jail. If the employee was found innocent the union had the right to go forward with the case if the union decides to do so. The union could still drop the case but most of the time the union would go forward with the case. This didn't mean that management had to resolve the issue but that the manager at step 2 had to hear the unions argument. The employee won in his court hearing and had the charges thrown out.

When this employee was setting up the deal with the postal inspector, of course the employee had no idea this person buying from him was a postal inspector, he had the buyer drop the money off at his house. This employee told the buyer he would meet him and told him where to park his car. The employee had his wife take the money so that now there was no money in his house. The postal inspector drove to the agreed upon location and before the employee got there he put the drugs out on the side of the street a block up from where he was meeting the postal inspector. He then drove up to where the inspector was waiting and told him there was something waiting for him at the next block. He then started to drive off but a few different cars came up after him and he was pulled over. This employee was arrested and charged with possession and sales. Yet the employee had no money in his possession, there was no money at his house, and this employee had no drugs on him when he was stopped. I guess this is one reason he won his case in court. The employee most likely had a good lawyer to represent him in court since again, he had all the charges against him thrown out.

I then set up a step 2 hearing with the manager of Motor Vehicle so we could go forward with this employees case. I really didn't think management would resolve the case even though the employee won his case already in court. I was wrong. The manager agreed to bring this employee back to work effective the beginning of the next pay period. A couple of days before the employee was due to come back to work management sent him a notice and told him not to come back. The employee was being placed on administrative leave with pay. Since the employee was getting paid there wasn't too much for me to do. I talked to the manager of the Motor Vehicle Craft and was told he had no choice. Someone higher up in management didn't like the settlement so while management was trying to decide on what to do the employee was getting paid for not working.

This employee went and got a job at Ryder Truck Company and was getting two checks every two weeks. This went on for approximately eighteen (18) months.

In between this time the union had their elections and I lost the election for the Clerk Craft President position and went back into the post office at the Sunset Post Office.

Sometime after the eighteen months management brought the same charges against this employee again. The officers in the union at this time dropped this employees case and he was fired by the Postal Service. Maybe I am wrong but I couldn't see how the same charges could be brought up again. The union didn't argue for this employee so it came to an end. I would think this employee had a good law suit against the union for not properly representing him.

I guess that's the difference between myself and some other union officers. I didn't want to know if an employee was guilty or not. If I was going to give it my best shot then it wouldn't matter. I was in the union to represent the employees the best way I could. Some of the other union officers didn't do that, like the ones who dropped this employees case. I know I had nothing to be ashamed of when it came to representing the American Postal Workers Union.

For what it's worth, this employee did do everything he was being charged with. He did sell drugs to an under cover postal inspector. He did take money that he never had to pay back, and he got away with it all. That is until he lost his job at the post office.

CHAPTER 13

HOW I DEALT WITH MANAGEMENT & MORE

DEALING WITH MANAGEMENT WAS no easy task. As a union steward and officer in Miami I had to deal with so many different supervisors, managers, labor relation representatives, and Postmasters. I would tell the shop stewards that you had to know when to jump in managements shit and when to back off. If a union steward went into a grievance and did a lot of yelling all the time that steward would get nowhere. I never yelled in a hearing. I would get mad and sometimes let my mouth get carried away with me, meaning the use of foul language, but not when I was presenting a grievance. I would tell the shop stewards not to let management upset you enough that it made you cuss at them, and then I would do what I told the steward what not to do. I would let myself get upset and get into a good argument with the supervisor or manager, but, once again, never raised my voice or use the foul language during the actual grievance presentation.

It is understood that when a union steward or officer is dealing with management either in a discussion or a grievance that the union official is equal to management. To me the union steward or officer is always equal to management and when presenting a grievance is above management. Employees are always told that they should show the supervisor and or manager respect. To me that supervisor or manager must earn respect. There are some good supervisors and managers, just not enough of them. There are also a lot of supervisors and managers that think their shit doesn't stink. I often wondered what rock some of these supervisors and managers crawled out from. I would tell some supervisors to not let their tie choke off the oxygen to their brain, and some I would tell them it was too late. The tie had already choked the oxygen to their brain and they became stupid.

When I first started presenting step 2 grievances it was in labor relations with a labor representative for management. The secretary for labor relations at that time, 1984, was Toby Lowe, The labor representatives I dealt with were Steve Murray, Peter Marcoux, Mike Yagodnik and Dan Smith. The manager of labor relations at that time was Allan Bame. Later when Peter Marcoux left Miami I believe this is when Joe Berezo came into labor relations. At some point Dan Smith transferred to Georgia. Then I believe Luis Cadavid came into labor relations, and also Toby Lowe went from secretary to become a labor relations representative. After Alan Bame left as manager of labor relations he was replaced by Steve Murray. When Mike Yagodnik left labor relations, he continued doing the same job but worked for the district manager handling the hearings for management for employees just from the General Mail Facility. After Steve Murray moved up to manager of labor relations I believe this is when management brought Rick Avery into labor relations. When Mike Yagodnik left labor relations I believe he was replaced by Maria Villar. Later Rick Avery and Maria Villar were married and both stayed in the labor relations department.

These were the labor relations representatives for management that I and other union stewards and officers presented grievances to at the second step. Also the labor relations representatives presented arbitrations for management.

The only labor relations representative I really had some heated arguments with was Mike Yagodnik. Mike Yagodnik was also the only one working in labor relations that was a union officer in the American Postal Workers Union. It is amazing how people forget where they came from. I have a real hard time understanding how people can say they believe in the union and then go from being a union officer into management. When Mike Yagodnik was a union steward he was a good representative of the union.

When I first met Alan Bame he would ask me why I don't wear a suit or a tie like the officers of the letter carriers union do? I would tell him I didn't want to look like management and that so many supervisors that did wear a tie would let that tie chock the oxygen to their brain and they became stupid. Alan didn't like my answer but would ask me the same question the next time he saw me. Alan finally quit asking and we got along great. While I was a union steward and officer Alan Bame was the best manager in labor relations that I dealt with. Dealing with the labor relation representatives was a lot better then dealing with the manager and supervisor on the workroom floor. The labor representative knew the contract and it made it easier to deal with management when they knew what they were doing. The labor relation representative didn't always settle when the union was right but I don't believe I had too many arguments with them. Of course, most of the time, I didn't settle grievances when I knew management was right. We either settled the case, with some language, or we would appeal the case to step 3 or arbitration.

The Miami Area Local would try to have labor-management meetings once a month. Sometimes we could get things taken care of without a grievance and other times we could use the date of the labor-management meeting for the start of a grievance. A grievance had to be filed within 14 days.

There was this one labor-management meeting where I set this manager up, sort of. I guess it depends on what set up means. The manager, Oscar Rodriguez, was over the stations and branches, like the postmaster today. Oscar was the type that said whatever he wanted no matter who it was to. He would yell and cuss but worked well with the union without any real problems.

At the labor-management meeting I asked Oscar Rodriguez what does a window clerk do if a customer verbally abuses them? Oscar said that the window clerk should excuse themselves and get the supervisor to handle the situation. I thought this was a good answer. Now for the set up. I asked Oscar what does a window clerk do if physical abused, if a customer grabs them or even hits them? Oscar said he would jump the counter and hit the customer back. Alan Bame, the manager of labor relations, was at the meeting and almost had a heart attack. Alan told Oscar he couldn't tell the union that. The whole room started laughing when Oscar gave his answer to the physical abuse a window clerk might get. Of course I never got a straight answer to my question.

Dealing with the manager or the supervisor that didn't know the contract like they should made presenting the grievance a little more difficult. The supervisor would ask me to show them where they were wrong. I would tell the supervisor that I was not there to train them, and for them to find the answer on their own. I wasn't there to help management, especially if it would hurt the employee I was trying to defend and win their grievance.

There was this manager that worked at the Ocean View Post Office that I just couldn't get along with. This manager started out as an acting supervisor at the Snapper Creek Post Office and then moved up to supervisor and manager pretty quick.

When this manager was an acting supervisor at the Snapper Creek Post Office he had marked this employee awol (absence without leave) for being late. When this employee called me and I checked the leave slips I saw that there was two leave slips for awol. The employee didn't know about the first one because the acting supervisor had approved the leave for this employee and then went back later and changed the approved leave to awol. When we went into a meeting with this supervisor, the employee and myself, I told the supervisor that I was going to call the postal inspectors to report this supervisor for falsification. Of course this was not really falsification but was altering a leave slip. But the supervisor didn't know the difference between falsification and altering, or so it seems. I got both awol charges removed and the employee was given approved leave.

Like I said before this acting supervisor later moved up and later became manager of the Ocean View Post Office. This manager never wanted to deal with the union so when the union made an appointment with this manager he would try to cancel the meeting or wouldn't be there when the union showed up. This wasn't just me he just didn't want to deal with but any union steward. I had heard some of the stewards saying when they went to meet this manager the manager wouldn't be at the post office.

This one time I came to Ocean View to meet with this employee and then to meet with this manager. I had the meeting set up way in advance. When I went to present the grievance to this manager he was getting ready to leave and told me he had forgotten our meeting and he had to leave. Of course I let this manager piss me off enough that I told him what I thought of him. I use every cuss word I could think of on him. This manager called labor relations to report my behavior and talked to Mike Yagodnik. When this manager told Mike that we had a meeting scheduled that he wasn't going to keep Mike Yagodnik started to understand why I was upset. The manager then hanged up the phone on Mike Yagodnik. I then looked like the good guy. It didn't matter at that time that I just finished cussing this manager out. I ended up talking to Mike Yagodnik when he called the Ocean View Post Office back. Mike Yagodnik was mad the manager ended their conversation the way that he did. Mike Yagodnik then talked to the supervisor at the Ocean View Post Office who ended up settling the grievance which was a letter of warning. I got the letter of warning removed completely from the employees file.

I also fired the shop steward who worked at the Ocean View Post Office. While I was having my argument with the manager this shop steward came up and told me I shouldn't be using that language on the manager. If the shop steward had done their job I wouldn't have had to present the grievance in the first place since the shop steward should've handled the grievance. The shop steward was right in the sense that I shouldn't have let this manager piss me off enough to cuss his ass out on the workroom floor. But even if I was wrong the shop steward is suppose to stick with the union and not let management know that we didn't agree on something. The shop steward could've talked to me later when we might have been alone. When I got back to the union hall later that day I had a letter sent to this shop steward letting them know they were no longer needed.

This was just one of a number of times I got into big arguments with management and ended up using foul language. There was this one supervisor, a black man, that I got into an argument with and I said you guys are all alike. I, of course, was talking about management. This supervisor said I made a racial statement. That was the furthest thing from my mine but it made me think that I had to be a little more careful dealing with some supervisors and how I say things to them. I didn't care about the use of my fowl language but I had to defend everyone and wanted to be more careful if people thought I was making any kind of racial statements.

Sometimes I didn't even realize that I use bad language. In June 1996 I went back to work in the post office, at the Sunset Post Office. I was later asked to be an alternate shop steward by the president of the Miami Area Local at that time, Donna Rivera Harris. I was to cover the Sunset Post Office and also the Olympia Heights Post Office.

This one day I was at the Olympia Heights Post Office writing a grievance when another employee came up to me and told me she had jury duty that was scheduled on her day off. She told me the manager wouldn't give her a revised schedule. I told her not to worry that I would take care of her problem. The manager at Olympia Heights was a real nice guy, Rick Suarez, and I thought I could get him to resolve the problem with the revised schedule. When Rick Suarez walked by I told him about this employee having jury duty and he told me that he doesn't revised schedules. I asked him if he was going to fuck this employee out of her day off? The next thing I knew Rick Suarez was telling me to leave the building or he was going to call the police. I didn't even realize what I had said. I told the manager I was writing up a grievance and I wasn't going nowhere until I finished. I had the right to be there.

I always told the shop stewards when I was an officer that if they were at a post office and had the right to be there, writing or presenting a grievance, and they were told to leave then they better not leave. I would tell them if they did leave when told then I didn't need them as a shop steward and that they could just keep walking. I would also tell them not to get stupid and get arrested but to let the police walk them out if it came to that.

When Rick Suarez got to his office instead of calling the police he asked me to come into his office. I told the manager that he was already mad at me and that if I came to his office I would most likely get him more pissed off. Rick Suarez called the union instead and got the president of the union on the phone, Donna Rivera Harris, and then asked me again to come to his office. This time I came into his office. I didn't care for Donna Rivera Harris but she was the president of the Miami Area Local. The manager had the speaker on the phone and we talked and Donna told the manager I was sorry for what I said. I spoke up and told Donna I was not sorry since I'm not even sure what I said. I then told the president I would take care of the problem with the manager and hung up the phone. I then talked to the manager, Rick Suarez, and then realized what I had said. The manager, like I said before, was a real nice guy but didn't like the foul language. I told the manager I would be more careful in the future in what I say. I told him next time I would use the word screw. The manager looked at me as if I was crazy. But I was able to settle the grievance I had written up and also got Rick Suarez to agree to get another employee to change days off with the employee that had jury duty so that she didn't have to work on her day off. A day or so after this I was fired as a shop steward from the president of the Miami Area Local. I guess she didn't like my experience and the way I dealt with management.

Sometimes managers and supervisors look for trouble from the union. When the shop steward at the Sunset Post Office, Rick Pujol,

Rick previously worked at the Snapper Creek Post Office, handed the manager of the Sunset Post Office a request for documentation form and the manager refused to sign the form but walked away with the form the manager was looking for trouble. I couldn't keep quiet and had to tell the manager what a stupid little shit he was and called him all sorts of other names. This was after I had requested the request for documentation form back from the manager and he just kept walking away with it. The manager ended up giving the shop steward, Rick Pujol the request form back, along with the documentation Rick had requested. But this should have been done before I had to say anything.

Sometimes when I met with a supervisor or manager to talk with them or to present a grievance I would keep my dark sunglasses on, where the supervisor or manager wouldn't be able to see my eyes. It depended on who I was dealing with. I loved to play with managements mind. To me when I dealt with management, it was like a game. Whoever played the best won.

There was the time when the main post office, the General Mail Facility, got this new manager in charge of tour 3. I went to meet this manager and I was polite to him. I took my sunglasses off and introduced myself to him. I told him if he needed anything that he thought I could help him with to give me a call.

Approximately a month later I was told by another manager that this manager in charge of tour 3 didn't like me. I said I didn't understand. I had only met this manager once and I was very polite, not my usual self. This other manager said that the manager in charge of tour 3 sees me coming into the General Mail Facility with my dark sunglasses on, talking to his supervisors and not taking off my sunglasses. I told this other manager that from then on I would never take my sunglasses off, even when I talked to the manager in charged of tour 3.

This same manager that was in charge of tour 3, some time later, got busted for sexual harassment and was fired from the Postal Service. He was brought back to the post office as a regular employee in another city but didn't stay too long. He had quit the post office altogether.

One time I received a call from an employee at the Tamiami Post Office telling me that the supervisor must be working the registry cage. This employee, Fernando Del Sol had a bid position where he worked at the Tamiami Finance unit in the morning and then after lunch went to work at the Tamiami carrier annex to work the registry cage.

Sometimes management would tell Fernando to stay at the finance unit and the supervisor would work the registry cage. When this happened Fernando would file a grievance and get paid for the time the supervisor worked in the registry cage.

This one day Fernando called the union hall and told me that, again, he was told to stay at the finance unit. I called the Tamiami carrier Annex and the supervisor answered the phone. I asked him who was working in the registry cage. Without saying anything I thought the supervisor hung the phone up on me. I started to get mad but then another employee picked the phone up and asked me if she could help me, the supervisor had put the phone on hold. I asked the clerk who was working the registry cage and I was told that she had been working in the cage. This was a Friday and was this employees scheduled day off. The problem was the time was at approximately 4:00 P.M. and this employee started working on this day at 4:00 A.M. I asked her if indeed it was her scheduled day off and was told it was. I then asked how she was still working when she had been there since 4:00 A.M.? She told me to figure it out and she put me on hold. Now I really was starting to get mad. When the supervisor came back to the phone I asked him what kind of games they were playing? The supervisor told me I didn't have to be rude? Now up to this point I didn't think I was being rude. I was just trying to find out why Fernando Del Sol was not working his bid job and who was working the job. I was also, now, trying to find out why this other employee was still working that day after 12 hours, especially since it was this other employees scheduled day off. I then told the supervisor I was not rude until now. I told him I would show him rudeness I called him a fat fuck and hung the phone up on him. The next day I went and filed two grievances. One to get Fernando Del Sol paid and the other to get the other employee paid additional time. I found out that the other employee, to help management out, went to lunch for four hours. This an employee cannot do just to help management out and to prevent another employee from doing their regular scheduled job.

Sometime later, after I was no longer working for the union and working at the Country Lakes Post Office this same supervisor, who I had called a fat fuck, was my supervisor for a short time. I knew I had to be careful what I say. I cannot cuss at my supervisor, of course I shouldn't be doing this in the first place. But as I said before some supervisors and managers look for trouble.

One day as I was working my window position at the Country Lakes Post Office and this same supervisor stood behind me for a good ten to fifteen minutes. He didn't say anything to me but the fact he was just standing there bothered me. I know my job and didn't need anyone watching me for that long period of time. Of course, as my supervisor, he can tell me to do a certain job and most of the time there would be no question on my part, I would do the job asked of me.

On this one day in question after the supervisor was standing there for as long as he did I told him I was going to the bathroom. I walked by the manager, Charlie Smith, and told him if this supervisor continued to stand behind me I would be going to the bathroom five times a day. I came back to my window and a few minutes later the supervisor walked away. I then went on my morning break. After I had walked away for a few minutes the supervisor called me to tell me to pull my cash drawer and lock it in the vault so another employee could work my window. I told the supervisor that the whole time he stood behind me and didn't say a word to me he should've told me then to pull my cash drawer before I went on break. The supervisor knew the break schedule, since he was the one who made the schedule. Since I had already gone on break I wasn't going to come back to the window now to pull my cash drawer. The supervisor wrote me up and called for a shop steward for a pre-discipline discussion.

Mike Knowles was the shop steward that represented me in the pre-discipline discussion. In the discussion the supervisor said that he gave me a direct order to come back to the window and pull my cash drawer. I told the supervisor that he was a liar and that had I been given a direct order I would've come back to the window. I filed an EEO on the pre-discipline discussion and for harassment. I had Al Pereda, another clerk at the Country Lakes Post Office and a former shop steward, represent me. Al Pereda did most of the talking in a meeting for my EEO against this supervisor. All I did was tell the supervisor that this was me. I was not going to change for him or nobody else. We could get along and he will see that I'm a good worker or we can fight and he will see that I can do just enough to get by. I never was given any discipline for not coming back to the window and had started getting along better with the supervisor. The same supervisor didn't work much longer at the Country Lakes Post Office. I don't know if that was his choice or the managers decision.

I think some managers do stupid things on purpose to upset the union. I don't really get upset as much as I just can't handle stupid people that do stupid things. Of course some people would say that I'm stupid for cussing at these managers and supervisors and these people would be right. But oh well.

There was another incident where this employee working at the Father Felix Verela Post Office called me up and told me she was denied annual leave even though nobody from the window section had annual for the time she wanted off.

In the local agreement the Miami Area Local had with management the clerks that work at the stations and branches have two sections for leave and overtime purposes. The distribution clerk that have no window position are in one section and the window/window distribution clerks are in another. Therefore at lease two clerks, depending on the amount of employees at a station or branch, could have off at the same time.

When this clerk called me I told her I would call the manager and talk to him. This same clerk called me back a short time later and asked if I had called the manager yet. I told her no but I was going to that day. When this same employee called me a third time, yes some clerks I represented were stupid also, they think I didn't have anything to do but wait for their phone call, I told her again I was calling. I called the manager up and told him I received a phone call and asked if he had a copy of our leave policy? When he told me he didn't I told him I would fax him a copy of the leave policy that was signed by the union president and the postmaster and I would call him in the morning.

The next morning I called this manager of the Father Felix Verela Post Office back and asked if he received the leave policy I faxed to him and when he told me he did I asked if he read the policy. Again he told me he had. I asked him then if he understood that when an employee from the window section and an employee from the distribution section put in for the same time off that both were to be approved? This manager told me he understood the leave policy but that he wasn't going to approve this employees leave. Maybe if I had an employee that worked for me that was such a pain in the ass as this clerk was maybe I would understand more. I told this manager that the employee was entitled to the leave and I was told that he didn't care that the clerk could file a grievance but he was not going to approve the leave. I then asked the manager if he was stupid or something? When the manager asked me what I said, I said that he was a fucking idiot and hung the phone up. I then called the area manager, Manny Molina, and got the leave approved for this employee. I guess I should've called the area manager in the first place but I thought it was an easy situation to resolve and would give the manager a chance to take care of the problem.

Manny Molina called me a couple of days later and told me I couldn't keep cussing at the managers the way I do. Of course I told him I know I shouldn't and would try to control myself but when his managers do such stupid things it makes it hard for me not to blow up.

I know with the years I worked as a union steward and a union officer for the Miami Area Local, over twenty (20) years, I represented a lot of employees. I saved some employees their job and I taught a lot of shop stewards ways to write and present grievances.

I didn't expect the shop steward to be like me in the way I dealt with management, but I did expect the shop steward to know how to handle themselves in a grievance or a hearing. Everyone has their own style. Whatever works as long as the employees receive good representation. Of course this didn't happen all the time. I'm sure some of the employees I represented didn't like the results. I guess you can't please everyone all the time. Sometime stewards were fired or asked to quit because there were a lot of complaints from the membership.

After the 1995 elections and I lost the position I was trying to get elected for which was the Clerk Craft President. I should've ran for the same position I held before the election which was the Executive Vice-President, but for some reason I decided to run for the other position.

I remained a shop steward until June 20, 1995. I had a bid position at the Sunset Post Office with the hours of 7:30 A.M. to 4:00 P.M. and Saturday-Sunday as my scheduled days off. After the 1995 election and I was still a shop steward this was still my schedule. Since the newly elected officers that took office on April 1, 1995 wanted to let me go as a shop steward and didn't want it to look like I was fired they tried to get me to quit. I was offered a full time steward position with the hours of 1:00 P.M. to 9:30 P.M. and Sunday-Monday as scheduled days off. I wasn't going to except this position with these hours, and I wasn't going to give up on my Saturday as an off day. I was offered this position on June 9, 1995. I was sent a letter dated June 20, 1995 by the General President, Donna Rivera-Harris, informing me since I failed to except the offer of a full time steward position I was being decertified as a shop steward.

Working at the Sunset Post Office was different then when I worked at Snapper Creek Post Office when I first bid to a station. I was now a full time window clerk. I also had a supervisor that had been a carrier supervisor at the Snapper Creek Post Office when I had worked there. When Sunset Post Office, a new post office, opened this supervisor went there and became the clerks supervisor.

She wasn't a bad supervisor but was a pain in the ass. Since I worked at the end of the window section, the wall was to my left, I was able to lean things against the wall, like a broom. When the custodian that worked at the Sunset Post Office would finish sweeping the front of the post office, before the window section opened for customers, I would ask the custodian to leave the broom and would put the broom up later when I took my break. The supervisor would come to work at 10:00 A.M. and when she would come up to the window section to check on the clerks I would tell her not to forget her transportation home and point to the broom. She would walk away saying that I never stop.

The supervisor started staying away from the window, or maybe just staying away from me. She would stay in her office and if she needed to talk to a clerk she would call then over the microphone.

On April 3, 1997 I excepted a position as an alternate shop steward at the Sunset Post Office and on May 15, 1997 I was asked to cover Olympia Heights Post Office as a shop steward. Both letters were sent by Donna Rivera-Harris. This didn't last long. I guess my style didn't fit the General Presidents style of representation and I was decertified again as a shop steward. The shop steward that replaced me didn't write up hardly any grievances even though there were grievances to write and was later busted for misappropriation of postal funds.

It's funny in a way that I had so many battles with supervisors and managers at different stations, but had no problems with some of the top managers in the Miami Post Office. When I went to see the manager of personnel I never had a problem. Sometimes the manager, Estrella Alam, would be meeting with some of her employees and would still take the time to talk to me or make a phone call to find some information for me. Sometimes Estrella would ask me what happen, I heard you had a problem at one of the stations. I would then tell her my side of the problem. She was a very good person to work with.

Manny Molina, the Area Manager in the South had an open door policy. If I came by his office, most of the time, even if he was on the phone he would invite me into his office so we could talk.

The Postmaster of Miami that I dealt with more than any other, Jesus Galves, was another that if he was in his office and I came by would invite me in so we could talk.

So it shows I wasn't that hard to get along with, most of the time. If I felt I was right I wasn't going to back down on any grievance or for anyone I was representing.

Shop stewards and officers of the union, not just the Miami Area Local, but all the unions should know that the union is the membership. Without the membership there would be no union. Therefore the membership should be provided with the best union representation possible. Members of the union get upset and drop out of the union. This hurts everyone not just the union. If the union doesn't have the membership then the union will not have the money to represent the membership the way the membership deserves to be represented. I tell members all the time instead of dropping out of the union if the member is that upset and fills that they were treated that badly then when election time comes around to make sure to vote. If the member drops out of the union then they give up their voting rights and the same officers get elected or worse. The membership gets what the Miami Area Local got in the 2004 elections. Unfortunately a lot of members of the Miami Area Local don't bother to vote. It is easy to complain but when the member doesn't take the time to vote then the members shouldn't be complaining. What's worst is that it's so easy to vote. The ballot comes to the members house and it doesn't cost to mail the ballot back. All it cost is some time to read, ask questions from members that know a little of what's going on, and to mark their ballot.

Now with the selling of the union building and the Miami Area local having a chance to walk away with maybe as much as three million dollars the officers now in office are going to be hard to defeat and the representation will remain the same. The present General President is going to try, along with others running for office, to take credit for putting the Miami Area Local in a good situation financially. But if it wasn't for Judy Johnson and the executive board at the time that Judy Johnson was president, and I was the Executive Vice-President, then the union wouldn't have own the building and land to sell.

Chapter 14

CALLING THE POLICE

THERE WAS ONE THING I couldn't control as a union steward and officer and that was my mouth. I would let management upset me and I would tell them how stupid they were but I would, a lot of times, use profanity.

I had the police called on me six times I can remember and only used profanity on two of those occasions. I was told many other times that the police were going to be called, but don't believe the manager or supervisor followed through. A lot of the times the Area Manager would be called and he would tell me I can't keep cussing at the managers. I would tell the Area Manager I only cussed at the stupid ones and that I would try to be more careful. I had a rule with my shop stewards and that was if they had union business at a post office and had a disagreement with management and were told to leave then they were not to leave, at least not right away. If the police were called then the steward was to wait and if need be to have the police escort them from the building. I would tell the steward if they were told to leave and they left when told then they could keep walking because I wouldn't want to keep them as stewards.

I would tell management I wanted to try to resolve the different grievances and try to get along. I would tell them we can either get along or we can fight, because I like a good fight once in awhile.

The first time I had the police called on me was at the Quail Heights Post Office. I was pretty mad when I received a call from a clerk that worked at the Quail Heights Post Office and told that they had been put on emergency suspension because they had an alleged shortage of their stamp stock.

I called the Quail Heights Post Office and found out this employee had an alleged shortage of just over $600.00. They previously had an overage of almost the same amount. I told the supervisor that I was coming to the post office and what documentation I needed. I also told the supervisor that if management thought the employee was stealing then they should have sealed the employees stamp drawers and call the postal inspectors. The supervisor told me it was the manager that put this employee off the clock.

As it turned out I got stuck at the union office that day and couldn't get to the Quail Heights Post Office until the next morning.

My intention, after arriving at the Quail Heights Post Office, was to fill out a request form for the documentation I needed and then leave. Just after I arrived at Quail Heights I heard a supervisor tell the window clerks, over the loud speaker, to go to the break room for a meeting so I went into the break room too. Just after I walked in and said good morning to some of the clerks the manager of the station asked me to come out of the break room to talk to him. I told him I wanted to hear what the supervisor had to say and I was told the supervisor wouldn't start without me. When I went out of the break room the manager told me in the future if I was going to come by his post office then I was to call ahead of time. I told the manager that if he had a problem with me being there then that was his problem and he should handle it. I then walked back into the break room. The manager then told all the window clerks to go back to work. They never had their meeting. After having a few words with the manager, I didn't use any profanity, I then walked out of the break room and into the back of the post office and finally filled out my request form for documentation.

There was a shop steward for the maintenance craft that worked at Quail Heights and I asked him to go with me as a witness that I was giving this request to the manager. My plan was just to get this manager to sign my request form and make a copy and then leave. When we walked up to the manager he told the shop steward to go back to work and he refused to sign my request form. I figured I would call the labor relations department, the ones that would hear a lot of grievances when the grievance got beyond step 2. At this point I figured I might as well piss the manager off more than I already have so I walked into his office to use his phone. He sent a supervisor into the office to unplug the phone. I guess the manager didn't have the balls to do it himself. I just walked back again to the back of the post office and went into the timekeepers office to use the phone there. As I was walking to go use the phone I heard the manager tell the supervisor to call the police. I was going to call the labor relations department but instead I called the steward area at the General Mail Facility and told

George Pagliery, the chief shop steward, to get down to Quail Heights because I needed a witness.

Before the police arrived I got a call from the labor relations department and also the area manager. I don't know if the supervisor or the manager called them, but it made little difference to me. The labor relations representative, Mike Yagodnik, told me if I was to leave he would make sure I got all the documentation I requested. Mike Yagodnik was a union officer from the Special Delivery craft prior to going into management and knew I wouldn't leave. I told him there was no way I would let it look like management was throwing me out of the post office, especially since I haven't done anything wrong for the police to be called. I didn't even use any profanity for a change.

When the Area Manager, Les Ogdon, came to the Quail Heights Post Office, since I told him over the phone I was not leaving until the police arrived, he again tried to get me to leave. A short time later my stewards arrived, George Pagliery and another shop steward, and at almost the same time a policeman came in from the front door. George Pagliery, thinking a little better then I did asked Les Ogdon if we could go to his office and settle the issue of management calling the police. The Area Manager told the policeman that it was a mistake to call and that he was not needed. After the policeman walked out we made the arrangements to go to the Area Managers office to settle our problem about the manager calling the police.

When I walked out of the post office with George Pagliery the policeman was still sitting outside in his car. I asked him if we walked back inside could he come in and walk us out. I told him it would look good on my labor charge against this manager. The policeman told us that he didn't even have jurisdiction to come inside the post office and if the post office insisted that he make me leave then he would have to call his sergeant to see what he was suppose to do. I guess I won that battle.

As for the employee that was put off the clock both the supervisor and the employee made a writing error when conducting the audit showing the overage. Instead of writing down the 192 dollar stamps they wrote down 912 dollar stamps. Somehow when writing what they counted they put the 9 in front of the 1 so it made the employees audit way over. I'm sure either the supervisor or the employee counted the stamps and the other wrote down the number. They were suppose to make separate counts and write down what they counted and then checked the figures together.

When the second audit was conducted, with a different supervisor, approximately three weeks later the count was done correctly but it showed the shortage. The employee was out of work for one week and got paid for this without a grievance. I don't remember the manager saying he was sorry for being a wrong and calling the police.

There was another time when I was at the Homestead Main Post Office investigating an alleged shortage for an employee when the police were called. An employee at the Homestead Post Office had an alleged shortage of her stamp stock of approximately $6,400.00.

Prior to this shortage there was another employee working at the Homestead Post Office that got caught stealing. I figured that with a known thief at the post office there was a possibility this employee took stock from the lady with the alleged shortage.

When I got to the Homestead Post Office I told the employee that unless we find some security violations we do not have a very good case. I told the supervisor I wanted to do a complete security check. I wanted to check all the employees keys for the stamp stock against every other employees stamp drawer. The supervisor told me he didn't have a problem with that request, but I would have to check with the acting Postmaster.

The acting Postmaster of Homestead was from Miami and I knew I would have a problem with him. I had a problem with this acting Postmaster when he was in Miami working as the manager at the Flagler Post Office. I went into his office and told him about the security check I wanted to do and as I expected I was denied the opportunity to check the employee's keys. The acting Postmaster told me that was management's job and in fact they do security checks all the time. It was then I knew I was getting nowhere with the acting Postmaster and had to do something drastic. I told him that I would put my request for documentation (a security check) in writing, file a grievance and do a labor charge. As I was leaving the Postmasters office I said I was use to dealing with assholes. This set him off. I didn't call him an asshole, but we both knew in reality I did. I was told to leave the post office and I said I was as soon as I filled out my request for documentation.

The police were there faster then what I expected. The Homestead Post Office was just a few blocks away from the Homestead police station. I was told I had to leave or I would be arrested for trespassing. Of course I was escorted out of the building with the police apologizing for making me leave. I never got to do a security check but did file a labor charge and a grievance for the shortage and a grievance for the denial of documentation.

The labor charge really didn't do much good. I was told the labor charge would be held pending the outcome of the grievance on the denial of documentation. The grievance on the denial of documentation wasn't going anywhere. Even if management wanted to give the documentation it wouldn't have done me any good. Just approximately three months after the incident with the police escorting me out of the Homestead Post Office hurricane Andrew hit Homestead and destroyed the post office.

As for the alleged shortage for the clerk the case went to arbitration and the union won the case thereby relieving the employee of any responsibility. The main reason the union won the arbitration was because management failed to provide the requested documentation.

I guess it was worth me upsetting the acting Postmaster and getting escorted out by the police so the union could win a $6,400.00 shortage.

I had the police called on me a few more times. Two times from the manager at the Sunset Post Office and once at the South Florida Mail Processing Facility.

The manager at the Sunset Post Office was a royal pain in the ass. I called him a little shit and told him if he put his hand inside his shirt he would really look like Napolean. It was hard to deal with a manager like him. I tried not to take things personal but I did not like this man and I guess I cussed at him more then I should've. I believe he looked for trouble knowing I would get pissed off and tell him what I thought of him.

The first time the manager of the Sunset Post Office called the police he called the postal security police. What the manager didn't know was that I knew some of the security police officers that worked for the post office. When the manager called the postal security police I waited in the office where the window T-5 (the person that took the money at the end of the night from all the window clerks)worked at the Sunset Post Office. The manager waited just outside the office, I guess hoping the postal police would walk me out. Instead, when the postal police officer arrived at the Sunset Post Office and saw me he came over and shook my hand and asked how was I doing? The manager got upset and just walked away. I then told the postal police officer that the manager was an idiot and I left the post office.

The second time the manager of the Sunset Post Office called the police on me was when the shop steward that worked at the Sunset Post

Office, Rick Pujol, gave the manager a request for documentation to sign. The manager refused to sign the request form and started walking away with the request form still in his hands. I told the manager that if he was not going to sign the request form then just give it back to Rick Pujol and we could get the documentation from labor relations. The manager just kept walking away and didn't even answer me. I finally said "listen you little shit give me the fucking request form back". I finally got the managers attention. It seemed like the only thing he understood was when someone cussed at him. Of course he called the police. This time he called the Metro Dade Police and not the postal security police. Unfortunately I wasn't there when the police arrived. Maybe I should've just let Rick Pujol handle the situation. Rick had more patients then I had. I had to leave to go to a scheduled meeting but Rick stayed and got the request form finally signed. When the police arrived at the Sunset Post Office they were told I had already left.

One of the last times I had the police called on me was again at the Quail Heights Post Office. This time it was a different manager and I didn't have to cuss at anyone to get them upset.

I had to go by the Quail Heights Post Office to pick up some documentation that I needed for a grievance. I had just a few days before found out my daughter was having a baby girl. Since I had dated a letter carrier that worked at Quail Heights I wanted to tell her about the good news. I walked in the post office and walked right by the manager and a supervisor and walked up to the carriers case, Karen a lady I had previous dated was working at. I told Karen about my daughter that was going to have a baby and walked away. It might have taken me a minute at the most. When I walked back passed the manager she told me in the future I was to call ahead of time before coming by the post office. I thought déjà vu, here we go again. I told the manager if she had a problem then she would have to deal with it. I started to walk to the timekeepers office when the manager told me to leave. I thought, at first, when the manager told me to leave that she was only talking about the carrier section. I told the manager I was picking up some documentation for a grievance then I was leaving. I just kept walking away and she told me she was going to call the area manager, Manny Molina. I told her when she got the area manager on the phone to let me talk to him. The manager, most likely, thought I was being a smart ass. I knew if I had talked to Manny Molina, I got along good with him, nothing would have happen. I'm not sure if the manager had called the area manager but had told me again to leave or she was calling the police. That's when I knew for sure the manager wanted me to leave the building. I had already picked up the documentation I requested and was walking toward the door to leave. When the manager told me again she was calling the police I had to turn around and stay since there was no way I was going to be threaten by her calling the police.

I walked to the break room and started looking over the documentation I requested and waited for the police. When the police arrived there were four policemen and I made a commit that they must really fear the postal workers since that many policeman came into the post office. Talk of disrupting the work force. When the police came in most of the employees wanted to see what was going on and stopped working. The first policemen didn't like my commit and told me I had to leave or I would be arrested. I told the policeman that I didn't have a problem leaving but that I had to be escorted out. The policeman said that wouldn't be any problem. I was escorted out and was asked if I wouldn't mine having my car searched. I had nothing to hide and figured I would use this in my charge against the manager.

I filed an EEO (equal employment opportunity) against the manager. George Pagliery represented me in the EEO hearing. It was really a mediation hearing which is part of the EEO process. George Pagliery representing me told us how the unions were started and the fight the unions had to go through just to get respect and protect their rights. It was interesting to all of us. I believe this was the selling point to resolving the EEO. The manager and the mediator was as interested in hearing George as I was.

I asked for a written apology and wanted it in writing that I would enter a post office at any time as long as I didn't cause a distraction. The manager agreed to settle the EEO with an apology and started treating me with more respect, or so it seemed. She later was promoted to Postmaster of Miami Beach and we seemed to have gotten along pretty good. The manager, after some time, was promoted again and left the Miami District.

I believe as I have gotten older I think I've controlled my temper a little better and avoided unnecessary arguments and tried to control my profanity. I still can not handle stupid people but I guess that's life.

After not being a union shop steward or officer I really had to watch what I said to management. After I started working at the Country Lakes

Post Office there were five managers or acting managers that I worked for. I was able to keep my mouth closed enough not to get into trouble. Most of the managers saw that I was a good worker and had no problem doing what was asked of me.

When I first starting at Country Lakes Post Office on February 1st 2003, Paulette Thomas was the manager and Charlie Smith was the supervisor. This was the main reason I took a bid job to Country Lakes Post Office. The manager and supervisor were good people and ones I knew I could work with. I had Sunday and Tuesdays as schedule days off. After Paulette Thomas got promoted as the acting area manager of the West Charlie Smith took over as acting manager of Country Lakes. After Charlie Smith retired at the end of January, 2006, Paulette Thomas also retired in October, 2006. While I worked at the Country Lakes Post Office there were three other managers or acting managers. For whatever reason the people coming in as the manager didn't last there very long. Maybe one day there will be a manager that stays for a longer period of time.

CHAPTER 15

LAST CHANCE SETTLEMENTS

LAST CHANCE SETTLEMENTS ARE just what it says, a last chance for an employee to keep their job. This is a type of settlement of the worst kind for the employee and the union. When dealing with an employees attendance the last chance settlement was usually after a period of time that an employee failed to come to work and management followed progressive discipline. Almost all the time the employee had been issued a letter of warning or two, after being given a discussion, followed by a seven day suspension. Sometimes the union was able to get the seven day suspension reduced to a lower suspension and then the employee might be issued another seven day suspension. Next is a fourteen day suspension and then a removal. When the employee is issued a removal the union has always been able to get a settlement of a last chance for the employee. When we were lucky, or could come up with some good arguments or the employee had an excellent reason for missing work the union was able to get more then one last chance settlements.

Sometimes the last chance settlements were not for bad attendance, but because the employee had a drug problem and got busted before their attendance had gotten bad enough to issue them a suspension or removal. In these cases management went right to a removal without going through progressive discipline.

Sometimes an employee had a physical altercation and the union was able to save their job, but had to settle on a last chance settlement.

Like I said before the last chance settlement was the worst kind of settlement the union negotiated. The problem is that the union had no choice. Our backs were up against the wall, so to speak.

The employees with what management called unsatisfactory attendance have had this type of attendance over a long period of time, sometimes years, and now management expects this employee to do a complete turn around and have satisfactory attendance. A lot of the time the employee doesn't make it and gets removed from the post office.

It was easier to save an employees job that had a drug problem than someone with just unsatisfactory attendance. Someone with a drug problem would go into the hospital, or clinic, to get help and if they messed up again they would go back into the hospital, or clinic, and management would see they're trying to get help and wouldn't issue any more discipline.

I was lucky when I first started in the post office. First I only worked for just over six months before leaving for the Army, and also the post office back in 1969-1970 wasn't as hard core on attendance, at lease in the section I worked in. Also I made sure I did a real good job to keep the supervisor from saying anything about my attendance.

When I had to sign a settlement for a last chance settlement I did not feel good about it knowing there was a real good chance the employee would not live up to the agreement. When the employee made it through the terms of the last chance settlement, usually one year, it really made me feel good that I helped an employee.

I would have employees call me from the night shift to see if I could get management to sign off on a last chance settlement. There was one time an employee, grievant, called and after meeting with her I agreed to set up a meeting. The person in management that the union negotiated with for the employees that worked at the General Mail Facility was an former union representative, Michael Yagodnik.

When I met with the employee and saw the letter of removal she received I told her I thought the union could win the removal without a last chance settlement. This meant if the union couldn't settle the case after step 2 of the grievance procedure then the employee would go on leave without pay until the case is settled. Of course if the union lost the case the employee would not come back to work. The problem with this, and management knows it, is that most employee can't afford to be out of work with no money coming in so the union is forced to agree to the last chance settlement.

I had to meet with Michael Yagodnik I didn't know what his title was, to set up a meeting with the employee. Mike would hear all the step 2 hearings for management that the union presented for the employees from the General Mail Facility. Also the last chance settlements for employees at the General Mail Facility had to go to Michael Yagodnik.

Michael Yagodnik was real hard to deal with. Being a former union officer didn't make a difference. It was obvious he forgot where he started from. What he would do is schedule a meeting with the union along with the employee and have the settlement already typed up for the employee and the union to sign. He would always give a copy to the union and the employee and read the settlement to us so the employee understood what they were signing.

I didn't have too much of a problem with most of the settlement. The employee had to have satisfactory attendance for a period of one year. The employee had to take a fitness for duty, test for drugs, and if need be go to meetings with an EAP (employee assistance program) counselor. The settlement explained what was considered by management as unsatisfactory attendance. What I did have a problem with was the part of the settlement that said the employee agreed to drop any and all EEO cases that were pending. When I saw that in the settlement I asked if this meant any EEO pertaining to this removal? I was told by Michael Yagodnik that this meant any EEO that was pending. I told Michael Yagodnik that he could stick the settlement up his ass and when I got up from the chair I was sitting in the chair somehow went flying against the wall. I then walked out of the room. The grievant followed me out of the room and asked me to come back in and sign the settlement. She said she read the settlement and didn't care what it said. She said she couldn't afford to go out on leave without pay for anytime and felt that she could live with the settlement. She convinced me that she would have satisfactory attendance so I went back inside the office. Michael Yagodnik was mad but so was I. I told him I never saw a settlement that said anything about dropping all the EEO cases pending but since I didn't have a choice I agreed to the settlement.

I would go onto the night shift every now and then to check on the employee. The employee did satisfy the agreement and later went on to become a shop steward. I was happy I could help her even though I didn't like what I was agreeing to.

I've agreed to a lot more last chance settlements but most don't stick in your mind. After signing the settlement you just hope the employee makes it through the agreed upon time. Most of the ones I do remember are the ones that don't make it and end up being removed from the Postal service. Here are a few of the cases that have stuck in my mine.

Hurricane Andrew hit Miami and Homestead Florida on August 24th 1992. Approximately February 1993 I received a call from the manager of the Snapper Creek Post Office, Charles Smith, telling me one of his employees haven't return to work since the hurricane. I told him I needed something in writing and that he had to send the employee a written notice again. The manager told me he sent the employee two notices to report for duty and a notice to report for a investigative interview. This is a hearing where the employee along with the union are informed what the employee is being charged with. The employee also has the right to provide information that might keep management from issuing discipline.

Since the union did not receive anything in writing the manager had to send the employee another notice to report for the investigative interview. The union also had to receive a copy of the same notice sent to the employee. When the union received the notice there was also a date set for the meeting to try to see if we could come up with any kind of a settlement or to file our grievance and appeal it to the proper step.

Knowing this employee I figured he wouldn't show up for the investigative interview so I brought a shop steward with me. The manager, Charles Smith did what he had to do by notifying the union and didn't have to go any further in trying to notify the employee. When we got to the Snapper Creek Post Office the manager gave me a package that was almost complete for the employee. The employee was being charged with failure to report to duty as assigned. After talking to Mr. Smith for a short time I asked him to hold off on any decision until I had time to go by the employees house. After Mr. Smith agreed not to make a decision I went by the employees house along with the shop steward.

When we got to the employees house there was a new motor home in his front yard but the house had not been touched after being damaged from hurricane Andrew. The house had bars on the windows but had no screens on the windows. After looking in the house we saw two beautiful puppies laying in water. Since there was no screens on the windows rain water came into the house every time it rained. We, the shop steward and myself thought about taking the puppies. We could have pulled them out between the bars on the window. I made a little joke by saying "I can see the newspaper now, two union officers get busted for stealing a dopers dogs. We decided to leave the dogs where we found them.

At this point I figured it appeared the employee didn't care about his job so why should I. I told the shop steward I was going to write up a settlement that I know the manager will never agree to and if the employee didn't call the union to file a grievance then there would be no case and the employee would be removed from the Postal Service. It wouldn't be our problem.

The settlement I wrote was as follows;

The grievant will be given thirty (30) days from date of settlement to report back to work. If the grievant reports back to work within the thirty (30) days then the issue would be moot and no discipline will be issued. If the grievant fails to report back to work within thirty (30) days it will be considered that the employee has abandoned his job and he will be removed from the Postal Service immediately.

I gave this settlement to the manager, Charles Smith, and after reading the settlement Mr. Smith signed the settlement. I think I was in shock. I asked Mr. Smith if he read what I had written and he told me he believed in giving an employee another chance.

The employee did report back to work on the last day possible to satisfy the settlement and after working six hours left again. Approximately one month later Charles Smith called me up to set up another meeting. The manager was requesting a removal for the employee for violating a last chance agreement. I told Mr. Smith the employee didn't have a last chance agreement and had I known Mr. Smith was going to sign the previous agreement we had then we might have discussed a last chance agreement. Charles Smith wouldn't discuss a last chance settlement and issued the employee a letter of removal for abandoning his postal job. I had to take the letter of removal for this employee to the Area Manager to get a last chance settlement. Les Odgon, the Area Manager, agreed to a last chance settlement but the employee had to take a fitness for duty, a drug test, to see if he was clean or doing drugs.

After talking to the employee and telling him I could settle the case but that he had to take a drug test. I also told him we could put the drug test off for approximately six weeks, or however much time the employee needed. The employee told me he had no problem with drugs and that he wanted to take the drug test as soon and as early as possible. I asked the employee if he really understood what the settlement was calling for. If he failed the drug test he would be removed immediately from the Postal Service. The employee told me again he had no problem with drugs and that he was ready to come back to work.

After getting all the parties, Area Manager, employee and myself, to sign the settlement I took the settlement to the post office medical unit at the General Mail Facility and scheduled an appointment for the employee.

I had the drug test scheduled as soon as I could at approximately 9:00 A.M. and had the notice for the drug test sent to the employee. A couple of days later the employee called the union hall and wanted to know why the drug test was scheduled so early. I told the employee I did as he requested and had the drug test scheduled as early as possible. Again, he told me he didn't have a problem, he just wanted to know who had the test scheduled.

When the employee took the drug test he tested positive for marijuana and cocaine. The employee was removed from the Postal Service and never reported back. What I didn't understand was that this employee had the opportunity to enter a clinic or hospital and this would've saved his job. He had to know he was going to test positive on his drug test and yet he took it any way. Now after all these years, 13 years, this employee is trying to get his job back in the post office. Since I was no longer a union steward or officer I didn't have to deal with it.

Sometimes I found myself in a situation I wasn't sure how to handle. I had to ask for advise and then decide how I wanted to react to the advise I received. One case I wasn't sure how to react to and had to ask for advise and then I disregard it the advise I was given. Hopefully I'll never regret how I handled the situation.

The president of the Motor Vehicle Craft of the Miami Area Local asked me to talk to this mechanic that worked in the garage at the General Mail Facility. The employee had served a ten day suspension for having what management called unsatisfactory attendance. Now, after receiving the ten day suspension this employee had already been absent two more times,

This employee lived only a few blocks from me and somehow knew where I lived. We both lived in the Homestead area, in Leisure City.

One day I saw this employee, the mechanic from the post office, picking up his mail at the Homestead Post office. I talked to this man about his attendance telling him he had to be careful before he was issued a removal from the Postal Service. I told him if he did get a removal to call me and the worse I could get as a settlement would be a last chance settlement. I was told by this employee he was going to be careful and try to improve his attendance.

As I was leaving the post office, I had already gotten in my car, the mechanic came up to the car and told me if he was given a letter of removal he would become famous. I told him he could not tell me this since I had to represent him and didn't need to hear something like this. He told me he didn't mean to say this. Again, I started to back up my car so I could leave the parking lot and again he came up to my window of the car. He told me if he was going to get fired his name would be in all the newspapers. I told him again to think about what he was saying and left the parking lot.

I called the National APWU office in Washington D. C. and talked to one of the national officers and told him what was said and asked for advice, I was told I would have to report this to management. What I thought about was if I did report this employee for what he told me this employee would've been put on emergency suspension and another union officer would have to represent him. My main concern was what if I was the only person this employee told about becoming famous and I reported this and he came to my house where I have a wife and two children.

I didn't report what this man told me. What I did do was get the shop stewards at the garage together, there were three shop stewards, and told them if this employee ever gets fired and loses his case and is seen coming back to the garage, then the shop stewards had to try to get all the employees out of the building away from this man. I didn't tell the shop stewards what this man told me. I'm sure, maybe they could've guessed. One of the shop stewards asked me about management in the office down the hall and the offices upstairs. I told him that if he thought he had time to inform management then good. If he didn't have time, oh well.

As it turned out this employee was issued a letter of removal and I got the letter expunged on a procedural error on managements part. This employee then received another letter of removal and the best I could do was get him a last chance settlement. This employee has since been removed from the Postal Service and I haven't heard anything from this employee again. It's now been a good twelve years so I don't think anything will happen, but for awhile I wasn't sure what to think and just hoped I made the right decision. I did try to save this mans job but some people you cannot help if they cannot help themselves.

There was another employee, a maintenance employee who worked on the machines at the General Mail Facility, he did go into a drug clinic and was issued a notice of removal. I saw the case way beyond the time limit to file a grievance and when I asked the Maintenance Craft President he acted like he didn't know a thing.

After checking phone numbers I was able to find out where this employee was and had to go talk to a maintenance manager to get an extension for the grievance. I was able to get a settlement for this employee but he had to stay drug free. He was doing real good at the clinic and was even talking to others about staying drug free. This employee came back to work and was doing good for the first six months but then had a relapse. I had heard he was caught in a car doing crake cocaine. He never called the union and I never heard from him again.

There was another employee, the custodian at the Country Lakes Post Office, that just couldn't get it together. One day while driving to work, his scheduled reporting time was 10:00A.M., he was passing cars on the right side of the road, even going off the road to pass. Two unmarked policemen saw him and turned around to go after him. By the time the police caught up to this employee he had already pulled into the post office parking lot and was walking toward the building. The police cited him for careless driving, DUI (driving under influence), plus he had four joints of marijuana in his pocket. The employee was arrested and had to get bailed out of jail.

He had been drinking so much the night before that the beer was still in his system, and with the joints of marijuana in his pocket as he was walking toward the building sure didn't help him with his job.

This employee went into the South Miami Hospital and got clean. He claimed to quit drinking so maybe the hospital helped him a little. After a disciplinary interview I was able to get him a last chance settlement. The last chance settlement was for one year and he had to stay clean of drugs and alcohol.

The manager at Country Lakes Post Office, Paulette Thomas, kept telling me that I should talk to this employee since she felt he was still doing drugs. I respected Mrs. Thomas for talking to me instead of just taking discipline against this employee. Of course it didn't do me any good to talk to this employee since he wasn't about to quit the drugs.

One day before this employee was to get off from work he went and moved his truck from the back of the parking lot to the front. While sitting in his truck before he finished work he was rolling a joint of marijuana when the supervisor walked up to his truck to see what he was doing. He didn't even see the supervisor until she was right outside the window of his truck. The supervisor told him to come inside to the office, but instead after throwing the marijuana that he was rolling into a joint out the window he left the parking lot. He did come inside the post office to clock out for the day before he drove off.

One would think this employee would have enough sense to clean up the marijuana but he didn't. The supervisor got the post office camera and took a picture of the marijuana on the ground. The employee was then given another disciplinary interview and then a notice of removal. Paulette Thomas, the manager at the Country Lakes Post Office would not settle the case as I was trying to get him another last chance settlement. I called the Area Manager, Manny Molina, but couldn't get him to agree to another last chance settlement either. I then called the Postmaster of Miami.

When I called the Postmaster, Jesus Galvez, I had to get him in the right frame of mind. I asked Mr. Galvez if he liked baseball? He said he did. I reminded the Postmaster that in baseball the player gets three strikes before they are out. The Postmaster, Jesus Galvez, then asked me where I was going with this? I then told him about this employee and asked for another last chance settlement. It took me some time, but I got the Postmaster to agree to just extend the previous last chance settlement we had. The Postmaster told me to get with the area manager, Manny Molina, and write up another settlement using the previous settlement as a guide line. The employee went back into the South Miami Hospital and again went through a rehab program.

I'm not sure how long this employee stayed clean, if he was ever clean of drugs at all, but he didn't satisfy the last chance settlement. Part of the settlement was he had to go for random drug testing. One day the manager at the Country Lakes Post Office, Paulette Thomas, told him they were going for a random drug test. Even then the manager was, in a round-about-way, trying to help this employee. The employee reported to work at 10:00 A.M. and as soon as he came into the post office the manager told this employee that they were going for the random drug test. The thing is the manager didn't take the employee for a few hours. Paulette Thomas thought the employee had enough sense to sign a sick slip and go home before she took him for the drug test. If the employee did that and called me, I would have told him to try to go back to the hospital into rehab again. It would've saved his job, at lease for a little longer. When the manager finally took the employee to take the drug test, as expected he failed the drug test.

The manager had previously talked to me and told me they thought the employee was still using drugs. Paulette Thomas suspected the employee was using cocaine. I talked to this employee a few times and told him that management felt he was still using drugs and that he better be careful or he was going to get fired. I guess he thought he was going to get away with it forever.

The employee was given another disciplinary interview and another letter of removal. A grievance was written by the Maintenance Craft President, I refused to write any more appeals for this employee, and appealed to arbitration. The union took the case to arbitration because the employee claims he was asking for help and that he went to Paulette Thomas and told her he needed help and that he was going to go back into the hospital. The union lost the arbitration and the employee was removed from the Postal Service.

After getting removed from the Postal Service I talked to this employee, he called me to see if there was anything else that could be done, and I told him to put in for disability retirement. I didn't think he could get disability retirement but it didn't hurt to try. He did have some medical problems, most likely due to the years of drug use. The employee surprised me and did get disability retirement. He didn't get full benefits but anything was better then nothing at all.

There was another employee, a clerk that worked at the Coral Gables Post Office that I tried to help, and thought I got through to this employee about getting off the drugs, But he too couldn't stay clean. I did a last chance settlement for this employee and after a year the employee had all discipline removed from his file. I really felt good that I saved this man his job and that he got off the drugs. He stayed clean for the whole year and even went almost another year before he fell off the wagon again.

I was working at the Sunset Post Office after losing my election for the Clerk Craft President position in 1995. Between June 1996 and September 1998, when I was reelected as the Executive Vice President of the Miami Area Local, the employee that I thought was clean and staying off drugs and out of trouble was disciplined and fired from the Postal Service. It didn't happen overnight. Management had to follow progressive discipline before this employee would be fired again. Because the employee started having real bad attendance again management started issuing discipline. This means he was given a letter of warning, a 7-day suspension followed by a 14-day suspension and then a removal. I don't know who represented this employee but I heard he had a last chance settlement and failed a drug test.

Chapter 16

SEX, SEXUAL HARASSMENT & DISCRIMINATION

There was, and mabe still is, so much discrimation and sexual harassment going on in the post office that it's unbelievable. The sex in the post office are stories I heard about but don't have first hand knowledge.

There was a mother and daughter that work together at the General Mail Facility that were called the silver foxes. Both of them had their hair dyed silver. There were rumors that both played around a lot. The mother was married and was caught in bed with another man by her husband. The husband killed his wife and then himself. The daughter either resigned from the Postal Service or transferred out of Miami.

There was a rumor that this manager at the South Florida Mail Processing Facility was caught with the secretary on the desk in his office. The secretary was rumored to having this managers baby. I don't know if this secretary was still married, her husband was a manager at another postal facility, but at some point she divorced her husband, or her husband divorced her. Either way they were divorced.

Then there was a man and woman, both married to different people, working at the Airmail Facility. While the man was casing mail the woman was on her knees between his legs. As far as I know they didn't get discipline for their activity, unless being sent to work at the General mail Facility is considered discipline. I guess while the man was getting some head he was casing a lot faster.

When I worked at the Snapper Creek Post office there was a custodian that also worked there that seemed to know a lot about other people. We had a manager that was rumored to be a ladies man. We had a supervisor that worked at Snapper Creek, she was a good looking lady. One day the custodian said that this supervisor had the managers baby approximately eight years ago. I didn't really think much about this not knowing if it was true or not. Of course I really didn't care either. One day I was in the break room and the supervisor was in there too talking about her eight year old son. His first name was Dennis, the same as the managers.

Then one day the custodian said that she heard the manager was caught by this other supervisors husband while the manager was sleeping with this supervisor. This was not the same supervisor that was alleged to have the managers son. The custodian had said that the manager was hit in the face by the ladies husband. I just laughed and said right. How would this custodian know this.

The manager never in the years I knew him wore sunglasses. After the custodian said the manager was hit in the face he came to work one day and had dark sunglasses on. He then took off on leave for a couple of weeks. I just laughed trying to figure out how she, the custodian, knew so much about this manager.

The supervisor later left her husband and married this manager that alleged got caught sleeping with her while she was still with her former husband. It was obvious there was a lot going on between the manager and this supervisor while she was married to this other man.

There were all kinds of stories where people were getting caught by the postal police having sex in the parking lot at the General Mail Facility.

I remember there was this one supervisor who got caught having sex with a female employee and was moved from the day shift to the night shift. This same supervisor gave me a discussion for leaving the building on my break, to go to the Miami Postal credit union. I guess this supervisor thought it was alright to fuck in the parking lot while on the clock, but not go to the credit union while on break.

I don't know what the divorce rate is in the post office compared to other companies but I do know a lot of divorce people working in the post office.

Unfortunantely there's a lot of sexual harassment in the post office. Sometimes the manager or supervisor is asked to resign from the post office before any action is taken. Sometimes the manager or supervisor is fired, but most of the time the manager or supervisor is put back to craft or just moved to another section of the post office.

There was this 204B supervisor at Snapper Creek Post office that was charged with sexual harassment and he was moved to the Allapattah Post office. I guess that was his punishment. While at the Allapattah Post

Office he was accused of coming up behind a female letter carrier and grabbing her breast. A sexual harassment charge was filed and for some reason was later dropped. From the Allapattah Post Office this supervisor went to the Coconut Grove Post Office. I didn't hear of any problems at the Coconut Grove Post Office but for some reason he was sent back to the Snapper Creek Post Office. When I saw this supervisor at the Snapper Creek Post Office I called the Area Manager and told him I wanted this scum of a supervisor out of this office. I made sure this supervisor heard me make the call. He was sent to the Normandy Post Office on Miami Beach. Maybe management thought he would be safe there. It wasn't long before another female employee, this time a clerk, filed a sexual harassment complaint against this supervisor. The last place I know of that he worked at was the Flagler Post Office. I had heard this supervisor was fired once but won his case and was brought back to work. Maybe it was the time the lady at the Allapattah Post Office dropped her complaint. It would seem like this supervisor didn't learn anything from when he was fired since he had at least one other charge after he came back to work. It also appears he had some friends in upper management.

Then there was an acting manager of the Snapper Creek Post Office that was fired from the post office after going to a MSPB (merit system protection board) hearing. The shop steward that was representing the employees on the sexual harassment case was a letter carrier. The letter carrier shop steward started an investigation when four female letter carriers complained of sexual harassment from this acting manager. The shop steward went back twenty years in his investigation. This was the time the acting manager started in the United States Postal Service. Seven women came forward to testify at the MSPB against this acting manager. One of the complaints was fifteen years old. Not only did the acting manager get fired for sexual harassment but the area manager was put on leave, I'm not sure if he was ever fired, for alleged lying trying to protect this acting manager but did lose his position as the area manager and is now a manager at one of the stations in Miami. It's too bad cause this area manager was great for me to deal with. I could go to his office to discuss any problems we had. I could get settlements from him that others wouldn't settle.

When Boca Raton merged with the Miami Area Local a sexual harassment case was brought to Judy Johnson. One of the top managers in Boca Raton had been harassing women and men for years before the case was brought against this manager. I don't know if it was that the employees were scared or embarrassed to bring complaints forward of sexual harassment against this management. When Judy Johnson started to hear some of the things said about this management she started an investigation. This top manager went to a hearing and was fired from the Postal Service.

This was just a few of the many incidents involving managements sexual harassment of employees. One would think that when a manager is fired that others would quit the sexual harassment of employees but it continues even today.

The worst case for the union to be in is when there are two craft employees involved. Both employees have to be represented if any grievance is written so the union has to be careful not to take sides.

There was a time at Olympia Heights Post Office where this employee was always making remarks to female employees. This was directed mostly at one employee. He would bark into the microphone, so everyone working there could hear, when this employee walked by. One day while wearing a union apron he lifted the apron and told the female employee that he had something for her. She walked over to him and grabbed him between his legs and told him there was nothing there. Both employees called the union. The female employee wanted to file a grievance for sexual harassment and the male employee wanted to file a grievance for assult. I had to go to the Olympia Heights Post Office to talk to these employees. I talked to one at a time and then talked to them together. I convinced them not to file a grievance and told the male employee he had to stop the harassment. This seemed to have worked. Both employees have since left the Olympia Heights Post Office to work at another postal facility in Miami. The male employee received a bid job south of Olympia Heights Post Office and the female employee received a bid job north of Olympia Heights Post Office.

There was another incident with this same male employee, prior to the last incident, where he walked up to this older woman. This employee, the older woman, was the secretary of the Area Manager who had his office at Olympia Heights Post Office. The male employee asked her if she knew why men liked older women? He then proceded to tell her older women with no teeth can give good blow jobs because they can gum the man. This female employee was so upset and called the union yelling. I went out to talk to the male employee and he apologed to the older female employee. Judy Johnson had to talk to the female employee.

There was another incident at the Perrine Postal Store where a female employee filed an EEO (equal employee opportunity) against the post office because she claimed a male employee sexually harassed her. I talked to both employees, one at a time. The woman that filed charges went out of work for some time and management was suppose to investigate the claim of sexual harassment. When the female employee returned back to work the male employee was sent, temporary, to another post office to work. The union was in a rough position. The female employee claimed the male employee had pushed her against the wall and tried to kiss her. The male employee claimed it never happened. The union cannot believe one employee over the other employee without any proof. That was also the problem with the post office investigation. There was no proof that the incident happened or not. The question was why would someone make this up? The male employee, a former supervisor, was quiet and never had any kind of problem. After a long period of time the two employees ended up working together again, I don't think they worked together without another employee working at the same time. The male employee later received a bid job to another post office.

The worst case I remember was when a female employee who had gotten a bid job on the LSM (letter sorting machine) and happen to walk by a male employee one day and said hello and smiled. The male employee started writing love letters to the female employee. When she complained to the union, George Pagliery talked to this male employee and asked him to quit writing the love letters. He didn't deny writing the letters and he did quit for awhile. Then he started writing the love letters again to this same female employee. Again she complained to the union. As far as I know she didn't inform management about the love letters. I, along with George Pagliery went to talk with this male employee. We told him to back off and quit writing the letters. We told him sooner or later she was going to tell management about the problem and when management wrote him up we would have to defend him. We told him we might even win a case of sexual harassment against him but that he knew he was wrong and had to stop writing the letters. I had heard he stopped for awhile and don't know if he ever started writing the letters again. He went home from work one day, he worked the night shift, and put a gun in his mouth and pulled the trigger. I felt like we, the union and myself, really messed this one up. I don't know what I could've done but felt I should've done something to help this man.

There was an incident reported from Portland, Maine, where a federal jury awarded $5.5 million to the family of a woman who was driven to suicide by what she had claimed was harassment and discrimination by her bosses and underlings at the Postal Service. Judith Coffin, a 12 year postal employee, accused her co-workers of calling her ugly. Circulating a caricature of her and leaving a suggestive poem for her at her job at a processing center.

Judith Coffin's family accused the employees that worked under this woman of botching jobs or missing deadlines to sabotage her career because she was a woman.

Her family also said the Postal Service discriminated against Judith when she was reassigned from her job as manager.

Judith Coffin was a diabetic and overdosed on insulin. She left a suicide note blaming the Postal Service.

This is just one such incident. One can only wonder how many more incidents of this nature arise and are not reported. I know in Miami there have been a number of suicides by both craft employees and management. The question is how many of these suicides were due to harassment or discrimination.

It was reported in the pasper, USA TODAY, on May 8th 2000 that the United States Postal Service spent $52,000.00 to settle a discrimination complaint against a top agency official who was accused of promoting a woman with whom he allegedly had a sexual relationship.

The Vice President of area operations for the Southeast signed the settlement in January 1999, according to the confidential agreement obtained by USA TODAY. Several days later the Postal Service issued a $52,000.00 check to the complainant and her lawyer.

The complainant is a senior Postal Service Manager in Jacksonville, Florida. She charged in an internal Equal Employment Opportunity (EEO) that she was bypassed for a top job in favor of a woman with whom, she said, the Vice President of area operations for the Southeast had a personal relationship with.

The Vice President of the Southeast area described the allegations as untrue and insulting. He is one of ten area Vice Presidents in the Postal Service and makes $145,000.00 annually. Prior to being promoted to

Southeast area Vice President he served as district manager for the Suncoast District in Tampa, Florida.

The EEO files show that in the capacity of district manager for the Suncoast District, on December 22nd 1997, he passed over the complainant for a senior managers job in favor of a woman who held a job three grades lower in the Suncoast District. The EEO was first filed on February 4th 1998. Ten days later she was appointed to a senior management post in Jacksonville, Florida, the identical job she sought in Tampa Florida. The Postal Service said she won the job in a competition with others. However, the complaintant said had it not been for the Southeast area Vice Presidents sexual relationship with the successful candidate in Tampa, she would not have had to move to Jacksonville, approximately 200 miles away.

The complainant had sought $250,000.00 in damages. After mediation the case was settled on January 11, 1999 for the $52,000.00.

The EEO documents show that the Southeast Vice President maintained in the proceeding that he acted properly in appointing the other woman to the Tampa post.

Postal Service officials said the Southeast area Vice Presidents decision to settle shouldn't be taken as a sign he had admitted the charges. The Postal Service claim that it was a business decision to avoid costly and time consuming litigation.

It was reported in the USA TODAY newspaper on May 23rd 2000 the Southeast area Vice President will retire after 40 years of postal service. His retirement was effect June 3rd 2000. Was he guilty of the discrimination charge that was filed against him? You be the judge.

Warren being sworn in as State Clerk Craft Director "2000"

Honeymoon in Las Vegas

2nd wife, Brenda an me—June 19, 2004

Warren and Jeff at National Convention in "2000"

First wife Teresa and me—June 23, 1973

Teresa and me at a wedding reception in the late 70's

Sam Wood—President S.W. Area Local
With Clerk Craft Director at State Convention 2002

Bernie and Wayne Wetherington at State Convention in 2002

Brenda and Warren at wedding reception of friends

*Mr. and Mrs. Pearlman celebrating their honeymoon
in Las Vegas in 2004*

*Jeff Pearlman elected as State Secretary Treasurer and
Warren Pearlman elected as State Clerk Craft Director*

Judy Johnson, President of Miami—July 25, 2001
Warren Pearlman—Executive Vice-President

Warren Pearlman in hotel room at State Convention 2000

CHAPTER 17

MISAPPROPRIATION &
POSTAL THIEF IN MANAGEMENT

POSTAL THIEF OR MISAPPROPRIATION, is it the same? It appears when there is misappropriation in management it's either authorized or the manager will be asked to resign from the Postal Service and of course not have to pay any money back to the post office.

When I'm talking about management and the way misappropriation of Postal funds are authorized I'm talking about upper management, The vice presidents or top officers of the United States Postal Service.

It must be understood what I call misappropriation might not be called the same by other people. There is one thing I really believe and that is, there is a double standard in the way higher level managers are treated compared to the working force of the postal service. Of course there are exceptions. There have been some incidents where a postmaster had been indicted, sentenced and even had to pay money back to the Postal Service. But if the postmaster is from a large city like Chicago or Atlanta, or the manager is an Area Vice President or a top financial officer then it appears it's alright to go on a spending spree and spend a lot of money that belongs to the Postal Service and the worse that might happen is that higher level manager, Vice President, Finance Officer, will have to retire from the Postal Service with a very good pension.

Again, what I call misappropriation, sometimes, is not misappropriation. It should be misuse of postal money. The Postal service is losing money and is in financial trouble. But this has not stopped the Postmaster General and the Vice-Presidents of the United states Postal service from receiving large salary increases.

In December 2006, the United States Congress voted to give the postal Board of Governors the authority to increase the pay of up to

12 United States Postal Service officers. The increases were given to the following officers of the USPS; Postmaster General from $186,600.00 to $258,840.00, an increase of only 39%. An Executive Vice-President from $186,000.00 to $235,000.00, only a 26% increase. Another Executive Vice-President from $186,000.00 to $215,000.00 an increase of 16%. The list goes on, another Executive Vice-President from $183,100.00 to $225,000.00 a 23% increase, Another Executive Vice-President from $183,100.00 to $215,000.00 a 17% increase, a Senior Vice-President from $177,800.00 to $215,000.00, a 21% increase, another Senior Vice-President from $183,100.00 to $215,000.00 and finally a Vice-President from $177,800.00 to $205,000.00 or a 15% increase. I guess you have to fill sorry for the Vice-President, he only received a 15% increase. I wonder how many bargaining unit employees would like to receive only a 15 % pay increase.

I might of gotten off track a little with the misappropriation, or what I call misappropriation talking about the salary increases for the Postmaster General and his Vice-Presidents so back to what I really believe is misappropriation.

In the Atlanta Journal it was reported on July 30th 1997 that the new Postmaster of Atlanta, Georgia, spent $40,000.00 for the swearing in ceremony. The Postmaster, the first black woman to hold the Atlanta Postmaster position, was alleged to have spent $15,000.00 bringing her family to the ceremony, and another $20,000.00 on a video of her life.

The Atlanta Postmaster had previously worked in Miami, Florida as manager of all the retail operations in the Miami District.

Prior to the Atlanta Postmaster spending this kind of money for a swearing in ceremony the Chicago, Illinois, Postmaster had huge expenditures on redecorating her office.

When the chairman of the board of Governors was questioned on the money spent for the ceremony of the Atlanta Postmaster he responded that a swearing in ceremony has historically been a community event where the public is invited to meet their new Postmaster. The event may also include refreshments.

So who ends up paying for this $40,000.00? Not the Postmaster. Was she ever charged with misappropriation of postal funds? Do you think she ever had to pay any of this money back? I don't think so. But she's a Postmaster from a big city and Postmasters from big cities spend money, sometimes the wrong way.

It was reported by the Associated Press on April 22, 2000 that the top Finance officer of the U.S. Postal Service retired after a report sharply criticized almost a quarter of a million dollars in relocation expenses were paid to him and another official.

The top finance officer was paid $142,311.00 in moving expenses. His payment included $12,075.00 for transportation of household goods, $37,275.00 for real estate costs, $25,000.00 for miscellaneous costs such as new rugs and plumber's bills, $28,961.00 to cover withholding taxes and $39,000.00 in a relocation income tax allowance. For this amount of money you might think this top officer of the Postal Service moved a great distance. He moved 15 miles, but his new residence was 2 ½ miles closer to a post office training center and Dulles International Airport. I guess moving this much closer to the post office training center justifies the $142,311.00 spent for relocation.

So if nothing was done wrong why did this top financial officer retire? According to the Postmaster General at this time the chief financial officer retired so the agency can move onward without any unnecessary distractions.

I guess this is why the Postal Service also paid the man who succeeded the top financial officer $105,817.00 for his relocation. After all he did move futher away then the man he succeeded. The new top officer moved 22 ½ miles from his home that was 26 miles from work to one that is six miles away. Why? So it would save him 30 minutes commuting time each way daily. The $105.817.00 was broken down to $7,256.00 for moving household goods, $31,573.00 for real estate costs, $25,000.00 for miscellaneous expenses, $24,455.00 for withholding taxes and $17,533.00 for relocation income taxes.

A report from the post office's Inspector General criticized the payment for the moving expenses of these top two officers since both of them moved less than 50 miles and continued working in the same offices. The payments exceeded those offered by private industry, and were not approved by the postal board of governors, and could be perceived as a way to circumvent the statutory limits on compensation.

Counting relocation benefits as income would have boosted the pay of both men to about $250,000.00, well over the cap of $151,800.00 in effect at the time.

I guess these payments for relocation is not considered misappropriation since they were approved by the Postmaster General. But then maybe that's why there's a different Postmaster General. Think either of these top level officers of the postal service paid any of this money back? I don't think so. But then why should they. It was approved by the Postmaster General.

Another top Postal Service officer retired after a review of his conduct came to light. The vice president of area operations for the Southeast Area misused a government car and frequently arranged his business meetings in Tampa, Florida, where he has a home. The Southeast area Vice president is based in Memphis, Tennessee. The questions about his travel was disclosed in USA TODAY on May 8, 2000, along with the fact the Postal Service spent $52,000.00 to settle a discrimination complaint against the area Vice President in January of 1999. The area Vice President retired on June 3, 2000, one year before the Postmaster General left his position.

Did anyone of these men have to pay any of this money back? I would be really shocked if they did. I guess if they did pay any money back then that would for sure be considered misappropriation and we wouldn't want that, would we?

There have been, which might come as a shock, some postmasters, managers and supervisors actually charged with thief and sentenced to jail time. They even had to pay money back. I will tell you about some of the reported cases that I have found through the years.

It was reported in the Philadelphia Inquirer on June 19, 2000 that the former postmaster of the Oaks Post Office in Upper Providence, Montgomery County, was indicted by a federal grand jury on theft and embezzlement charges involving tens of thousands of dollars.

The former postmaster faces 98 counts of false reporting of money and one count of embezzlement. According to documents the former postmaster embezzled $60,202.92 between October 17, 1995 and November 14, 1997 from his stamp stock, the main stock at the post office, and money he received from customers. The U.S. Attorney's office also alleges that the former postmaster failed to report the receipt of more than $35,000.00 from postal customers and falsely claimed to have disbursed more than $11,000.00 to customers as rebursements from the sale of money orders or bulk mailings.

If convicted the former Postmaster faces a maximum possible 169 year prison sentence and a $10,900.00 fine, the First Assistant U.S. Attorney had said.

According to the Postal Inspection Service public information officer the former Postmaster probably could have continued his illegal activity for a while longer, but in 1997 he was put on paid administrative leave for threatening a customer. Because a new acting Postmaster was put in charge a routine audit was conducted.

You have to wonder how long this man was on paid administrative leave. The fact that this former Postmaster was alleged to have threatened a customer and was still getting paid shows the double standard of the United States Postal Service. If a bargaining unit employee made a threat they would be put on emergency suspension, 16.7 of the collect bargaining agreement, without pay. If the bargaining unit employee was put on emergence suspension and they were a veteran then after 14 days would start getting paid again until 30 days after a notice of removal was issued.

- In a reported article from the Fresno Bee dated November 1, 2000 it was reported that a former postmaster was sentenced to eight months in custody, four months in a halfway house and four months of home detention for stealing approximately $60,000.00 from the U.S. Postal Service. The former postmaster was also ordered to pay back the money he had taken. The former postmaster pleaded guilty to taking money from January 1, 1993 to August 22, 1996 while he was postmaster in the Tulare County Community but claims that he only stole about $20,000.00. The U.S. District Judge ordered the former postmaster to pay back the $60,000.00, the amount that the Assistant U.S. Attorney and federal investigators said he took.

- In an article taken from the Daily News it was reported that a former window clerk and temporary supervisor at the Philadelphia main Post Office has admitted stealing more than $715,000.00 in cash receipts over a 31 month period.

The theft was discovered after officials learned that the former temporary supervisor was buying a large number of money orders without filing currency transaction reports. It was reported he wrote money orders totaling $691,286.00. An additional $24,286.00 in mostly hundred dollar bills was found in his apartment.

It was reported that full restitution had been made. This former window clerk and temporary supervisor was facing a prison term in the three to four year range.

• In yet another case it was reported in the Union Tribune on April 26, 2005 that a U.S. Postal Service manager who stole more than $430,000.00 from work pleaded guilty to theft charges in a San Diego, California federal court.

The manager was an accountant at the Carmel Mountain Processing Center where he was in charge of handling checks for the sale of undeliverable mail to recycling companies.

The manager has retired after 33 years with the Postal Service and has agreed to pay back the money he stole over the past three years. The manager is free on a $40,000.00 bond and is scheduled to be sentenced on July 25, 2005.

• Then there is the Miami case. The case started off as just a disappearance of a husband and wife, both managers. The husband was manager of support services where he oversaw all of the U.S. Postal Service purchasing and contracting operations in South Florida. He was responsible for negotiating and awarding all supply and service contracts and blanket purchase agreements and reviewing contract performance. The wife manager of information services managing the computer systems for the post office. She was responsible for verifying the invoices submitted by the vendors.

They both called in sick on February 9, 2000 and when they didn't show up for work on February 14, 2000 the District Manager claims to have called the postal inspectors because he was worried something might have happened to them.

Because of the managers disappearance and the fact they had access to millions of dollars in Postal Service funds there was reason for a full blown investigation and an audit by the South Florida Postal Inspectors.

When the managers disappeared they left behind a 6,300 square foot house that sits on an acre of land in the Pine Tree Estates section of Parkland. According to the contractor it cost a little over $1 million to build the house. Not too bad for a pair of postal managers making approximately $140,000.00 a year combined. This is one reason postal inspectors were so interested in finding out where the couple went to and why they left.

It also appears the postal inspectors were on to the managers. The managers departments where they worked was audited and the audit turned up discrepancies in record keeping. This was several years prior to the managers disappearance.

At the same time of the managers audit the IRS was investigating a Miami accountant who just so happen to be working with the managers. After this accountant pleaded guilty in New York to money laundering, IRS agents in Miami started looking through the accountants files.

It would appear that the managers knew they were under investigation and therefore made themselves disappear.

When the postal inspectors talked to neighbors of the managers they found out that the husband told everyone a different story about where he worked. He never told any of his neighbors that he worked for the Postal Service. He told some neighbors he was in the mortgage business, and others the computer business. He even told others he didn't work but his wife did.

It was reported in the Miami Herald on April 12, 2000 that after the investigation was started the managers were being charged with receiving more than $1 million in bribes from two Weston computer companies whose contracts they supervised. I guess we now know why the managers disappeared.

The managers lived in Venezuela for the two months that they were reported missing. According to postal inspectors they rented an upscale apartment in downtown Caracas, Venezuela, bought a new car and vacationed throughout the Caribbean.

The couple had just returned from a trip to Venezuela's Margarita Island and were about to jet off to Aruba when Venezuelan authorities, working in conjunction with the U.S. Postal Inspectors, nabbed them in the lobby of the Hotel Santa Fe in downtown Caracus.

Because the couple were on foreign soil authorities had to let the Venezuelans make the arrest. The couple were detained for having entered the country under false names. That was grounds for deportation. U.S. authorities accompanied them on the flight back to Miami.

The managers pleaded not guilty to a kickback and bribery conspiracy and was set to be in a Miami Federal court for a bond hearing.

The Postal Inspectors, four inspectors claimed to have worked around the clock on the case, wouldn't say how they tracked the couple to Venezuela. The inspectors did say that they used their knowledge of the couple's personal habits, especially the wife's exercise regimen to pinpoint them. The couple had signed up in a posh health club under false names.

When the couple went for their bond hearing they changed their plead from not guilty to guilty. They confessed to using $3.2 million to fund a lavish lifestyle.

According to confessions from all parties involved, the South Florida businessman who ran the two Weston computer companies began offering gifts to the wife. He had offered her camera equipment, jewelry and designer clothing in exchange for contracts. The two managers would go on shopping sprees. They bought motorcycles, cars, a speedboat and hundreds of thousands of dollars worth of sterio equipment.

The wife would then bill the United States Postal Service for nonexistent goods she claimed to have ordered from the computer companies. The postal service would then pay the businessman who would then pass on huge cash kickbacks to the managers.

The couple eventually built their lavish dream house with a Jacuzzi waterfall, marble staircases and an elevated toy train set that chugged from room to room.

The accountant, who had previously pleaded guilty, had handled nearly $700,000.00 for the managers. The accountant is also the one who tipped the managers off that the authorities were moving in and getting real close to them.

The night before the managers disappeared they threw a party for family and friends. The managers made an unusual display of hospitality. They invited guests to take in their possessions suede chairs, lamps and Harley-Davidson Fat Boy motorcycles. I know if I was invited to a party and was told I could take home expensive gifts I would be very suspicious.

The U.S. District Judge sentenced the managers to the maximum allowed, 71 months behind bars. The judge also fined them each the exact amount they had accrued in pensions and unused vacation time, which added up to thousands of dollars. The husband had over 30 years and the wife over 20 years in the postal service.

The managers were not the only ones to plead guilty and to be sentenced to prison. The accountant was sentenced to 27 months. The businessman who owned the Weston computer companies was too ill to be sentenced. He was 80 years old. His companies was fined instead. Also an architect pleaded guilty to paying more than $70,000.00 in bribes to the husband in exchange for $3 million in contracts. This was reported on November 1 2001 in the Miami Herald. The architect faces up to five years in prison. Then a Miami construction contractor pleaded guilty to mail fraud. He paid $70,000.00 in bribes to the husband in exchange for approximately $9 million in construction contracts. He also faces up to five years in prison. Also it was reported on January 2, 2002 another Miami contractor pleaded guilty to making payments to the husband in return for construction services and materials contracts.

The two managers were not the only postal employees involved with this case. A former architect and engineer for the Postal Servive in the South Florida district pleaded guilty to two counts of conspiracy to receive gratuities. He was sentenced to six months probation with home confinement and ordered to pay $20,000.00 in restitution to the Postal Service. Also the former manager of Maintenance at the General Mail Facility and the South Florida Mail Processing Facility and his wife, who was the bid clerk at the General Mail Facility, were either forced to retired or resigned from the Postal Service because they had some involvement in this case.

- According to a story printed in the Riverside, California, Press-Enterprise on January 21, 2001, an audit by the Inspector General revealed that United States Postal Service executives cheated the public by misappropriating chauffeurs and limousines in excess of 520 times over four years. It was reported that the chauffeurs and limousines were used to give rides to spouses and for delivering packages without postage.

The study was conducted in 2000, when the Postal Service was almost $200 million in the red and clamoring for the one-cent postage hike that went into effect on January 12, 2001.

According to the report only the Postmaster General is allowed the use of a chauffeur for office-to-home travel. Other executives are authorized use of official vehicles and drivers at certain management levels and while on official business.

There were nine unidentified executives mentioned in the report with the biggest abuser using a chauffeur 460 times over a two year period.

A Representative from Tennessee, said the chauffeur service is definitely an abuse of power. The representative from the House Of Representatives went on to say that all these executives with the Postal Service who have used the chauffeur service should be made to reimburse the Postal Service and the biggest abuser should be fired.

The Deputy Postmaster General of the United States Postal Service disagrees. He wrote to the auditors and said that although some use of official vehicles and chauffeurs was inappropriate it did not rise to the level of willful, that to his way of thinking is required for prosecution, suspension or firing. The Deputy Postmaster General went on to say that some of the executives had retired and or made appropriate restitution.

Since some of the executives have retired, with full benefits, I guess then that was alright for them to abuse their power of authority. Just my opinion.

A postal spokesperson said that the auditors did not check the reasons for why the executives used the chauffeurs to get home or to the office. He surmised that they may have found using a USPS chauffeured limousine was cheaper than a taxi. According to the postal spokesperson executives were required to make restitution of $362.00 for two of the incidents.

- In a report dated November 17, 2004 it was reported the United States Postal Service Vice President and consumer advocate who is the subject of an Inspector General investigation will retire in February, 2005. The Postal Service claims that the Vice President and consumer advocate made the decision to retire on her own and that there was no connection to the Inspector General's investigation.

The Inspector General's office was looking into whether the Vice President tried to influence a contract award. The Inspector General's office had questioned Postal Service employees about whether in 2002 the Vice President improperly aided a company bidding on a $635 million contract to manage seven call centers. A report prepared by a Postal Service attorney in March, 2003 concluded there was compelling evidence that the Vice President leaked sensitive information to the company which was the incumbent contractor.

The consumer advocate's office analyzes Postal Service performance and customer satisfaction.

The Inspector General's office denied a freedom of information act requested by the Federal Times for access to investigation documents and reports.

So once again a top official, this time the Vice President and consumer advocate, gets to walk away with no punishment, unless you consider retirement a form of punishment.

- In news reports from the Washington Times and the Washington Post it was reported that a Inspector General of the United States Postal Service agreed to retire after a federal investigation affirmed charges that the Inspector General abused her authority, wasted millions of taxpayer dollars and mistreated subordinates in her office.

According to the report in the Washington Post it claims the retiring Inspector General hired a team-building consultant at $3,000.00 a day, held eight hour working lunches which was called mind-numbing. Employees accused the Inspector General of trying to hide meeting expenses and of authorizing a purchase of a $4,500.00 executive treadmill in headquarters that had a full gym. She was also accused of overspending for a $6.6 million computer program.

- In a report dated January 21, 2005 a New Jersey Postal Inspector from Ridgewood, New Jersey, was sentenced in the United States District Court in Camden, New Jersey, to 10 months in prison, fined $10,000.00 and ordered to pay $16,000.00 in restitution for his guilty plea in August 2004. The New Jersey Postal Inspector admitted that beginning in late 2003, he was engaged in the investigation of credit card fraud schemes. The Postal Inspector used his position to access a United States Postal Service mail depository from which he stole several individuals credit cards. The Postal Inspector then used those individuals personal information to obtain additional credit cards in their names and charged more than $19,000.00 worth of merchandise. If we can't trust a United States Postal Inspector then who can we trust? It seems that the

United States Postal Service picks and decides on who to really punish and who gets to just retire with no punishment.

• It was reported that a former United States Postal Service contracting official was sentenced to nearly four years in prison February 11, 2005 for accepting more than $770,000.00 in bribes.

The former official, a printing specialist, pleaded guilty to taking bribes and other payments from people associated with printing companies seeking preferential treatment in contract considerations. The former contracting official also admitted to laundering money. He was sentenced by the United States District Court for the District of Columbia to 46 months in prison and will have to forfeit the money, a Chevrolet corvette, a Rolex watch and his home.

• There was a supervisor in Miami that has stolen money and continued working as a supervisor. Of course he hasn't been caught taking any money but everything points in his direction. Maybe I shouldn't say he was stealing money, but this is what I believe.

I was called to the Olympia Heights Post Office by the window technician (T-5) because she was to be questioned by the postal inspectors about a missing $1,000.00.

At the end of the day the window technician (T-5) counts all the money, checks and cashed money orders that the window clerks have turned in. After counting the money it must be verified by a supervisor, or another employee, to make sure the count is correct.

After counting the money this one day the T-5 gave the money to the supervisor who was sitting at her desk and while the supervisor was supposedly counting the money the T-5 was doing some paper work on the computer. She wasn't watching the supervisor count the money. The supervisor was suppose to sign his name or initial that the money was verified. This supervisor told the window technician that the money count was correct. Without looking at the deposit slip the supervisor was suppose to sign the T-5 put the money and the deposit slip into a registry pouch and dispatch the pouch to the registry clerk who in turned gave the pouch to the truck driver. Everyone who touches this registry pouch has to sign for it.

Approximately one week later the Olympia Heights Post Office received a call and was told a $1,000.00 was missing. When the manager of Olympia Heights Post Office asked the supervisor if he verified the money the manager was first told that it wasn't him but later said it was, he forgot, and since his initials looked different then they normally are the supervisor claims that he was in a hurry that day.

When the T-5 was questioned by the postal inspectors she was asked to take a lie-detector test. I informed the employee that the union advises employees not to take a lie-detector test. The T-5 didn't have a problem with the test, and I couldn't talk her out of it. I went with the T-5 to the Postal Inspectors office and waited outside the office while she took the lie detector test. Of course the window Technician passed the test. I don't know if the supervisor took a lie-detector test or not.

When I did some investigation on the case I found out that when this supervisor was at a Miami Beach post Office money was missing. When this supervisor worked at the Ludlam Post Office money was missing. The missing money at the other post offices was not as much as the $1,000.00 that was missing from the Olympia Heights Post Office but the fact was there that when this supervisor was a closing supervisor at other post offices money was missing.

I guess it could be a coincidence that money was missing everywhere this supervisor worked. It doesn't mean that he took any of this money but to me it seems the Postal Inspectors would look that much harder. Especially since this supervisor said at first that he didn't verify the money at Olympia Heights Post Office on the day when the $1,000.00 was missing.

I don't know where this supervisor is now working, and don't really care, but there's a saying once a thief always a thief. Maybe one day he will be caught.

The girl that was the window technician at Olympia Heights Post Office when this $1,000.00 went missing has also left Olympia Heights and bid to a different post office. Even though she was cleared of any wrong doing with the $1000.00 that was missing she was upset the way she was treated by the Post office.

- On July 17, 2006 the Federal Times reported that a former Vice President for public affairs and communications for the United States Postal Service was under fire for alleged sexual harassment, misuse of funds, and abuse of power before the former Vice President resigned from the Postal Service.

The former Vice President for public affairs and communications resigned on June 30, 2006, 11 days after an Inspectors General report into his conduct. The report detailed more than $46,000.00 in questionable spending along with numerous accusations of sexual harassment, intimidation and improper conduct.

It was reported that in one three-night stretch in 2004, the former Vice President ran up $8,252.00 staying at a Washington D. C. hotel suite, less than nine miles from his home.

In one evening the former Vice President spent $3,486.33 for steak dinners and a bar hopping binge for himself and other postal employees in 2005. He also tipped two waiters $1,511.66 following a seafood dinner for 20 employees and business partners in 2003.

I bet there were no bargaining unit employees among the 20 employees that had dinner with the former Vice President.

The Postmaster General had announced that the 51 year old former Vice President was leaving the Postal Service to pursue other career opportunities.

The former Vice President for public affairs and communications had 30 years in the Postal Service and had been in his position as Vice President since October, 1999.

Even after the former Vice President resigned on June 30, 2006 he continued to be on the Postal Service payroll as a consultant until September 1, 2006 when the former Vice President removed himself from the payroll and took the remainder of his earned vacation pay.

As the Vice President for public affairs and communications his annual salary was $164,000.00 and he earned $53,000.00 in vacation pay.

On September 1, 2006, a spokesman for the Postal Service had confirmed that the former Vice President was still on the payroll after the Federal Times began asking questions in mid August as to why the former Vice President was still on the payroll. The spokesman contains that the former Vice President was still on the payroll so that he could receive his vacation pay in installments.

Also on September 1, 2006 the Postal Service said it would not seek any reimbursements for the more than $46,000.00 in questionable spending from the former Vice President.

A Postal Service spokesman said the Postal Service decided to reconsider its expense policies after the Inspector general released the report on the former Vice President.

The new Postal Service expense guidelines was released on September 13, 2006 that capped individual dinners at $50.00. The Postal Service has also limited tips to 20 percent. Also all expense claims must be approved by one's supervisor before they will be honored. The former Vice President was able to approve his own expenses. The Postal Service said that any purchases outside the guidelines set on September 13, 2006, will not be reimbursed.

Of course the bottom line, another top United States Postal Service official walks away with no punishment, gets paid for all of their alleged vacation time, and receives, I'm sure, a really good pension.

CHAPTER 18

MISAPPROPRIATION AND POSTAL THIEF BY POSTAL CLERKS

WHEN I WAS IN office as the union Clerk Craft President and the Executive Vice-President of the Miami Area Local one of the worst jobs I had was meeting with the employees who got caught stealing. Since I covered the stations and branches in Miami and Homestead, most, if not all, of the clerks that were caught stealing were window clerks.

The window clerks worked on what was called an IRT and later the POS 1 replaced the IRT. When the window clerks worked with the IRT money orders were printed on a money order machine. A lot of the clerks that were caught misappropriating Postal Service funds were taking money orders out of sequence, and after selling the money order the clerk was keeping the money order voucher and the money and attempting to pay for the money order at a later date.

The Postal Inspectors called this kiting, I called it taking a interest free loan. Sometimes the clerk got so caught up in selling the money orders, keeping the voucher and money that they didn't get a chance to put the money back in.

After the Postal Service pulled out the IRT machines the POS 1 was put in. With the POS 1 there was no more cutting money orders on a machine, it was all done on the POS 1. There was also no way to take money orders out of sequence. The thief had to find another way to steal.

When the Postal Inspector came to the station to talk to an employee, and the employee asked for union representation I was sent most of the time. I had to talk to the employee to try to get an idea of what they were accused of before going into the office with them to talk with the Postal Inspector. I would then sit with the employee while the Postal Inspectors questioned them. As a union officer I couldn't interfer with the Postal Inspectors investigation but also had to keep the employee from saying too much that might hurt their case even more then it already was.

I found out real quick that almost all the time when the Postal Inspectors came in to talk to an employee that the inspectors already had enough evidence on that employee that it was too late to save their job. There were a few exceptions, but only a few.

Unfortortantly there was a lot of employees at different stations and branches throughout Miami, through the years, that were caught stealing. Some stations had more then one employee that was caught stealing. There are just over 40 stations and branches in Miami and there had to be close to 15 of those stations or branches where an employee was walked out for stealing.

In almost all instances the employee that was caught either stealing credit cards or for cutting money orders out of sequence were employees that I would not have ever suspected of wrong doing.

When I worked at the Snapper Creek Post Office as a shop steward, prior to being elected a union officer, there was a casual employee that was caught stealing credit cards. This employee would ask all kinds of questions about how the mail came into the station and how the mail was dispatched. He ask so many questions that I told other employees to be careful that this guy could be a Postal Inspector. I felt that if the post office wanted to put a Postal Inspector into the station the best way would be as a casual employee. When the Postal Inspectors caught this guy stealing I was really surprised. I would've never suspected this guy of stealing. It was a good learning experience.

One of the first cases I remember where I had to represent an employee for alleged stealing was at the South Miami Post Office. I was called out there because an employee had a shortage of just over $7600.00. Prior to the shortage the employee was AWOL (absence without leave) for three days and when he came back to work he told the supervisor he had to go to New York to bail his brother out of jail. This was approximately six weeks before the shortage.

When I met this man I told him I had heard that he went to New York to bail his brother out of jail. He told me he didn't have a brother in jail, that he just made the story up. I asked him if he put anything into writing about a brother in jail? I was told he didn't. We went outside on the platform so we could talk without other employees around. I told him that when the Postal Inspectors talk to him not to say anything, when asked, about a brother. Also he had to call me when the Postal Inspectors come out.

I didn't have much time to talk to this employee because a supervisor came out to the platform where we were talking and said he was needed in the office. Talk about timing. The Postal Inspector, there was only one, had just gotten there. I thought there would be two Postal Inspectors. One being the nice guy, and the other being a hard ass.

We went into the office and I introduced myself to the Postal Inspector. I was the Clerk Craft President of the Miami Area Local at this time. The Postal Inspector surprised me when his first question to the employee was "did you steal this money?" Then the Postal Inspector said he heard that the employee went to New York to bail his brother out of jail. The employee didn't answer, just like I told him, and I said that his brother in New York had nothing to do with this case. The Postal Inspector just gave me a real dirty look and told the employee that I'm just a union representative and not a lawyer. The Postal Inspector never asked the employee again about any brother so I accomplished what I was trying to do. The Postal Inspector had a job to do and so did I. I was there to represent an employee to the best of my ability, and I think I did that.

It was obvious the Postal Inspector didn't have any evidence that the employee did anything wrong except he had a large shortage. Had the Postal Inspector had some evidence of wrong doing the employee would've been put on emergency suspension without pay by the manager of the station or a supervisor.

I started my investigation which was to check other employees keys against the grievant' stamp drawer and I found two different employees had keys that open the stamp drawer of the employee I was representing. Management still denied the grievance, because it was so large and because the Postal Inspector was investigating.

Management then did what they were suppose to do, they changed all the locks and keys for all the stamp drawers. Management then put the employee back on the window. I asked why since he was under investigation and was told the Postal Inspector wanted the employee to work the window. That made sense because the Postal Inspector wanted to watch the employee to see if he could catch him in the act of stealing.

Approximately three months later the employee was audit again, window clerks had to be audited at least once every four months, and this time he had a shortage of approximately $5900.00. The employee was improving. He went from being short approximately $7600.00 to approximately $5900.00, and if the Postal Inspector was watching he didn't do a very good job. Since management had changed all the locks and keys on the stamp drawers I didn't really have much of an argument so I just appealed the grievance to the next step. This shortage also didn't help the previous shortage. The employee was again put back on the window and when audited again he had another shortage of approximately $3000.00.

After this audit, management requested a letter of warning, a discipline letter, since the employee was out of tolerance three times. The letter of warning was resolved so that if the employee was within tolerance on the next audit the letter of warning would be removed from his files. But if the employee was out of tolerance again the employee would have his bid taken away and sent back to the General Mail Facility as an unassigned clerk.

During this period of time, approximately six months, I assumed the Postal Inspector was still investigating this employee. I didn't hear anything from the inspector and there was no Postal Inspectors report. There was no reason for him to call me, and I wasn't going to call the Postal Inspector.

While this employee was having these shortages there was another employee at the South Miami Post Office that was also having shortages, just not nearly as large. Since management requested the letter of warning for the one employee they had to request a letter of warning for the other employee. This letter of warning was resolved the same way as the other.

This other employee helped management by not securing his stamp stock on at lease one occasion. I went to the South Miami Post Office to represent this other employee for a shortage. When I walked up to the window this employee was not there. The supervisor walked up to me and asked if I was there for this employee. After telling the supervisor, Paulette Thomas, I was, she asked if she could wait with me for the employee. I just told the supervisor that it was her station and who was I to say anything about her waiting for the employee. A few minutes later the employee came walking up and when he did Paulette Thomas asked him if those were his keys. I looked to where the supervisor was pointing and saw a set of keys hanging from the lock to the employees stamp drawer. I couldn't believe I didn't notice the keys hanging from the lock before the supervisor said something. I started to walk away and the supervisor asked me if I saw the keys hanging from the lock. I said that I saw nothing. The supervisor, Paulette Thomas wrote this employee up and requested a letter of warning for not securing his stamp stock and having the out of tolerance audits. This sure didn't help me when I wrote the grievance and said management failed to provide adequate security.

As it turned out both employees were short again on their next audit and both were removed from their bid assignment and sent back to the General Mail Facility.

After working at the General Mail Facility for awhile the other employee, that was also removed from his bid assignment at the South Miami Post Office, was arrested for a minor traffic incident. It was obviously a set up. There was an undercover policeman in the jail cell with this postal worker. After talking for awhile the undercover policeman talked the postal worker into selling him credit cards. Again it appeared obvious that the postal inspectors was onto this employee and most likely worked with the police to get this man into jail and then put an undercover policeman into the same jail cell.

Talk about being in the wrong place at the wrong time. The employee who had the large shortages came by the other employees apartment and heard him argue with this other man about credit cards. The other man was, the undercover policeman, saying he couldn't use the credit cards because they all had woman names on the cards. Since this guy was in the apartment of his friend the employee with the large shortages thought this guy must be alright so he sold him credit cards too. Ones with men names on them. Needless to say both employees were busted for stolen credit cards and fired from the post office. I wasn't involved with the handling of any case for the credit cards.

Some time later I saw the Postal Inspector that was investigating the South Miami shortages and I asked why this employee was never caught stealing and why he remained on the window. The Postal Inspector told me he never told management to keep this man on the window, so he wasn't watching him. Also the reason the employee was never caught stealing was because the Postal Inspector couldn't prove that he was stealing because all the records management had, 1412's, were missing. The 1412 was a daily log of all the transactions an employee did on any peticular day.

On December 2, 1988 the manager of the Riverside Post office telephoned the postal inspectors office to report numerous shortages of window clerks at the station. In total five clerks and the window supervisor were involved with exchanging stock before an audit and after the audit.

The supervisor in charge of the window at the Riverside Post Office was in charge of the window at the Coral Gables Post Office prior to coming to the Riverside Post Office. While at the Coral Gables Post Office she authorized a large sale of stamps with the customer paying with a check. The customer was a friend of the supervisor. The customer didn't have the funds to cover the check so the supervisor was responsible for the money. Another story I heard was that the supervisor received a check from a friend and tried to input the check, but the funds were not there.

I was not involved with this incident so I'm not sure which story is accurate but do know that the supervisor was responsible for the money. The supervisor should've been questioned by the Postal Inspectors then but it appears this supervisor had connections in the accounting department.

I was called and asked to count the stock of this one employee. I was covering the position of the Clerk Craft President at this time. The clerk was audited on December 1, 1988 and was in tolerance, having a shortage of only $28.28, but had been missing from work since the audit. On December 6, 1988 I sat with a supervisor from systems compliance, a part of accounting, and conducted an audit of this employees accountability. This employee was now short $9,784.60. Another employee at the Riverside Post Office was short $14,033.81. She was audited on December 1, and then again on December 6, 1988. Both of these employees were fired from their jobs with the post office along with the supervisor. The other three employees that had the shortages at the Riverside Post Office were later brought back to work. Their shortages were $2,213.65, $9,472.66 and $6,282.74. I guess these three clerks made a deal with the postal inspectors and even though they had to pay the shortages back they still kept their jobs.

This incident at the Riverside Post office set off a chain of surprise audits at different stations and branches throughout Miami.

At the Buena Vista Post Office the t-6, (window technician) a window clerk responsible for receiving the money from the other window clerk and turning in all paper work from the window on a daily basis, was going into her accountability and changing the amount she was accountable for.

When a window clerk was to have an audit of their stamp stock it was suppose to be without their knowledge ahead of time. In other words when a window clerk was to be audited it usually occurred when they first came to work and before they opened on the window. They were not to know the day before that they were going to be audited.

The t-6 at the Buena Vista Post Office appeared to know each time she was to be audited. The supervisor, without thinking, would tell the clerk not to open the next day because she was to be audited. The t-6 would go into her accountability and changed the figures so that when she was audited it looked like she had a good audit.

When the t-6 had this random audit, a surprise audit, she wasn't prepared. The audit was on April 20,1989 and when the audit was fishished the t-6 was short $10,808.02. When the Postal Inspector came out to interview this employee I was called out to represent her. The inspector showed me where the t-6, when she knew the supervisor was going to audit her, would go into the IRT and changed her accountability down to approximately $4500.00 and then would bring her accountability back to where it should have been which was approximately $12,000.00, after each audit.

The employee claimed she didn't do this that maybe someone else went into her accountability. She was placed on emergency suspention without pay and was later prosecuted. She received six monthe probation and of course loss her postal job and had to pay the money back to the Postal Service. Prior to being removed from the Post Office this employee resigned.

At the Coral Gables Post office the supervisor was getting ready to audit an employee when she noticed stamps in this employees stamp stock that were not issued by the supervisor. This supervisor at Coral Gables Post Office was the one who ordered the stamps for the station and also conducted the audits. After the employee had their stamp stock counted, the employee was within tolerance, there was a $50.00 tolerance for all window clerks, the supervisor called the postal inspectors. Instead of going to Coral Gables Post Office the postal inspectors went to the Miami Springs Post Office where the husband of the employee from the Coral Gables Post Office worked as the supervisor. He would provide his wife stamps from the Miami Springs Post Office before her audit and then she would give them back after the audit. It appeared they knew when she was to be audited, or it was a good guess. An employee had to be audited at least once every four months, an audit could be every day if management wanted to do this. But of course management would never have the time to conduct audits even on a monthly basis. As it gets real close to the four months an employee could almost pinpoint when the audit was going to be.

Both employees resigned from the Postal Service and I don't know if they ever went to court. I'm sure they paid some money back to the Postal Service.

At Miami Springs Post Office the employees were exchanging stamps before audits. The supervisor had already resigned and one other employee was fired from the Postal Service from the Miami Springs Post Office. Three of the employees that were put on emergency suspention came back to work.

Believe me, I don't think it's funny when an employee gets removed from their job from the Postal Service. But I have to tell this story. When the postal inspectors came to interview the employees at the Miami Springs Post Office a few different union officers got involved. George Pagliery, Donna Rivera-Harris, Judy Johnson and myself. When Judy was in the office with one of these employees with the postal inspectors the employee stated that he had given stamps to this other employee and didn't get the stamps back. Therefore he knew he would be short on his stamp audit. Judy tried to tell the employee that he didn't give the stamps to this other employee but had placed the stamps on the counter and this other employee took them. The employee said the other employee didn't take his stamps, that he did give the stamps to this other employee.

This other employee had talked to George Pagliery and had already resigned. She was a very pretty lady. I use to say that the employee that talked to Judy paid for the pretty lady. That was the most expensive piece of ass that he never got. He didn't see that he did anything wrong. I was able to get the man back to work but he had to pay for the shortage he had. Of course the reason he had the shortage was because he gave his stamps to this other employee.

At the Snapper Creek Post Office the t-6, window technician, was also the one who set postage meters for customers. When the customer would write a check to the Postal Service the t-6 would put that check into stamp sales and pocket the money. She got away with this until the Postal service started calling the customers with the meters and telling them there was no money in their account.

When I first heard about the t-6 from Snapper Creek Post Office being put on emergency suspention I tried calling her, I was friends with her husband, a mail handler that worked at the Ludlam Post Office, and left a message with her brother. When she called me back I was told she didn't do anything wrong and that she didn't need the union. When I got off the phone with this employee I told my wife that this employee was guilty. If I was put on emergence suspension I would want all the help I could get. The fact she told me she didn't need the union made me believe she was guilty. I was glad I didn't have to represent her.

At some later date this t-6 tried to get in touch with the union president, Judy Johnson, and ask for help. By this time the postal inspectors had already finished their report and the employee was told she had better get a lawyer since there was no way to save her job. I didn't get involved with the case after I was told the union wasn't needed. Her husband, who was a friend, quit talking to me. I guess he blamed me because his wife got caught stealing.

At Allapattah Post Office, Olympia Heights Post Office, Kendall Post Office and Edison Post Office clerks were caught cutting money orders and not paying for them until a later date, if paid at all.

The clerk at Allapattah had paid back all the money from the money orders she had sold except the last one. When the clerk was suspected of kiting money orders her stamp and cash drawers were sealed keeping her from paying back the money.

What these clerks were doing was to sell money orders to a customers, keep the money and the voucher and pay for them later, usually the next time they were to receive their pay check. This is what I called taking an interest free loan and what the Postal Inspectors called kiting.

All the employees that were caught taking these interest free loans were fired from the Postal Service and had to pay back some, if not all the money that was taken. The Postal Inspectors had to prove the amout through documentation.

The best I could do for these employees was to get management to agree to let the employee resign from the Postal Service with a clean record. This meant that on the employees personel file it stated the employee resigned for personal reasons.

Approximately May, 1989 there was a case at the Little River Post office where an employee called the union and said he felt someone was breaking into his stamp and cash drawers. I went to the Little River Post office and had the supervisor audit the employee and he came up with a shortage of approximately $300.00. I asked the manager to call the Postal Inspectors.

This same employee called the union again a few weeks later and this time he said he knew someone was breaking into his stamp and cash drawers. Again I went out to the Little River Post Office with a shop steward and again this employee was audited. This time he had a shortage of approximately $500.00. He told me at the end of each night he was counting his money. A window clerk kept only approximately $50.00 in their cash drawer. I was told when he counted his drawer that $10.00 was missing. Grievances were filed on both shortages that this employee had. Meanwhile other clerks were coming up with shortages but none said anything about someone possibly breaking into their drawers.

I had the shop steward call the Postal Inspector since I didn't want a thief stealing from other clerks. When I did talk to the Postal Inspector, unfortunately I was seeing postal inspectors too much with that many clerks getting caught stealing, I told him I thought the closing supervisor might be the one stealing.

When the closing supervisor was acting manager at the Surfside Post Office I went to investigate a shortage of this employee and found out through documentation that the locks on the employees stamp drawer were never changed. When any employee first get their stamp stock the locks have to be changed.

When I tried to copy the documentation the copy machine was not working. When I came back to the Surfside Post Office a few days later the documentation was missing. After going to the manager of labor relations, Alan Bame, and telling him about the missing documentation, I received the documentation a few days later. The employee at the Surfside Post Office was cleared of the shortage. I figured anyone capable of moving documentation was also capable of stealing.

I saw the Postal Inspector a couple of months later and I asked him why when management calls for him he comes out right away but when the union calls we don't hear a thing. The Postal Inspector told me if he was investigating he wasn't going to let the union know because the union would have to represent the employee that might be caught if it wasn't a supervisor or a manager. I took this to mean that the Postal Inspector was conducting an investigation. I saw the same Postal Inspector approximately one month later and the Postal Inspector told me when I said I thought it was the closing supervisor that might be the one who was breaking into the drawers that I wasn't too far off. Thinking like a union representative I figured the Postal Inspector found something on the supervisor.

After the Postal Inspector was called by the union and before I asked the Postal Inspector why we haven't heard from him another employee that had worked at the Little River Post Office was removed from his bid job because he kept having shortages. This employees job was the closing clerk at the Little River Post Office. I saw the Postal Inspector a couple of months later and he asked me if I had heard from the clerk that was removed as the closing clerk. When I told him I haven't heard from this employee he told me that this employee was walked out the building by the Postal Inspectors for stealing over $3300.00 in money orders and that the employee admitted to breaking into other clerks drawers. Right after the Postal Inspector told me about walking this employee out of the building I went to the General Mail Facility to check to see what time this employee was walked out of the building by the Postal Inspectors. I was told that the employee had been walked out weeks before this day. When the Postal Inspector told me I just figured that it just happened since the employee never called the union, even though we wouldn't have been able to help him much anyway.

The employee that had called the union to say someone was breaking into his stamp and cash drawers was relieved of the shortages. Also other clerks that had shortages also were relieved of their shortages.

The reason the employee was caught was because money orders were taken from other employees stock. Along with this employee a letter carrier was also involved and also a lady who didn't work for the post office. The employee breaking into the other employees drawers might have gotten away, at lease for a little time, if he had only taken cash but the money orders were traced back and when the clerks that had missing money orders reported them missing it was only a matter of time before someone got caught.

There was an employee that worked at the Quail Heights Post Office that had a shortage of just over $1100.00. I resolved the case and the employee was relieved of any responsibility due to the shortage, because management audited the employee late, past the four months. I don't know if this is why the Postal Inspector started to investigate this employee but not too long after winning this employees shortage I was called out to the Quail Heights Post Office for this same employee. He had said that he sold two money orders to two homeless people and because they couldn't write he wrote the money orders out for them. One of the problems, besides the fact it was hard to believe that a homeless person would have almost $700.00 to buy a money order, was that the money orders that were sold at this employees window was also cashed at his window. Also a $700.00 money order that was voided was then cashed by this employee. The employee ended up resigning. I worked out a settlement where he resign with a clean record.

I believe from the time I started as a union officer there were six employees caught at the Quail Heights Post Office of either cutting money orders and not paying for them, to selling stamps and not reporting the sale or writing bad checks.

One of the last cases I remember was from an employee that worked on the IRT from the Snapper Creek Post Office. The employee was a former shop steward and had approximately twenty years in the post office.

On September 2, 1998 I received a call from the Snapper Creek Post Office and was told this employee needed to se me right away. She was in the office with a Postal Inspector but knew to have someone call the union hall.

When I got to the Snapper Creek Post Office, I went with George Pagliery, I met a different postal inspector then the one I had previously dealt with. After introducing myself and the shop steward, George Pagliery, we took the employee outside the building so we could talk. We were told that she was about to get audited when she got an emergency phone call from her daughter and had to leave work. The next day she didn't show up for work and since her audit was due, if management was late on the audit the union would've won the shortage, management got the employees witness to open the key envelope, where a dublicate key for the stamp and cash drawers are kept. When the envelope was open there was no key for the employees stamp drawer so the drawer had to be broken into. The stamp stock was audited and the employee was short $11,102.45. The employee told us she didn't do anything wrong. Since it's management responsibility to control the dublicate key envelopes and the fact the key was missing I felt pretty good about this case. I believed the employee when she told us she didn't do anything wrong, afterall she was a former shop steward. I believed her not because she was a former shop steward but because I have known this employee for a few years and didn't believe she would do what it appeared she was being accused of.

When we went back into the office where the Postal Inspector was waiting I told him since the stamp drawer key was missing from the duplicate key envelope that he was talking to the wrong person. The

Postal Inspector agreed that we shouldn't be talking about the shortage of $11,000.00 but that we should be talking about the hundred stolen money orders. The Postal Inspector put a hundred money order vouchers on the desk with the top one being $700.00. I sat there for what felt like a long time looking at that stack of money orders and thinking $700.00 times one hundred would be $70,000.00. I'm not sure what color my face turned, red or white, as I was in a state of shock. This employee had just a few minutes earlier told us she didn't do anything wrong. The money order vouchers were in her stamp drawer. I didn't understand how she thought she wasn't going to get caught. I couldn't say anything but looked over at George Pagliery and I think he was as surprised as I was. When I finally regrouped I took the employee outside again. I think George was more upset than I was. I tried to keep my cool since I've had other employees that got caught stealing lie to me about doing anything wrong.

I asked this employee if she realized what had just happen inside the office with the Postal Inspector. When she didn't say anything, I told her the Postal Inspector hit me in my face so hard. She looked at me as if I was crazy. I told her that when the Postal Inspector put those money order vouchers on the desk, it was like he hit me. I told the employee to make some phone calls and get herself a good lawyer.

When we went back inside I told the Postal Inspector that the employee was willing to admit wrong doings but that she was going to get a lawyer. The Postal Inspector wanted her to put into writing what she had done and I told her not to. I told the Postal Inspector that when this employee got a lawyer and the lawyer wanted her to put something in writing then it would be out of my hands. The Postal Inspector then told me if he was the one representing the employee he wouldn't want anything in writing either. This was the only thing that made me feel good. I got a compliment from the Postal Inspector.

The employee was put on emergency suspension and got a good lawyer. She was sentence to jail time that her lawyer got suspended. She ended up with six months house arrest, and two years probation. She had to also pay back the money. The money orders added up to just over $24,000.00 and with the $11,000.00 shortage she had to pay back just over $35,000.00.

When the post office switched over from the IRT to the POS 1 and employees had no stamp accountability employees were getting caught unreporting stamp sales. They would sell stamps and not ring up the sale and pocket the money. When the post office, where the employee that got caught stealing was working at, came up with big shortages the Postal Inspectors started investigating. Clerks were caught stealing at the Kendall Post Office, Coconut Grove Post Office, and the Jose Marti Post Office just to name a few.

One of the first clerks that got caught after the Miami Post offices switched from the IRT to the POS 1 was at the Kendall Post Office. I believe George Pagliery handled that case.

From October 9, 1997 through September 1, 1999 the unit accountability of the Kendall Postal Store was audited a total of 22 times. Those audits have resulted in a net shortage of $82,539.33.

Besides the shortages what started this investigation by the postal inspectors was the fact that this employee over charged Publix Supermarket $1000.00. This employee was stopped on the way to his car by the Postal Inspectors on September 23, 1999 and brought to the managers office. The employee had a total of $2,275.95 in his pockets when brought to the office. The Kendall Postal Store was audited September 24,1999 and the results was a shortage of $8,735.66. This employee was put off the clock on emergency suspension on September 23, 1999. An audit was conducted again on October 12, 1999 and the results was a shortage of $493.60. The Postal Inspectors claim that this employee was responsible for $5,298.00. The odds are he got away with a lot more then what the Postal Inspectors could show through the documents. The employee was charged with embezzlement and under reporting stamp sales.

There was one employee that had gotten a second chance and I guess it didn't help. This employee was working at the Key Biscayne Post Office and had a shortage of approximately $300.00. This was when the window clerks were still working on the IRT machines. What this employee thought was if her next audit was an overage of the same amount then management would offset the shortage.

The employee would overcharge the customers on foreign mail and then put the postage on the package after the customer left the post office. The postage was less than what the customer paid. This employee after putting the postage on the package would bump the round date over the postage so it was hard to tell how much postage was on the package. Her problem was when the package went through the foreign section at the General Mail Facility and the clerks couldn't tell how much postage was on the package the Postal Inspectors were called.

Postal inspectors were going to the Key Biscayne Post Office with foreign packages pretending to be a postal customer and each time the wrong amount was charged to the Postal Inspector. This went on for a awhile, enough time for the Postal Inspectors to build their case.

After the Postal Inspectors interviewed the employee, I don't believe the union was called, the manager was called into the office. This is where the employee got a break. She was being charged with padding her account. She didn't actually steal money, the people who lost money was the customer. The manager told the employee that she was being fired and had the employee turn in her ID badge. The employee never was given a pre-discipline hearing.

Every employee that gets discipline must have a pre-discipline hearing and the union must be called. It doesn't matter that the employee might be guilty or not but everyone is entitled to know what they're being charged with and what discipline management is requesting. The Postal Inspectors cannot fire any employee. The Postal Inspectors make their report and turns this into the Postmasters office who then sends the report to labor relations who then sends the report to the the manager of the station.

When this employees case went to arbitration she won with full back pay. The arbitrator said in his decision "one has to consider which is worst the employee that steals .50 cents to $1.00 per transaction or management that cost the Postal Service thousands of dollars because of not giving the employee their right to a pre-discipline hearing.

The employee came back to work but was taken off the window for a couple of years. George Pagliery had to talk to Oscar Rodriguez, who was in charge of the stations and branches, to get this employee back on the window. I know George had to do some talking. She then was allowed to bid back to the window and went from the Tamiami Post Office to the Snapper Creek Post Office and ended up at the Quail Heights Post Office.

I use to tell this employee that she was famous. I told her two different bands wrote songs about her. I told her the Beatles wrote a song called dizzy miss lizzy and Led Zeppelin wrote a song called dazed and confused. She would just walk away from me.

I guess the main problem with this lady was she liked to gamble. Her downfall was when she won over $20,000.00 at bingo. I guess she thought she could keep winning. She was wrong. She gave back the money she had won and a lot more. She told me she was at the Indian village where they play bingo from 5:00 P.M. till 12:00 P.M. the next day. She had done this on more then one occasion. It was a disease.

This employee was the window T-5 at the Quail Heights Post Office and when the other employees turned in their money to her she would keep some of the money and write a check to the post office for the same amount. The problem was that she didn't have the money to cover the check she wrote to the post office.

When the checks started bouncing the Postal Inspectors were called. She had writted checks totaling $7000.00 that she couldn't cover. She resigned from the post office and the union made a settlement that when she resigned it was with a clean record. Of course she had to pay the money back to the post office.

There was another incident with a clerk at the South Miami Post Office. This employee had a shortage of approximately $600.00. One of my shop stewards filed a grievance and when it was denied appealed it to step 2 and then it was appealed to step 3 where I, after asking the shop steward to check with the employee, resolved the shortage. The settlement was to relieve the employee of half the shortage so that the employee would only be responsible for approximately $300.00. A few weeks later I went to the South Miami Post Office with George Pagliery, one of the chief shop stewards, and this employee was really upset with me for splitting her shortage. I told her that this is what I was told she would be happy with. This is what I was told by the shop steward that wrote the grievance at step one. I remember George Pagliery asking me if I could pull the grievance back and do something else. I told the employee I could call management in labor relations and get an amended decision, which would be a denial, and then appeal the case to arbitration.

A few hours later while at the union office the manager of the South Miami Post Office called me and asked if this employee talked to me while I was at the post office. Of course I told this manager if she considered yelling at me as talking then yes I talked to her. The manager then informed me that after George Pagliery and I had left the South Miami Post Office that the Postal Inspector came into the office and after talking to this employee walked her out of the building. It seems that this employee, while working at the South Miami Post Office had gone into the ladies bathroom one day and found another employees wallet and took a debit card and pin number from this wallet and used it on three different occasions at the credit union.

I guess this lady was lucky I split her shortage before she was caught stealing another employees debit card. Of course I never pulled the case back and this employee never called me. She did talk to another union officer, Betty Tsang, and her case was resolved where she resigned from the post office with a clean record. I don't know if she ever had to pay the other employee back for stealing the debit card and using it.

I spoke about the window clerks in Miami that I represented, or tried to represent for kiting money orders, not reporting stamp sales and writing bad checks. There were also a few clerks in Homestead that got caught stealing.

The first that I remember was a distribution clerk working at the Homestead Post Office. The employee had pockets sewn into the legs of his pants. This employee was stealing credit cards. This employee lived in North Miami, I think the only clerk that lived that far north of Homestead, and that's where the credit cards were being used. That's also the reason the Postal Inspectors started watching only this employee.

The Postal Inspector told me when this employee was seen throwing a credit card into his pocket that was sewed inside the leg of his pants, the Postal Inspector came out onto to work room floor and walked him to the office. When they got to the office this employee had three credit cards in his pocket. This employee was throwing so fast the Postal Inspector sent a supervisor to check this employees letter case and all the mail was thrown right. The Postal Inspector told me he was watching this employee all the time and didn't see the first two credit cards being put into his poicket.

The employee that was caught at the Princeton Post Office took a money order out of sequence, from the bottom of the money order pack, and sold it to himself. The only problem was he didn't pay for the money order. He tried to blame everyone except himself. This employee said that he had the money to pay for the money order and either he left it on the counter and a customer pick up the money, or at the end of the day he left it on the registry cart and a carrier pick the money up. Whatever happen really didn't matter much. The money order was sold sometime before he alleged to have tried to pay for it. Also he told the Postal Inspector that he gave me the money order voucher.

When I was reading the Postal Inspector's report I read that the employee gave the union steward, Warren Pearlman, the money order voucher. I immediately called the Postal Inspector on the phone and asked how he could write that in his report. I was told that the employee told him this. I knew what a money order voucher looked like and there was no way I would've taken the voucher.

One day while I was at the union office a man came into the office and asked for me. I figured he was an employee from the night shift that I didn't know. I soon found out that I was being issued a subpoena by the Postal Inspector to appear in court. This employee who refused to say he took money from his cash drawer and had cut a money order for himself without paying for it was being taken to court. He ended up being sentenced to jail for six months.

Then there was this employee who was stealing money from the express envelopes. On March 9, 1992 the Postal Inspectors escorted this employee to the Postmasters office. This employee was Spanish so the migrant workers that came into the Homestead Post Office would go to this employees window. The migrant worker would tell this employee that they wanted to send money to their country as fast as they could. He would give them an express envelope and tell them to put the money inside and then he would take care of it. He didn't tell them that they should buy an international money order. By the time the Postal Inspectors caught this employee he had been taking the money from the migrant workers for approximately six months. I asked the Postal Inspector why it took so long to get this employee and I was told they had to build their case. The Postal Inspectors initiated the investigation on January 13, 1992. I don't know how much money was stolen or if the migrant workers got any money back from the Postal Service.

When I went into the office with this employee and the Postal Inspector I didn't say anything except I told this employee to get a good lawyer. I don't know if this employee went to jail or how much money he had to pay the Postal Service. I don't think I cared too much.

To me it is worst when a shop steward gets caught stealing. It really makes the union look bad. While I was in office two shop stewards were caught stealing. One in Boca Raton and one at the North Miami Beach Post Office.

The shop steward in Boca Raton worked at a small post office across the street from the main office. He was the box clerk and when a customer paid their box rent this employee would put the money in stamp sales when it was a check, and then pocket the money. I helped the Business Agent in Boca Raton but didn't really handle the case. The last I heard the money that was stolen added up to over $15,000.00.

The shop steward at North Miami Beach Post Office had almost thirty years in the post office. I had a really hard time believing he was stealing. He said he didn't steal anything but ended up resigning from the post office.

The day the Postal Inspectors talked to him the employee left work early to go to the doctors. When he finished at the doctors and went to his car the Postal Inspectors were waiting.

The Postal Inspectors claimed that he had a package in front of his front seat in his car that had a tracking device. Also a ring was on his dashboard of his car. The Postal Inspectors said they saw this shop steward put a canvas bag into his car when he was doing the collection, picking up the mail from the mailboxes, in the morning. The problem I had with that is if the Postal Inspectors did see this employee put a bag of mail in his car then why did they let him drive off? The employee claimes he was working the parcels and found this ring at the bottom of the hamper. He claims he meant to turn it in but was in a hurry, he had a doctors appointment, and forgot to give it to the supervisor. He put the ring in his pocket. As for the box on the floor in the front of his car he says he did not know how that got there. The employee says he left his car door unlocked and someone could have put it there. I never heard anymore about the canvas bag that was supposedly put into this employees car.

As I said before I was involved with just about all the cases in Miami for the stations and branches and in Homestead. There were some employees that worked on the OCR that were caught stealing and I remember a couple of employees that got caught stealing food stamps from the mail but that was at the General Mail Facility and I wasn't involved with any representation or investigation.

On August 7, 1991 an employee that worked on the LSM at the General Mail Facility was caught trying to steal a whole tray of credit cards. The day before, August 6, 1991, this employee was observed putting this tray of credit cards behind some distribution cases inside a u-cart and covering the tray with some boxes. After the employee ended his tour of duty for the day the Postal Inspectors went to where this tray was hidden to make sure it was first class mail that contained credit cards. When the employee reported to work on the day in question, August 7, 1991 he was observed taking the u-cart out the door with the tray inside the cart. After he loaded the tray of credit cards inside his car he was approached by Postal Inspectors. Also found in the employees car was a loaded five-shot Smith and Wesson revolver with a speed loader. This employee was arrested and was sent to a federal prison in Pennsylvania for approximately nine months and then was sent to a half way house for a period of time.

In December 1997 the Postal Inspectors initiated an investigation of an employee working in the Business Mail Entry Unit (BMEU). On May 20,1998 the employee was arrested by the Postal Inspectors. On June 10,1998 a federal grand jury in the Southern District of Florida returned a ten count indictment against the employee. The indictment included seven counts of mail fraud and three counts of bribery. I don't know how much, if any, this employee was charged with taking or had to pay but a company that he was working with, the employee would under charge the company and get money in return, had a report that showed money that was sent to the Postal Service. In 1995 the company paid $518, 996.00 in postage. But in 1996 the company only paid $297,798.00 in postage and in 1997 only paid $243,134.00.

Can you imagine trying to provide extra customer service and by doing so do something that you most likely know is wrong? On July 11, 1997 while returning unclaimed parcels at the Goulds Post Office the two clerks working there came across an express parcel that was being return to sender because it was unclaimed. The problem was that the return address was a bad address. The express parcel was sent to the Goulds Post Office because this was the place it was mailed from. Since the parcel had been at the Goulds Post Office for over ten days and nobody came to inquire about the parcel the clerks thought instead of sending the express parcel to dead letter maybe if they were to open the package there might be an address inside so that the parcel could be delivered.

After opening the package I received a phone call from these same employees. When they told me what they had done I asked if they found drugs inside. I was asked then how I knew this. I figured if someone was to mail a package and put a bad return address then it seems to me what they were mailing was illegal. The clerk told me that they had called the Postal Inspectors and then were interview by the Postal Inspectors. I wasn't notified when the employees talked to the Postal Inspectors.

I was really surprise that these clerks would have done what they did. Opening accountable mail or any mail for that matter that didn't belong to the person opening the mail is against postal regulations. These were good clerks that never had a problem.

The clerks were given letters of removal for the opening of the mail. Trying to provide better customer service, but going about it the wrong way, got them in trouble. Lucky for them I was able to get their letter of removal expunged from their files and reduced to a letter of warning. The letter of warning was to be removed from their files in a period of time provided they didn't do the same thing again. I believe the time period was either six months or one year. Management could've pulled the removal completely without reducing it to a letter of warning but wouldn't. Since I knew these clerks would never open another package it really didn't matter if the discipline was held in their file as long as neither employee was trying to transfer out of Miami. No one reviewed their file or even looked into it. I believe the clerks were more scared of what they found in the package then what management would do to them. The same two clerks continued working together at the Goulds Post Office and never opened another package. They both have since retired from the Postal Service.

The thing about this is if they had never called the Postal Inspectors after opening the express package no one would have known about the drugs or the package at all.

Chapter 19

CHARGES & EMBEZZLEMENT BY UNION OFFICERS

THERE'S A BIG DIFFERENCE between embezzlement and bogas charges. A number of union officers from different locals around the country have been accused, charged and have been sentenced, some with prison time. Any employee working for the United States Postal Service can file charges against a union officer. Most, if not all the time, when charges are filed against a union officer the charges are brought up by a union member. Sometimes the charges are due to elections, someone doesn't like the results of the election. Sometimes the charges are due to missing funds or officers have taken part in illegal activities. Sometimes the charges are legitimate and other times there's no reason for the charges except for political reasons.

At every national convention a local or a member, usually a former shop steward or officer, from a local brings an appeal to the delegates at the national convention to be voted on. The appeals brought to the national convention are charges dealing with almost anything other than embezzlement. It seems most of the time it's because an officer was removed from office by the local. The delegates have the final word in an appeal process dealing with the union. Of course the local or member can take the issue to court and let a judge make a ruling if that member or local doesn't like the outcome at the national convention.

When the Department of Labor gets a call or charges are filed through the Department of Labor there's an investigation. If the charges are legitimate then one must consider the money that it cost the union in handling the charges. Is money well spent? Of course once the Department of Labor gets a call and decides to investigate, it will cost the union money, to at least time.

Sometimes when a union steward files a grievance and settles the grievance with management, the employee doesn't like the way it was settled and calls the Department of Labor. I had to take the time to meet with the Department of Labor on two different occasions because either I didn't file the grievance or the employee didn't like my settlement. On both occasions the Department of Labor said I was justified in the way I handled the grievance.

Sometimes charges are filed with the Department of Labor, or charges are filed against the local President or another officer and the charges are just for political reasons, and have no merit, and the charges are sent to the National Union. What I call dirty politics, then it should never happen. Of course there's no way to stop the dirty politics. Most of the time when the Department of Labor get involved with a local union it has something to do with the local's elections. Sometimes the National American Postal Workers Union gets involved, and again it's for political reasons.

The Miami Area Local has had the Department of Labor called, so it seems, almost every election. The Department of Labor ran at lease one election for the Miami Area Local because of charges.

When I was brought up on charges, along with the President, Judy Johnson, it was for political reasons which cost me my position in the union as the Executive Vice-President and cost the union a lot of money.

In reality the charges were brought up because Judy Johnson was questioning the finances and wanted a complete audit of all the books of the Secretary/Treasurer of the Miami Area Local. Not just what the Secretary/Treasurer wanted members to look at and what he might have handed over for an audit, but a full complete audit. Plus the fact Judy Johnson kept being elected President of the Miami Area Local and the only way to get rid of her was for Judy Johnson to decide not to run or for charges to be filed against her and hopefully get enough support for the charges to hold up and have Judy Johnson removed from office.

With Judy Johnson out of office someone else would take over as President. If the charges are upheld by the National APWU then the person being removed from office, in this case it was Judy Johnson, would not be able to run for election for a period of time.

This is what happen in the Miami area Local of the American Postal Workers Union. Also since I was the Executive Vice-President, I would have moved up to the position of President so charges had to be filed against me also.

A trial board was picked by the people removing Judy Johnson and myself from office even though the Miami Area Local had an elected trial board. It was obvious from the beginning that we were not going to get a fair hearing by the trial board that was picked by the same people that brought Judy and myself up on charges.

When the charges were appealed to the APWU National office the decision was final. No national officer came into Miami to talk to Judy or myself. I'm not really sure what they based their decision on. One thing is for sure the National APWU Officer who was appointed by the National APWU President to conduct an investigation failed to do so. I don't know if he was told to just go along with the charges against Judy Johnson and myself without checking to see if the charges had any merit. All I do know is that if the charges had been properly handled the charges would've been dropped. I could've appealed the decision to the National Convention but decided not to.

One has to consider it just part of the politics. A union steward is taught about due process from the same national union officers that forget what they teach when it comes to politics.

I heard, don't know for sure, that the Department of Labor was called and that the FBI was notified about Judy and myself. If this is true it's funny that I'm still here and nobody from the labor department or the FBI has tried to contact me.

I was taken out of office at the end of October, 2002, and went back into the Post Office on February 1, 2003.

For what it's worth Judy Johnson and myself was able to secure a lawyer and everything the local union brought forward was thrown out in a court of law. It cost us a lot. I had to max out my charge cards and ended up filing bankruptcy. I had good credit before all this happen. Of course the people that brought us up on charges used union funds to fight against Judy and myself.

This wasn't the first time charges were brought up in the Miami Area Local. Charges were filed with the Department of Labor over elections more then once. But it was the first time I had charges brought up against me. It hurts when you know that you are doing a good job representing the membership, know that you didn't steal anything and yet you are accused and thrown out of office because the ones who were behind the charges know they couldn't win in an election against Judy Johnson or myself.

Unfortunately there have been union officers of the American Postal Workers Union from different locals around the country that have been indicted for illegal activities and embezzlement.

I'm sure there're more locals where an officer has been charged or indicted but here are a few I have written about. Some of the charges and the amounts of money that was taken might surprise you. I know it open up my eyes. I'm only writing about the American Postal Workers Union. There's so many more indictments and charges from other unions then one can imagine.

- It was reported in the Federal Times on July 8th 1991 that the head of the American Postal Workers Union Chicago Local and his secretary/treasurer were indicted by a Federal grand jury on embezzlement and illegal loan charges.

It was reported that they were involved in an alleged scheme to use more than $84,000.00 in union funds for illegal loan's and for the president's personal use.

The president of the Chicago Local of the APWU was charged with 17 counts of mail fraud, embezzlement, authorizing an illegal loan, destroying and concealing union records and tax violations.

The Federal Times goes on to report that between January 1984 and April 1988 the President of the Chicago Local used associate membership dues to provide loans to postal employees at the union office. This was done through a Finance company where the owner of the company was also indicted.

The employees repaid the finance company through payroll deductions at an interest rate of 67.5 percent.

The President of the Chicago Local was also charged with illegally authorizing a $20,000.00 loan of union funds to himself, tax evasion, failing to file his income taxes for two years and filing false income taxes two other years.

The President of the Chicago Local was facing up to 69 years in Federal prison and $2,475,000.00 in fines.

The Secretary/Treasurer was charged with authorizing an unlawful loan to the President and failing to file her income tax returns for four years. She was facing five years in prison and fines of $105,000.00.

The President of the Chicago Local died in Federal prison.

- It was reported in the Federal Times on November 2, 1998 that two former officers of the Norristown Local were indicted by a federal grand jury.

The former President and Secretary/Treasurer of the American Postal Workers Union, Local 2233, in Norristown, Pennsylvania were indicted on October 8th 1998, on charges of embezzling nearly $54,000.00 from their local chapter's treasury and then attempting to conceal the theft.

According to the indictment filed in the U.S. District Court in Philadelphia the former President and Secretary/Treasurer wrote five extra salary checks worth nearly $16,000.00. The checks were written to the former President near the end of his term of office in 1995.

The former officers used the locals American Express card to charge personal purchases, including about $10,000.00 for stays at local hotels, nearly $8,000.00 for car repairs and a personal trip to Orlando, Florida for about 41,700.00.

The former officers also allegedly charged more than $7,600.00 for private purchases.

Before the former President was elected in 1992 the local held more than $300,000.00 in net assets including a $180,000.00 cash reserve. After the 1995 elections the local was $40,000.00 in debt.

- When a newly elected President was elected for the New York Metro Area Local of the American Postal Workers Union he decided to hire an auditing firm to look at the books of the previous administration. The audit covered the years 1997-1998. The findings were that the previous President and her administration allegedly misspent over $817,000.00 in union funds.

The audit found improper spending for personal travel, meals, clothing and liquor, as well as thousands of dollars paid out in allegedly improper bonuses.

The New York Metro Area Local was the local where former National APWU President Mo Biller was once President,

- On March 12, 2002 a former secretary/treasurer of the American Postal Workers Union, Local 761, in Nevada was indicted in the

United States District of Nevada. The former secretary/treasurer was indicted on two counts of embezzling $132,824.00 from local 761 of the APWU and $1,764.00 from the American Postal Workers Union Nevada State Association. Also two counts of making false statements in violation of 18 U.S.C. 1001.

On may 17, 2002, the former secretary/treasurer pled guilty to one count of embezzling union funds. She embezzled approximately $200,000.00 from the unions by making unauthorized payments by check and credit card to herself and her creditors.

On August 23, 2002 the former secretary/treasurer was sentenced to 18 months imprisonment followed by three years probation and was ordered to pay restitution in the amount of $193,337.33.

- On April 17, 2002, the United States District Court for the Eastern District of North Carolina indicted the former President of the American Postal Workers Union, Local 1616, on one count of embezzling $8,163.00 in union funds and one count of making false entries in union records.

On August 19, 2002 the former President of APWU, Local 1616, pled guilty to making false entries in the union records. He admitted making the false entries in order to conceal his embezzlement of union funds totaling $8,163.09.

On December 9, 2002 the former President of APWU, Local 1616, in Roanoke Rapids was sentenced to six months of home confinement followed by three years of supervised release. The former President was also ordered to make restitution in the amount of $6,734.00 and pay a $5,000.00 fine. The former President had previously made $1,700.00 in restitution.

- On July 25, 2002, in the United States District Court for the Northern District of Georgia, the former Secretary/Treasurer of the American Postal Workers Union, Local 2695, pled guilty to a three-count information charging her with embezzling $4,803.00 in union funds, theft of United States Postal Service funds in excess of $1,000.00 and access device fraud to obtain in excess of $1,000.00.

On October 4, 2002 the former Secretary/Treasurer of Local 2695 was sentenced to six months home confinement, five years probation, and 150 hours community service. The former Secretary/Treasurer was also ordered to make restitution of $2,200.00, pay a special court assessment of $300.00, and participate in both a mental health treatment program and financial counseling under probation guidance.

- On January 9th 2003, the District Court for the Western District of Louisiana charged the former Treasurer of the Louisiana State American Postal Workers Union with embezzling $34,800.00.

On May 16, 2003 the former Treasurer of the Louisiana State Union of the American Postal Workers Union was sentenced to 60 months of supervised release and ordered to pay $30,000.00 in restitution plus a $100.00 special assessment. The former Treasurer pled guilty to embezzling $34,800.00 in union funds on January 23, 2003.

- On April 6, 2004 a former Secretary/Treasurer of the American Postal Workers Union, local 968, was indicted in the United States District court for the Southern District of Mississippi. The former Secretary/treasurer was charged with one count of embezzling $14,483.50.

On June 1, 2004 the former Secretary/Treasurer of local 968 of the American Postal Workers Union pled guilty to one count of embezzling $14,484 in union funds.

On August 10, 2004 the former Secretary/Treasurer of local 968 was sentenced to three years probation with the first six months in a home confinement program. The former Secretary/Treasurer was also ordered to make restitution in the amount of $19,079.00.

- On February 3, 2005 a former Secretary/Treasurer of Local 11 of the American Postal Workers Union pled guilty to one count of embezzlement in the United States District Court for Nebraska. The former Secretary/Treasurer was charged with embezzling $113,377.00 from the local union.

On July 7, 2005 the former Secretary/Treasurer of the APWU, Local 11, was sentenced to six months imprisonment followed by three years of supervised release with a special condition of six months continuous home confinement. The former Secretary/Treasurer was also ordered to make restitution in the amount of $113,377.00

- On February 7, 2005 in the United States District Court for the Northern District of Iowa charged a former Secretary/Treasurer of the American Postal Workers Union, Local 2339, with embezzling union funds.

On March 2, 2005 the former Secretary/Treasurer pled guilty to one count of embezzling union funds and made restitution in the amount of $13,265.26 to the American Postal Workers Union, Local 2339.

On December 20, 2005 the former Secretary/Treasurer of the APWU, Local 2339, was sentenced to three months imprisonment and two years of supervised released. As a special condition of release, the former Secretary/Treasurer was ordered to serve three months of home detention.

- On August 18, 2005, in the United States District Court for the District of North Dakota a former Secretary/Treasurer of the American Postal Workers Union, Local 349, was indicted on charges of embezzling $34,919.90, making a false statement in a labor report, making a false statement to the Postal Service, and making a false entry in and the destruction of labor union records.

On November 28, 2005 the former Secretary/Treasurer of the APWU, Local 349, pled guilty to a two-count information charging him with embezzling union funds totaling $34,919.90 and one count of making a false statement to obtain Federal employees' compensation.

On February 27, 2006 in the United States District Court for the District of North Dakota, the former Secretary/Treasurer for the American Postal Workers Union, Local 349, was sentenced to three years probation, which included six months of home confinement with electronic monitoring and work release privileges. He was also ordered to pay restitution of $18,812.18 to the local and a $125.00 assessment.

- On September 22, 2005 in the United States District Court for the District of Wyoming, a former Secretary/Treasurer of the American Postal Workers Union, Local, 769, was indicted on 18 counts of embezzling union funds totaling $7,089.14, and one count of making false statement in a Labor Organization Report.

On December 9, 2005, the former Secretary/Treasurer of the APWU, Local 769, pled guilty to one count of embezzling union funds totaling $7,089.14.

On February 21, 2006, the former Secretary/Treasurer of the American Postal Workers Union, Local 769, was sentenced to three months time served and three years probation. He was ordered to pay restitution of $3,899.14 in addition to the $6,500.00 he had already repaid, plus a $100.00 special assessment.

- On February 17, 2006 in the United States District Court for the District of New Jersey, the former Secretary/Treasurer and former President for the American Postal Workers Union local 190 were arrested and indicted on three counts of conspiring to embezzle union funds totaling over $400,000.00. The indictment also charged that the former President and Secretary/Treasurer obstructed investigations by the American Postal Workers Union and the Department of Labor by destroying essential financial records.

The arrests and indictments followed an investigation by the OLMS New York District Office and the Office of the United States Attorney for the District of New Jersey. The former Secretary/Treasurer for local 190 had previously ran for the office of National General President of the American Postal Workers Union.

The former President and former Secretary/Treasurer of local 190 have since pled guilty to the charges files against them. The former Secretary/Treasurer has been sentenced to 20 months in prison and three years of supervised release and was also ordered to pay $783,931.00 in restitution. The former President of local 190 has still not been sentenced.

- On January, 18, 2007, a former Secretary/Treasurer of the American Postal Workers Union, Local 7065, pled guilty in

Federal Court for the Western District of Missouri to one count of embezzling $6,383.00 in union funds. The former Secretary/Treasurer was charged in December, 2006, with one count of embezzling $6,383.00 from approximately February 2003 to September 2005.

- On February 28, 2007 the former President and Treasurer were charged with embezzling union funds from APWU Local 238.

On May 23, 2007 in United States District Court of Kansas the former Treasurer of Local 238 pled guilty to conspiring to embezzle union funds. The former Treasurer and President co-signed checks that allowed the Treasurer to embezzle approximately $26,237.00 in union funds. The former President of local 238 pled guilty on May 30, 2007.

On August 17, 2007 the former Treasurer was sentenced to 6 months home detention, 5 years probation and ordered to make restitution of $26,236.94. The former President was sentenced on October 1, 2007 to 5 years probation for conspiracy to embezzle union funds. He was ordered to make restitution of $11,959.44 and serve 6 months home confinement.

- The former Southern Regional Coordinator was convicted by a Federal jury after less than a half an hour of deliberation.

The former Regional Coordinator was convicted of submitting false hotel receipts to the American Postal Workers Union from January, 2006 to June 2006. The Regional Coordinator had submitted a total of 13 false hotel receipts in excess of $10,000.00. Eleven of the receipts submitted for reimbursement from union funds were allegedly to be from the Hilton Garden Inn, New Orleans. The problem for the Southern Regional Coordinator was the Hilton Garden Inn, New Orleans was closed to the public from August, 2005 to April, 2006 due to wind, water and significant roof damage from Hurricane Katrina.

The former Southern Regional Coordinator was appointed trustee of the New Orleans Local office to deal with union related issues following the aftermath of Hurricane Katrina.

Every member of every local union of the American Postal Workers Union, or any other union for that matter, should have the trust from every elected officer from their local, state and national organization.

Unfortunately when a union officer is caught embezzling union funds that trust is broken.

There should be and has to be a full and complete audit of all union records from every local, state and national organization on a regular basis. There should be bylaws of every organization that state when an audit should be conducted either by elected trustees, an appointment of trustees and an outside auditing company.

The Florida American Postal Workers, in which my brother is the Secretary/Treasurer, is audited on a regular basis. Wayne Wetherington, an elected officer from the Gainesville Area Local in Florida, heads an auditing team that audit's the books of the state organization.

I know that in the American Postal Workers Union, Miami Area Local, an audit is suppose to be conducted by elected trustees twice a year. But this has not happen, but should.

It's not easy trying to run a local union. The President of any local has to have reliable officers and shop stewards to help in dealing with management and filing grievances on a day to day basis. Someone has to be responsible for making sure the grievances, that have been denied by management, are appealed to the next step in a timely manner. That someone is usually the President of the local.

The President and Secretary/Treasurer co-sign the checks written and must be held accountable for all the finances of the local. When an officer starts taking money that they didn't earn, embezzlement, then it really makes the whole union look bad. Management of the United States Postal Service doesn't hesitate to point out to employees when the local union has problems with their officers because of embezzlement or just the dirty politics.

Chapter 20

VIOLENCE & THREATS OUTSIDE THE POST OFFICE

STRESS AND VIOLENCE, ARE they related? The Webster's new universal unabridged dictionary gives the definition of stress as follows;

1. Strain; pressure; a force exerted upon a body, that tends to strain or deform its shape.
2. Urgency; importance; significance.
3. Tension; strained exertion; as, the stress of war affected all the people.

The Webster's new universal unabridged dictionary also gives the definition of violence as follows;

1. Physical force used so as to injure or damage; roughness in action.
2. A use of force so as to injure or damage; a rough, injurious act.
3. Great force or strength of feeling, conduct, or language, passion; fury.
4. To assault; to injure.

So again, I ask, is stress and violence related? I wish I had the answer. All I know is that some people get stressed out and turn to violence as the answer. Over the next few chapters I will go into some of the incidences of threats, robberies and violence by postal employees and against postal employees.

There are so many, too many to mention them all. Incidents of shootings by postal employees and former postal employees. There are also many incidents of violence against postal employees. Again I will mention some incidents to show that it's not only the postal employee that is out there shooting, or trying to rob the post office.

Over the years there have been three serial killers that worked at one time in the post office.

In London, England between the years 1938-1953 John Reginald Halliday Christie was one of England's most notorious serial killers. He had worked as a postman but was fired. However he didn't tell anyone he was fired and continued wearing his uniform and told people that he worked for the post office.

Over a period of thirteen years Christie killed eight women, including his wife, without causing suspicion. He buried some in the garden and others under the floorboards or in an alcove in the kitchen.

After Christie moved the new tenants noticed the odor of decomposing flesh and he was soon arrested. After his trial he was hanged in London on July 15, 1953.

David Berkowitz, the infamous son of sam, or the 44 caliber killer worked in the post office as a letter sorting machine (LSM) operator in Bronx, New York. Between 1976 and 1977 he shot about a dozen people sending New York City into panic. Berkowitz pleaded guilty to six counts of murder and eight counts of attempted murder. He was sentenced to a total of 365 years in prison. Berkowitz claimes he was ordered to commit the murders by a neighbor Sam Carr but said the messages were passed on by Carr's demon dog.

Robert Shulman was a postal worker who made a hobby of killing prostitutes. One women was found in December, 1994 on a roadside in Medford, Long Island New York. In April 1995, another women was found at a Brooklyn recycling plant and a third women on December 11, 1995 was bludgeoned to death and dumped in a Long Island garbage bin. There might have been another women in 1991 whose body was found in a Yonkers trash can, but was not part of the charges brought against Shulman. In July, 1999, Shulman was sentenced to death for his crimes.

Besides the serial killers that worked for the post office there's a lot of other instances of shootings by postal employees and shootings of postal workers. I'm sure the following are just a few such instances.

- On September 4, 1998 police came to the home of postal worker Edward Premo of Hartford, Connecticut after a neighbor accused

Premo of vandalizing her car. Premo was waiting for the police in his yard and opened fire with two handguns. The police officers were wearing bulletproof vests and were not hurt, but returned fire and hit Premo. Despite his injuries Premo was able to get his hands on a semi-automatic rifle and shot a third police officer. After Premo was arrested the bomb squad searched his trailer and discovered homemade explosives.

- October 6, 1998, Riverside, California, Fontana, letter carrier Joseph Neale shot the mayor, two councilmen, and three police officers. Nobody was killed but one of the councilmen was shot in the face and received 32 stitches to his tongue, lost a lot of teeth, and had his jaw bone rebuilt twice after the attack. Neale was sentenced on February 9, 2001 to 374 years in prison.

- It was reported in the Miami Herald on November 15, 1993 that a South Dade postal worker was accused of murdering a 14-year old football player and wounding two other youths. The postal worker was angry that the teen boy was friends with his stepdaughter, a cheerleader for the football team.

- On January 16, 1994 it was reported in the Miami Herald that an former postal worker in Cedar Rapids, Iowa, was charged with ambushing and killing a letter carrier as she was delivering a certified letter. The former postal employee, Ronald Downs, had an alleged grudge against the letter carrier so he mailed a certified letter to his son's house and waited for the letter to be delivered. He shot the letter carrier first with a shotgun and then with a handgun.

- A former supervisor in Jacksonville, Florida, was sentenced to 15 years in prison for her role in a failed conspiracy to murder two other postal supervisors. She was also given five years supervised release and fined $20,000.00.

- In the parking lot of the South Miami Post Office a former football player at the University of Miami shot his ex girlfriend, a letter carrier, and killed her before killing himself.

I came by the post office after I heard about the shooting and found out the phones on the workroom floor could not be used without a password, not even to dial 911. This was soon changed so that the phones could be used. Calling 911, in this case, wouldn't have saved the letter carriers life but employees have to have use of the phones for emergencies.

- In another incident involving a South Miami letter carrier Barry Baist, a 21-year employee was killed by his estranged wife as he was delivering mail. They were embroiled in a bitter custody battle for their son. Barry Baist was standing outside his postal truck when his wife, they were separated, drove up and as she got out of her car fired several rounds. When the gun malfunctioned she walked back to her car and returned with another gun and emptied it into her husband as he layed on the ground. She then returned to her car and waited for the police to arrive.
- It was reported in the Miami Herald that a man called 911 and reported that he shot and killed his wife, Tania Morales, a postal employee that worked at the General Mail Facility in Miami, Florida. The man, who may or may not be the husband to Tania Morales, was being held at the Miami-Dade county jail on second-degree murder charges, an offense for which there is no bond. Because there were no witnesses to the murder the man got off saying he shot Tania in self defense. He was twenty years younger then Tania and rumor had it that Tania was getting ready to kick him out of her home.

According to Florida Supreme Court guidelines, the use of deadly force is justifiable when necessary to prevent death or great bodily harm.

- There was another incident where a female letter carrier that worked at the Sunset Post Office in Miami, Florida was killed outside her home. The letter carrier had been dating another letter carrier but when she decided not to date him anymore it obvious upset him enough to take her life and then his own. The murderer was waiting outside the women's home when she came home with her children and her date. The man she was with took the children into the home so that she could talk to the person that killed her.
- There was a Special Delivery Messenger that worked at the Air Mail facility in Miami, Florida that I represented. This man got upset because someone parked in his desiniated parking space for

his postal vehicle. When he came into the post office to fine out who had parked in his parking space he got into an argument with the female messenger who had parked in his parking space and who he claims to have cussed at him. After going to his supervisor to report this incident the employee claims that the supervisor told him she didn't have time for him. The employee then claims that he walked to the managers office and was told to see his supervisor. This is when he made an alleged threat and was put off the clock. After leaving the building he came back in to retrieve some personal mail he had left at his case. He then left the building again and drove to the front of the post office where he sat and claimes to have been writing out some checks to pay bills. The problem was that he had a gun on his front seat.

When the postal security police came up to his car and saw the gun he was arrested. One of the charges in his removal was that he had a gun on postal property.

When I appealed the case to arbitration some of my arguments were that the Air Mail Facility was not on postal property since it was a lease building. Also the fact that he came back into the building. I argued that if the employee wanted to do something he had a chance right then. My arguments didn't satisfy the arbitrator and the employee lost his case and he was removed from the postal service.

The case was presented in arbitration by the Southern Region National Business Agent for the Special Delivery Craft. I was in the arbitration to assist. The national business agent called me sometime after losing the arbitration and told me the man that we defended killed someone in an argument.

If this was true, to me it was only hearsay, then maybe it was good that we lost. I always wondered why he had the gun on his front seat. Was he waiting for this other employee? He told me the gun was in the glove box of his car and his checkbook was under his gun. He had to move the gun to get to his checkbook. I still wonder why the gun wasn't put back into the glove box. I also wonder if he was planning to harm this other employee he had the argument with?

- In another incident in Miami, at the General Mail Facility, an employee who had worked on the OCR belt had previously applied for a supervisor position. When he was passed over by a Hispanic female he made comments that there was a Cuban connection in the post office. This employee was an older American male. One day while working on the OCR belt with another employee, an Hispanic male, he reach for a tray of mail and his shirt pulled up enough that the other employee saw this man wearing a holster. When the Hispanic employee asked what he was wearing he told him his gun holster with two guns. A few minutes later the Hispanic employee said he was going to the mens bathroom. He didn't want to panic right after seeing this man wearing the guns in fear the man might do something. As he walked away he immediately went to the office to report the incident. When the postal inspectors came down and walked this man out of the building to his car they found a rifle or shotgun in the trunk of the car. This employee, obviously, never returned to work.

A couple of cases that the Miami Area Local took to arbitration were from the South Florida Mail Processing Facility. The union lost both cases.

- An employee was issued an proposed removal on February 8, 1999 and a removal on April 30, 1999. The employee participated in the armed break-out of her son from the Everglades Correctional Institute in Miami. The employee was apprehended immediately but her son wasn't captured until the following day after a car chase that resulted in the death of an innocent citizen. On May 10,1999, the employee pleaded guilty to one felony charge and served thirteen months in jail.
- The other case was when an employee was given a removal on December 17, 2001. The incident that led up to this employee being removed from the Postal Service started on February 15, 2000.

On February 15, 2000, this postal employee was arrested and charged with kidnapping with a weapon, aggravated battery with a firearm and aggravated assault with a firearm. This employee was in jail from February 15, 2000, the day he was arrested, until April 24, 2000. When he was released from jail he was placed under house arrest prior to his court date.

When he went to court he accepted a plea bargain that got him two years of community supervision and then after completion of the two years five years of federal probation.

After being released from jail he contacted his supervisor at the post office which resulted in a proposed indefinite suspension.

Why the kidnapping and assault and battery? The employee claimes he tried to protect his mother against her boyfriend.

There have been a number of robberies or attempted robberies at post offices thoughout the Miami Area. I'm going to only mention a few,

- When an employee reported to work at the Edison Post Office on Northwest 62nd Street in Miami there were two gunmen waiting. The opening clerk arrives at approximately 7:30 A. M. to work the box mail before the window section opens. The two gunmen handcuffed the postal employee and demanded that she open the safes and cash drawers. A neighbor saw what was happening and flagged down a police officer.
- The Motor Vehicle driver that was picking up the last dispatch at the Goulds Post Office received a big surprise. As he was walking back to his truck a robber came up dressed in full ninja gear with a sword. The ninja worrior told the driver to give him the registery pouch, which indicates it was an inside job. No robber, unless they work for the post office or have someone, spouse, parent or friend, would know to ask for a registered pouch.

The closing clerk at the Goulds Post Office, at the time, was brought to the Quail Heights Post Office to be questioned by the Postal Inspectors. Since this employee didn't ask for union representation he was in the office with the Postal Inspectors all by himself. I tried to get in but had a few words with this one Inspector, not good words, and then talked to another Inspector outside where this employee was being questioned.

This employee then took a lie detector test and failed the test. The Postal Inspector I was talking to outside the office told me they didn't think this employee was involved with the robbery but had to rule out all possibilities.

After a long period of time I heard the Postal Inspectors arrested a man who was the boyfriend of an employee who had worked at the Quail

Heights Post Office but had been fired, or resigned, for some missing money.

Sometimes a serious situation like a robbery could turn out looking a little funny. I know if someone at the Gratigny Post Office had a video camera and recorded the attempted robbery they could've been on the funnies home videos.

- On August 28, 2001 an armed man with a .38 calibre revolver came inside the Gratigny Post Office and demanded money from the clerk working at the end of the counter. The problem for the robber was when he asked for the money the clerk disappeared. The clerk ran through some curtins that separates the window section from the back of the post office. The armed gunman then went to the next clerk who just dropped to the floor. With the counters the way they are the clerk could not be seen unless the robber jumped onto the counter. The robber then went to the third clerk who went into hysterics, causing the gunman to panic and run away empty-handed. The third clerk had to be taken to the hospital for an apparent anxiety attack but nobody was seriously hurt.
- While a letter carrier was delivering mail on Friday, January 31, 2003 two men were following her with intentions of robbing the postal carrier. When the police officers arrived two men were breaking into the postal truck. One of the men tried to run away but was caught and the other man climbed inside the truck. Armed with two handguns the man forced the postal letter carrier to drive through residential neighborhoods.

As the truck drove onto a main street the letter carrier obeyed the speed limit and stopped at red lights. As the letter carrier drove the mail truck, with the gunman knelt behind her with two guns, dozens of police officers chased the postal truck. Police blocked cross-traffic to keep the postal truck's path unhindered, and 48 Miami area schools were locked down. TV helicopters flew overhead broadcasting the chase.

Finally after a couple of hours the police officers threw spikes onto the road and flattening two tires on the truck. The postal truck stopped in an intersection and was surrounded by the police swat team. The gunmen used mail to block the view through the windows of the postal truck.

After approximately two hours the postal letter carrier was released and about one hour later the gunman backed out of the truck and was arrested. He was to be charged with federal and state charges of attempted murder, kidnapping and armed robbery.

- On March 2, 2007, the Norland Post Office was robbed at the end of the business day. It almost had to be an inside job, meaning someone who works at the Norland Post Office or a previous employee or maybe just someone who was given information. The man that robbed the Norland Post office went straight to the window technicians (T-5) office after the window closed but before the money was given to the registry cage. The robber made off with over $43,000.00. Also the robber was wearing a post office uniform.

CHAPTER 21

VIOLENCE & SHOOTING BY POSTAL EMPLOYEES

GOING POSTAL IS A myth, a bad rap, according to the head of a commission that was hired to study postal violence. There is far less on-the-job homicide in the Postal Service than at the work places of other employees, and the term "going postal" is unjustified and unfair, according to a commission formed to study aggressive behavior at the post office.

Joseph Califano, the head of the commission was the former Secretary of Health, Education and Welfare in the Carter administration. Mr. Califano went on to say "postal workers are no more likely to physically assault, sexually harass or verbally abuse their co-workers than employees in the national work force. Joseph Califano was the president of the national center on addiction and substance abuse at Columbia University.

The commission was established in 1998 by the Postmaster General at the time, William Henderson, as part of an effort to make employee relations his number 1 priority.

Prior to this commission being hired on postal violence in 1998 a previous Postmaster General, Marvin T. Runyon, changed how the United States Postal Service was handling employment applications.

It was reported on August 6, 1993 that the Unites States Postal service would start doing a lot better job of screening new employees. The Postmaster General Marvin Runyon said it was expected that at the beginning of 1994, before a new employee is hired by the Postal Service, complete background checks would be made to include criminal records, to include the local police records. Also employment records, military records and where appropriate driving records. The Postmaster General also pointed out that there may never be a complete solution to the problem of violence but doing a more intensive search of future employees past will help decrease the violence.

Before the change in background checks of future employees there were 15 shooting incidents in 10 years that I will be writing about. Since the change in background checks of future employees there have been eight shooting incidents over a lot longer period of time. It is obvious to me the change in hiring practices has helped.

In the March, 2006, Florida Postal Worker, there was an article written by Tony Neri, the Maintenance Craft Director for the American Postal Worker Union of Florida. In this article Tony states "there is a distinct difference between being crazy and being insane". I couldn't agree more. I know I'm a little crazy. To work for the union, and work for the union for a long period of time, I worked for the union for over twenty years, you have to be somewhat crazy. It really is a thankless job, yet I wouldn't have traded those years for nothing.

As Tony Neri questions in his article, the employees in the post office that brought guns into the post office and shot and killed fellow employees, were they crazy before they started working for the post office and then went insane? Were they already insane? Or were they normal, if there is such a thing as normal, and after working for a period of time go totally insane? Most of the employees that went on shooting sprees inside the post office had a lot of time as postal employees, years of time to go insane. Well as Tony Neri states in his article he has no words of wisdom. Sorry, neither do I. I wish and pray that the killings and the shootings stop. I've prayed for the families of the employees who were killed, and I've prayed for the families of the killers. Yet I don't have any answers or suggestions.

As I previously mentioned most of the employees, or former employees, that went on a shooting spree had a lot of time in the Postal Service. But not all. In one incident there was an employee with 1 year in the post office and was 27 years old. There was an employee who was 31 years old, another employee was 37 years old with only 4 years in the post office. But for the most part the postal workers that went on shooting sprees were over 40 years old and some over 60 years old. Some of the employees were military vets that served in Vietnam.

So the questions has to be asked again, were the shooters and or killers insane before they started working in the post office or did working in the post office make them insane? You will have to make your own opinion. Over the years, the postal shootings;

- <u>August 19, 1983, Johnston, South Carolina.</u> Three months after he resigned as a postal worker, after 25 years, Perry Smith charged into the Johnston Post Office with a shotgun and began firing at workers, who fled the building. Perry Smith followed them wounding two and then killed the local Postmaster.
- <u>December 2, 1983, Anniston, Alabama.</u> James Howard Brooks walked into the office of the Anniston, Alabama Postmaster and shot him dead, then wounded another supervisor. Brooks had been involved in a long dispute with supervisors.
- <u>March 6, 1985, Atlanta, Georga.</u> Steven W. Brownlee, who had worked for the Postal Service for 12 years, opened fire in a mail sorting area of the main Atlanta, Georgia Post Office, killing two employees and wounding a third. He was then overpowered by fellow postal workers who held him until the police arrived.
- <u>May 31, 1985, New York, New York.</u> David Perez, a letter carrier entered a New York City Post Office and pulled a rifle from a mailbag and attempted to shoot a supervisor, A postal cerk came to the supervisor's aid was shot and wounded. Perez held the supervisor hostage for two hours before surrendering.
- <u>August 20, 1986, Edmund, Oklahoma.</u> Patrick Henry Sherrill, a part-time letter carrier in Edmond, Oklahoma, brought three guns to work, two .45 caliber pistols and a .22 caliber, and fired only fifty rounds, killing 14 people and wounding seven in less than 15 minutes. Sherrill had over 300 rounds of ammunition. He fired a final bullet into his own head killing himself. This incident led to the term "going postal".
- <u>June 29, 1988, Chelsea, Massachusetts.</u> Dominic LuPoli killed a co-worker in the parking lot of the post office where they worked. After fleeing LuPoli committed suicide.
- <u>December 14, 1988, New Orleans, Louisiana.</u> Warren Murphy, a mail handler, shot his supervisor in the face and killed him. Three others were wounded and he held his girlfriend hostage for almost 13 hours before surrendering.
- <u>March 25, 1989, Poway, California.</u> Donald Mace, a 44-year-old letter carrier, walked into the Poway, California Post Office and put a 38-caliber revolver to his head and killed himself.
- <u>May 9, 1989, Boston, Massachusetts.</u> Alfred J. Hunter, a Boston mail handler killed his wife. He then stole a two-seater Cessna

airplane and sprayed the post office where he worked with an ak-47 automatic rifle for three hours before the police persuaded him to land the airplane and surrender.

- August 10, 1989, Escondido, California. John Taylor shot his wife to death in their home. He then drove to work to the Orange Glenn Post Office dressed in his letter carrier uniform where he killed two fellow letter carriers and wounded a third. He then killed himself. John Taylor was just three years from retirement.

- October 10, 1991, Ridgewood, New Jersey. Joseph M. Harris, a fired postal worker, killed his former supervisor with a samurai sword and shot her boyfriend to death at their home in Wayne, New Jersey. He then went to the Ridgewood Post Office where he killed two mail handlers. After a four hour or more standoff with the police he surrendered.

- November 14, 1991, Royal Oak, Michigan. Thomas McLlvane was fired from his position as a letter carrier for alleged insubordination. McLlvane had vowed revenge on his supervisors. Six days after hearing that he loss his arbitration on his removal he armed himself with a sawed-off .22 caliber rifle and went to the Royal Oak Post Office where he opened fire, killing four supervisors and wounding five employees before killing himself.

The Postmaster General, Anthony Frank, announced that the Royal Oak Postmaster, Daniel Presilla, had been suspended with pay pending an investigation.

Anthony Frank said that Presilla's policies were quite autocratic and that Presilla had gone overboard at times, but stopped short of blaming Presilla for the shooting.

Danny Presilla started in the post office in Miami, Florida, as a Distribution clerk and once ran for the position of president for The Miami Area Local.

- June 3, 1992, Citrus Heights, California. Roy Barnes, a 60 year old postal worker put a .22 caliber pistol to his chest and killed himself in front of co-workers in the Citrus Heights, California, Post Office.

- May 6, 1993, Dearborn, Michigan. Larry Jasion, a postal mechanic with 24 years in the Postal Service, entered the postal garage in Dearborn, Michigan, carrying a shotgun and a pistol. He killed another mechanic and wounded a supervisor and the administrative clerk before killing himself.

- <u>May 6, 1993, Dana Point, California.</u> Just four hours after the postal shooting in Dearborn, Michigan, Mark Hilbun, a postal employee with 38 years killed his mother and her dog. He then went into a Dana Point, California post office and shot and killed a letter carrier and injured a clerk. Hilbun then left the post office and continued his shooting spree wounding three more people before being captured a day and a half later.
- <u>July 10, 1995, City of industry, California.</u> Bruce Clark, a 22-year postal employee punched a supervisor in the back of the head. When the supervisor left to report the incident Clark also left and return with a paper bag. When the supervisor asked Clark what was in the bag Clark withdrew a .38 caliber revolver and shot the supervisor twice. Clark's co-workers subdued him until the police arrived. The supervisor died from the gunshot wounds.
- <u>August 29, 1995, Palatine, Illinois.</u> Dorsey Thomas, 53, walked up to another postal employee and fired five rounds from a .380 caliber semi-automatis pistol wounding the employee. Thomas then went to the lobby of the post office and fired twice at another employee wounding him. In the confusion Dorsey Thomas managed to get to his car and he drove home. Police arrested him shortly after he arrived at his home.
- <u>December 18, 1996, Los Vegas, Nevada.</u> Charles Jennings shot and killed his former supervisor in the post office parking lot. Jennings had learned a few days before that he had lost an arbitration on his removal from the postal service. Jennings received a life sentence with no possibility of parole.
- <u>SEPTEMBER 2, 1997, MIAMI BEACH, FLORIDA.</u> Jesus Antonio Tamayo was working at his window position at the Miami Beach Post Office when his ex-wife and a friend came into the post office. While his ex-wife was in line Tamayo left the counter and went to his car then came in the lobby doors and without saying a word pulled one of two .357 magnum handguns out of a fanny pack and critically wounding his ex-wife and her friend. Tamayo then went back out the lobby doors and tried to get back into the post office by the employees enterence but someone had

locked the doors. Tamayo then walked to the nearest tree and killed himself.

I had represented Jesus Tamayo on several grievances when he worked in Homestead, Florida. Jesus worked in a one man post office in Naranja, Florida until the post office closed and then he worked at the Princeton Post Office which is part of Homestead. I was really surprised when I heard about the incident in Miami Beach with Tamayo. But then I did not know anything about his personal life.

Tamayo had to file an EEO to get a transfer with his seniority from Homestead, Florida to Miami Beach, Florida. Tamayo had over twenty years in the post office.

- DECEMBER 18, 1997, Milwaukee, Wisconsin. Anthony DeCulit, after being at work for over two hours, pulled out a 9mm handgun and shot his supervisor wounding her in the eye. When another postal worker tried to help the supervisor DeCulit shot and killed the employee. DeCulit then fired and wounded another employee as they were trying to flee the area. When another postal employee confronted DeCulit and tried to talk DeCulit to put the gun down instead Anthony DeCulit put the gun in his own mouth and killed himself. DeCulit was only 37 years old.
- DECEMBER 24, 1997, DENVER, COLORADO. David Jackson, a former postal employee, entered the Denver General Mail Facility and pulled out a gun. He took seven postal employees hostage. After approximately 10 hours Jackson surrendered.
- APRIL 17, 1998, Dallas, Texas. Maceo Yarbough, a letter carrier with 1 year in the postal service, fatally shot a postal clerk after they had argued in the break room of the Northaven Post Office. Yarbough fled the scene but was apprehended after a short time. The postal clerk had 15 years in the postal service.
- JANUARY 31, 2006, GOLETA, CALIFORNIA. Jennifer San Marco, a former postal employee who was granted an early retirement for medical reasons in June, 2003, shot and killed her next door neighbor on the evening of January 31, 2006. She then drove to the mail processing plant where she used to work and killed six postal employees and wounding another before killing

herself. The following day the wounded postal employee died from their wounds. This shooting is thought to be the deadliest workplace shooting by a women in the nation. It was also the nations bloodiest shooting at a postal installation in nearly 20 years. San Marco used a 9 MM handgun, reloading at least once. It was just a matter of time before a women shooter joined the men that were involved with postal shootings. Jennifer San Marco was 44 years old and had only 6 years in the Postal Service.

From the list of the employees, or former employees, mentioned above they worked mostly as letter carriers. There were some Clerks and a couple of Mail Handlers. Most of the men, one women, that went on these shooting sprees were fired employees.

Has the stress from the job caused these shooting sprees? I guess everyone handles stress differently. I believe there's more pressure on letter carriers than other employees which could cause more stress. I'm saying this from what I observed in Miami, Florida.

Maybe I've been one of the luckier employees. I've had some really lousy managers and supervisors. But I've also had some good supervisors and managers that knew how to treat people. I don't think I was ever stressed out in the jobs I worked at in the Postal Service, at lease not to the point that I ever thought of getting even. But I guess everyone handles their situation differently. I've never been issued any notice of removal or threated with removal. How would I react after working in the post office 37 years if I were to get a removal notice? I cannot really answer that question truthfully. I would like to think I would leave and not look back but one never knows until they are faced with a removal. I retired on June 2nd 2007, from the Country Lakes Post Office in Miami, Florida, so I never had to be faced with this problem. Hopefully there will be no more shootings in the post office and employees that are stressed out will be able to handle it differently then going on a shooting spree that only leaves more stress for the family of both the victims and the shooters.

CHAPTER 22

WORKPLACE VIOLENCE OTHER THAN THE POST OFFICE

I WORKED IN THE United States Postal Service for over 37 years and never thought as my job being like a family. The manager or supervisor, in a service talk, would say we are a family here and I would say to myself, "I wouldn't treat my family the way the post office treats it's employees". But in a way maybe management was on the right track when they said we were a family.

I would hear people complain about the wait they had in the post office before getting to the counter with their package or to buy stamps. But did you hear people complain when they were in a bank on pay day and had to wait, or a grocery store. There's a saying, you can bad mouth your family but don't let anyone else outside the family do it.

This brings me to the subject at hand. Violence in the work place. When there was a shooting in the post office it was big news, and still is. The story is usually on the front page of many major newspapers across the nation. Another postal worker goes postal. But in realty there were, and are still, less shootings in the post office than at other places of business. Between August 1983 and April 1998 there were 22 shooting incidents, where someone was killed, in the post office that were reported. Two of the incidents reported was the gunman killing themselves. There was one more shooting incident in the post office reported in the papers almost eight years later, January 31st 2006, after the previous shooting. In those 23 shooting incidents 58 people were killed, including the shooter, and 30 people were wounded. But it is worse in other places. Schools are one of the worse when it comes to shootings and taxi drivers face the highest homicide rate. Most victims overall are retail workers.

Only a handful of workplace murders make the headlines, except the local newspaper or television. But, as said before, a postal shooting is reported nationally.

When there's a shooting in a place of business you don't hear that an employee went factory. You hear that an employee went postal, even if it has nothing to do with the post office. I guess it just sounds natural.

In a report dated July 9, 1996 from the Virginian Pilot, who got their information from the Associated Press, they said that the highest homicide rate were taxi drivers, and most victims overall are retail workers. When you think of workplace violence, a postal employee wielding a semi-automatic pistol may jump to mind. But the reality is much different. The most likely to be killed are cab drivers, and most victims work in retail, according to a study released on July 8, 1996.

At a workplace violence conference on November 17, 2004 it was reported by NIOSH, National Institute for Occupational Safety and Health, taxi drivers are 60 times more likely to be murdered on the job than workers in any other profession. Also according to NIOSH taxi drivers have the 3rd highest rate of assaults. The report goes on to say the accuracy of this figure is greatly compromised by the fact that approximately 75% of attacks on taxi drivers go unreported.

In another report published in the Daily Gazette on February 10, 2006, Swarthmore, Pennsylvania, by an independent group of Swarthmore college students, it states that driving a taxi is one of the most dangerous professions. The report goes on to say that taxi drivers generally represent a largely disadvantaged community. An example is New York City where there are 100,000 cab drivers and 90% are immigrants. Approximately 60% of cab drivers are from either an Indian, Pakistan or Bangladesh background. Maybe this is why most of the attacks on taxi drivers go unreported.

In a report dated January 5, 2005 by Kim Wells, Executive Director of the Corporate Alliance to End Partner Violence (CAEPV) it reported on the number of workplace homicides. In the report by Kim Wells it was reported that in 2003 homicide in the workplace took the lives of 631 people. In 1994 there were 1,071 workplace homicides reported, 56% of the victims worked in retailing or other service industries, 179 were retail supervisors or proprietors and 105 were cashiers. It was reported 86 taxi drivers were killed in 1994.

On April 19, 1995 in downtown Oklahoma City, Oklahoma, the Oklahoma City bombing took place. The bomb attack on the Alfred P. Murrah Federal Building was the most destructive act of terrorism on American soil until the September 11, 2001 attacks. The Oklahoma blast claimed 168 lives, including 19 children under the age of 6, and injured more than 680 people. The blast destroyed or damaged 324 buildings. The bomb was estimated to have caused at least $652 million worth of damage.

The government started keeping track of the homicides in the workplace in 1992. From 1992 the number of homicides in the workplace were; 1992-1044 homicides, 1993-1074, 1994-1080, 1995-1036, 1996-927, 1997-860, 1998-714. 1999-651. 2000-677, 2001-643—this figure excludes fatalities from the attacks of September 11, 2001, 2002-609, 2003-632, and 2004-559.

Then there's the school shootings. School shootings committed by either a student or intruders from outside the school campus have occurred more than one might exspect. There was even a song written by Neil Young called Ohio, about the Kent State shootings on May 4, 1970 when the National Guard opened fire on a group of protesters. The students were protesting the announcement from President Richard Nixon that the United States would be invading Cambodia.

There's so many school shootings, to mention them all would be impossible. So I will only mention a few notable shootings at schools from elementary to Universitys.

- Cleveland School massacre. The Cleveland School massacre occurred on January 17, 1989 at Cleveland Elementary School in Stockton, California. The gunman who had a long criminal history shot and killed five schoolchildren, and wounded 29 other schoolchildren and one teacher, before committing suicide. The gunman victims were predominantly Southeast Asian refugees.
- University of Iowa shooting. The University of Iowa shooting occurred at the University of Iowa in Iowa City, Iowa on November 1, 1991. The gunman had killed four faculty members and one student. He later seriously wounded another student before he committed suicide.
- Lindhurst High School shooting. The Lindhurst High School shooting occurred on May 1, 1992 at Lindhurst High School

in Olivehurst, California. The gunman, 20 years old, who was a former student at the school killed three students and one teacher, and wounded nine others before he surrendered to police. On September 21, 1993 the gunman was found guilty on all charges against him and was sentenced to death.

- Westside Middle School massacre. The Westside Middle School massacre occurred on March 24, 1998 in Jonesboro, Arkansas. A total of five people, four female students and a teacher, were killed. Nine students and one teacher were injured. The shooters were two students, 13 years old and an 11 year old, both boys. They were shooting in an ambush style from the woods in camouflaged clothes. The boys had planned to run away as they had food, sleeping bags, and survival gear in their van. The night before the shooting the boys loaded up the van, belonging to the mother of the 13 year old boy, with camping supplies, snack foods, and seven weapons, which were stolen from the 11 year old boys grandfathers house. In their attempt to run back to the van after their shooting they were captured by the police.

- Columbine High School massacre. The Columbine High School massacre occurred on April 20, 1999, at Columbine High School in Columbine, an unincorporated area of Jefferson County, Colorado. Two students embarked on the massacre killing 12 students and one teacher. They also injured 21 other students directly, and three people were injured while attempting to escape. The two students then committed suicide. It was the deadliest massacre for an American high school.

- West Nickel Mines School. The West Nickel Mines school is an Amish one-room schoolhouse in the Old Order Amish community of Nickel Mines, a village in Bart Township of Lancaster County, Pennsylvania. On October 2, 2006 a gunman took hostages and eventually shot ten girls, with their ages ranging from six years old to 13 years old, killing five of the girls before committing suicide inside the schoolhouse. The West Nickel Mines school was torn down after the shooting and a new one-room schoolhouse, the New Hope School, was built at another location.

- Virginia Tech massacre. The massacre on the Virginia Tech campus occurred on April 16, 2007. There were two separate attacks by a single gunman more than two hours apart. At approximately 7:15 A.M. at West Ambler Johnston Hall two students were killed. While police and emergency medical services units were responding to the shootings the gunman went back to his dormitory room, the gunman was also a student at Virginia Tech, and changed out of his bloodstained clothes. The gunman appeared at a nearby post office and mailed a package of writings and video recordings to NBC News. The package was postmarked 9:01 A.M. The gunman then walked to Norris Hall. In a backpack the gunman was carring were several chains, locks, a hammer, a knife, two guns, nineteen 10 and 15 round magazines and almost 400 rounds of ammunition. The gunman entered Norris Hall on the Virginia Tech campus and chained the three main entrance doors shut. The gunman placed a note on at least one of the chained doors claiming that attemps to open the door would cause a bomb to explode. The bomb threat was never called in, even though someone found the note. The second shooting occurred between 9:40 A.M. and 9:51 A.M. where 30 more people were killed and 25 people were injured before the shooter committed suicide. The Virginia Tech massacre is one of the deadliest shooting incidents by a single gunman in United States history, on or off a school campus.

In 23 shooting incidents in the post office 58 people were killed, including the shooter in some incidents. Also 30 people were wounded. In the seven school shootings I wrote about, 75 people, mostly students, were killed, including the shooter in some of the incidents. There were also 101 people, mostly students, injured.

Maybe working for the United States Postal Service isn't an unsafe place to work. Maybe sitting in a classroom, not knowing when someone might walk into the room with a weapon, is more of an unsafe place to be. That's a scary thought. Hopefully there will not be a next time. But if there is maybe people should think before saying someone went postal. Just a thought.

CHAPTER 23

OFFICE OF INSPECTOR GENERAL & POSTAL INSPECTORS INVESTIGATION

THE UNITED STATES POSTAL Inspection Service is one of the oldest law enforcement agencies in the United States. The mission of the United States Postal Inspection Service is to protect the United States Postal Service, its employees and its customers from criminal attack, and protect the nations mail system from criminal misuse.

United States law provides for the protection of mail. Postal Inspectors enforce over 200 federal laws in investigations of crimes that may adversely affect or fraudulently use the United States mail, the postal system or postal employees.

The office of Inspector General (OIG) of the Unites States Postal Service was created by Congress in September, 1996 by amending the inspector General Act of 1978 and the Postal Reorganization Act of 1970. The Inspector General Act provides that the OIG may conduct audits and investigations in the Postal Service as it considers appropriate. Prior to the 1996 legislation, the Postal Inspection Service performed the duties of the OIG. The Inspector General, who is independent of postal management, is appointed by and reports directly to the nine Presidential appointed Governors of the Postal Service. The OIG does not report to the Postmaster General nor is the OIG under the Postmaster General supervision.

The primary purpose of the OIG is to prevent, detect and report fraud, waste and program abuse, and promote efficiency in the operations of the United States Postal Service. The OIG has "oversight" responsibility for all activities of the Postal Inspection Service.

In a letter dated March 22, 2005 the United States Postal Service informed the national office of the American Postal Workers Union that the responsibility for investigating certain types of employee misconduct, internal crimes, is being shifted from the Postal service Inspection Service to the Office of Inspector General.

The American Postal Workers Union sent a request for information to the United States Postal Service trying to understand the reasoning for the change to the OIG from the Postal Inspection Service. The postal Service stated that the agents of the OIG will comply with article 17.3 as it relates to an employee request for a shop steward or union representative during the course of an interrogation. The Postal Service response did not satisfy all the concerns of the APWU. The APWU questioned whether the change was proper because it has been past practice consistent with applicable regulations, collective bargaining agreements, and settlements that Postal Inspection Service agents are the law enforcement officers who conduct interrogations of bargaining unit employees regarding an internal crime investigation. Also the fact that the OIG does not report to the Postmaster General, nor is the OIG under the supervision of the PMG, and the APWU contractual relationship is with the PMG and not with the Board of Governors, whom the OIG reports their information to.

The bottom line is still the same. If any Postal Service employee is called into an office by either the Postal Inspection Service or the OIG, that employee should know to request a union representative and not to say anything or sign anything while waiting for the union to show up. It wouldn't matter if the employee is guilty of a crime or innocent, the employee is still entitled to a representative, either a union officer or shop steward or a lawyer.

My dealings with the Postal Inspectors was very limited. Everytime, except once, I was called to represent an employee that had been called into the office by the Postal Inspectors was for either a very large shortage the employee had while working the window, or for misuse of money orders, or both.

The one time I was called to represent an employee, that was not dealing with the window, who had been brought to the office of the Postal Inspection Service, was a gun issue. The employee was accused of pointing a gun at two other employees in the parking lot and the Postal Inspectors were called. I talked to the employee outside the office and I was told that she had no gun and she didn't point no gun at anyone. When we went back into the office with the Inspector waiting for us the Inspector asked the lady if she would give him permission to search her car.

Since the lady had no problem with the Postal Inspector searching her car we all walked to the parking lot where her car was parked. I remember thinking, while we were walking to the car, I hope there's no gun in that car. As it turn out there wasn't any weapon in the car belonging to the lady and the Postal Inspector ended his investigation.

I have never had any dealings with anyone from the Office of Inspector General. And as far as I know have never seen any agent from their office.

As I said before the Postal Inspectors investigate and enforce over 200 laws directly or indirectly affecting the United States Postal Service, some of which are assaults and threats, robbery and burglary, mail theft, embezzlement, workers compensation, counterfeit money orders and money laundering, narcotics, mail fraud, child pornography, mail bombs and anthrax, and many many more crimes. I never stopped to think much about what the Postal Inspectors investigated, other than the times I had to deal with them in the post office trying to defend an employee.

The first semiannual report to Congress from the Office of the Inspector General was for fiscal year 1997, October 1, 1996 through March 31, 1997.

Karla Corcoran was sworn in as the new Inspector General on January 1, 1997. Prior to this date the chief Postal Inspector had served as the Inspector General for the United States Postal Service since 1988.

The Postal Inspection Service continues to conduct investigations of crimes, issue warrants and subpoenas, make arrest for Postal Service offenses and present evidence to prosecutors for criminal and civil action.

I am writing about only a few of the investigations by the United States Postal Inspection Service that have led to prison time. These were taken from the reports to Congress from the office of the Inspector General, 1996-2007.

Assaults and Threats.

- On January 14, 1997 a former letter carrier at Dana Point, California was found guilty on August 6, 1996 of two counts of murder and related charges for the May 6, 1993 homicide of one employee and attempted murder of a second employee. The former letter carrier was sentenced to seven consecutive and two concurrent life sentences. He was also fined $10,000.00.

- In New Jersey an employee arrested by Postal Inspectors for the August 1996 shooting of a supervisor at the Patterson Vehicle Maintenance Facility pleaded guilty in September, 1996 to assault with intent to commit a felony and assault with a dangerous weapon to do bodily harm. On February 21, 1997 the employee was sentenced in Federal Court to five years and three months imprisinment. He was also ordered to undergo a mental health evaluation.

- An inmate at a Maine prison was sentenced to 21 years and 10 months in prison for mailing threatening communication. The sentenced to be served consecutively to his identical September 1996 sentence on eight similar counts. The inmate mailed threatening communication to President Bill Clinton, and the Governors of Maine and New Jersey.

- A postal clerk convicted in September, 1996 of shooting two postal employees at the Palatine, Illinois Processing and Distribution Center was sentenced in Federal Court on December 5, 1996 to a term of 16 years in prison.

- On January 6, 1997, a letter carrier in Washington D.C. was robbed at gunpoint by two assailants. One of the suspects was arrested on February 14, 1997 and plead guilty to one count of armed robbery. On April 2, 1997 he was sentenced to 24 years in prison with a 19 year suspended sentence, plus a mandatory five year prison term to be followed by a three year drug treatment program at a secured facility. The second suspect was arrested on February 19, 1997 and also pled guilty. He was given a nine year suspended sentence, two years probation and 100 hours of community service.

- On November 12, 1996 a Postal Inspector in the Sacramento, California area, who was attempting to arrest a man for whom a federal arrest warrant had been issued, was hit by the car the man was driving as he tried to flee. The man pleaded guilty in Federal District Court to assaulting the inspector and was sentenced on these and other charges to 43 months in prison, 36 months supervised release and court ordered restitution of $57,314.00.

- A man was sentenced in Federal Court in Tampa, Florida for assaulting Postal Inspectors with his vehicle while they attempted to arrest him for violating a conditional release that was the result of an earlier Postal Inspection Service related conviction involving a credit card scam. He was sentenced to nine and-a-half years in prison plus an indictment for impending and resisting arrest.

- On December 19, 1996 in Las Vegas, Nevada, a former employee who lost his arbitration on his removal, shot and killed the Labor Relations Specialist who was the advocate for the United States Postal Service in the arbitration. The shooter was convicted of first degree murder on December 5, 1997 and sentenced to life without the possibility of parole.

- A non-employee who attempted to assault postal police officers with a razor as they escorted him from the Morgan General Mail Facility in New York City was sentenced to 33 months in prison.

- The leader of a Houston, Texas gang, responsible for over 30 attacks of postal vehicles was sentenced to 27 months in federal prison and ordered to make restitution in the amout of the forged checks he wrote.

- After an Postal Inspection Service investigation seven members of the "constitution court of we are the people" in a Tampa, Florida Federal Court received sentences ranging from six months to 15 years. They were charged with 60 crimes, including extortion, mailing threatening letters and obstruction of justice. The defendants believe they are the direct descendants of the authors of the constitution and are exempt from the laws of the United States. The threatening letters were sent to Federal Judges, United States Attorneys, court clerks and members of juries.

- An Ohio Federal Judge sentenced a man to 28 months in prison and three years probation to include mental health and alcohol rehabilitation counseling. Postal Inspectors found that the man mailed a videotape to his girlfriend containing at least 10 threats to kill her and her mother.

- A customer entered a Colorado postal station with a loaded shotgun to complain about his mail service. The customer was arrested by Postal Inspectors without an incident. The customer was convicted in Federal Court on three counts of assault and sentenced to three years in prison and three years probation.

- An individual was sentenced to 29 years in prison for attempted murder, aggravated battery with a firearm, armed violence and aggravated discharge of a firearm, for the shooting of an Illinois letter carrier.
- An individual was convicted of assaulting a Federal employee and using and discharging a weapon during a crime of violence. The shooter, who was found to be mentally ill, but not legally insane, was incarcerated without bail and faces a mandatory ten-year sentence on weapon charges and additional ten years on assault charges.
- A man was sentenced on March 26, 2001 to five life terms without parole and an additional 110 years in prison for murdering a letter carrier in Chatsworth, California, and shooting other individuals on August 10, 1999, at a Jewish Community Center in Granada Hills. He was also sentenced to serve two consecutive terms of life in prison and ordered to pay $690,294.00 in restitution.
- A New YorkCity man was sentenced in February, 2001 to 16 years in prison for the aggravated assault of a Postal Police Officer. Postal Inspectors determined the officer had been performing routine perimeter patrol at the Morgan General Mail Facility on June 2, 2000 when he was struck on the head without warning or provocation, by a man wielding a 24-inch steel pipe.
- A Philadelphia, Pennsylvania man was sentenced in November 2000 to 14 years and six months in prison for shooting a city letter carrier in Prospect Park, Pa. Postal Inspectors alleged he struck and critically wounded the carrier with a high-powered fifle as she delivered mail on her route. The man was ordered to pay restitution of $261,054.00 to the Postal Service to cover workers' compensation payments and medical expenses incurred due to the carrier's disabling injuries.
- Following a competency hearing on September 5, 2001, a New Jersey man was found not guilty by reason of insanity for his assault of a Bergenfield, New Jersey letter carrier. The carrier was intentionally hit by the defendant's car on January 31, 2001, and was then stabbed in the back. The letter carrier suffered a broken leg and stab wounds, but returned to limited duty in late February, 2001 and to full duty in May. His attacker was diagnosed as paranoid schizophrenic and determined insane at the time of the

assault. He was ordered committed to a mental institution for long-term psychiatric treatment and hospitalized until deemed no longer a danger to himself or others.

- A man was sentenced in June 2002 to more than 10 years in prison and three years supervised release after shooting a Los Angeles letter carrier on March 7, 1997. The shooter fled and remained a fugitive for four years, until he was arrested in July 2001 by Postal Inspectors from the Southern California Division's Major Crimes Team. The shooter must also pay restitution of $9,707.00 to the carrier.

- Two men who had been arrested by Postal Inspectors were sentenced on June 17, 2002, after entering guilty pleas to the May 2001 kidnapping and sexual assault of a Tennessee postmaster. The judge ordered the maximum sentence of more than 40 years in federal prison for one of the assailants and more than 26 years in prison for his cohort.

- A man convicted in 1981 of murdering a postal contractor in Eatonville, Florida, in October 1979 was executed at the Florida State Prison on December 9, 2002, after numerous postponements. The postal contractor was abducted from a contract postal station after 37 postal money orders were imprinted. Postal Inspectors found the postal contractor with 16 stab wounds and severe injuries that resulted from being run over by a vehicle multiple times.

- A man was sentenced in August 2005 to 33 months in prison for assaulting a federal employee and another 84 months for using a firearm in a crime of violence.

- In February 2005, a suspect was sentenced to six years in prison after pleading guilty to the September 24, 2002, stabbing of two postal employees. The incident occurred when the suspect was denied access to the Milton R. Brunson Postal Station in Chicago, Illinois.

- A man was sentenced in Georgia to life imprisonment in January 2006 for assaulting and attempting to murder a federal employee and using a firearm in the commission of a crime. The man shot a letter carrier seven times in the arm and abdomen, The shooter than drove to the Snellville, Georgia Police Department where he confessed to the shooting. The shooter stated he shot the letter carrier because the carrier was a federal employee. The shooter had medical bills totaling more than $90,000.00 and was in fear of losing his home. He felt he would be treated better in federal prison than to be homeless. The shooter believed the easiest way to be prosecuted would be to kill a federal employee.

- A former letter carrier was sentenced to life in prison in July 2006 in Baker City, Oregon. He received a mandatory minimum sentence of 25 years for murdering his supervisor and an additional 10 years for the attempted aggravated murder of his postmaster. On April 4, 2006, the letter carrier ran over his supervisor with a postal van in the parking lot of the Baker City Post Office. The carrier then ran into the post office looking for his postmaster. When he was unable to locate the postmaster he ran back to the parking lot and shot his supervisor repeatedly, killing her.

Robbery and Burglary

- In Phoenix, Arizona an individual was sentenced to 42 years and six months in prison for the September 1995 robbery of two letter carriers and the attempted murder of one of the carriers.
- On December 2, 1996 an individual responsible for the armed robberies of five Southern California letter carriers was sentenced to 106 months in prison.
- A man who robbed the North Hollywood Chandler California Postal Station was sentenced to serve nine years and nine months in prison and ordered to repay the Postal Service $2,070.00, which was stolen during the robbery in July, 1996.
- On January 23, 1997 a former 10-year veteran police officer believed responsible for 10 post office robberies in West San Gabriel Valley, California pleaded guilty to two counts of robbing a postal facility and one count of using a firearm in the commission of a violent crime. He was sentenced to 10 years and 10 months in Federal prison.
- A postal employee, his brother, cousin, and a friend were sentenced to prison terms ranging from 51 months to 68 months for the sledge hammer robbery of an MVS driver at the back dock of a postal facility in Upper Arlington, Ohio.

- An individual was indicted for the June, 1996 murder of the Ruby, Alaska Postmaster and armed robbery of the Ester and Ruby Post Offices in Alaska. To avoid the death penalty the man pleaded guilty on July 25, 1997 to killing the Postmaster and was sentenced to life in prison plus 30 years without parole.
- A man responsible for the robbery of the Sumner, Texas Post Office was sentenced to life in prison. He also received a 20 year sentence for the burglary of the Brookston, Texas Post Office and two additional 20-year sentences as enhancements resulting from a criminal record that includes 11 prior felony convictions.
- In Birmingham, Michigan two men responsible for robbing the post office were each sentenced to nine and-a-half years in prison and restitution of $102,985.00.
- A man founf guilty of robbing and murdering a Motor Vehicle Service Operator, in January 1993, was sentenced to life in prison without parole. He was also sentenced to 25 years on gun charges that were to be served consecutively and ordered to pay $81,000.00 in restitution. The money will be taken from his prison wages.
- In march, 1998 a man convicted of the armed robbery of the Lynwood, California Main Post Office and the attempted robberies of the Long Beach East Station Office in February amd March 1996 was sentenced to 15 and-a-half years in prison.
- One of two armed robbers who stole $25,100.00 in official remittances from a postal driver and a clerk at a Birmingham, Alabama facility was sentenced to 75 months in Federal Prison and 60 months of probation. The other robber was sentenced to 130 months in prison and 60 months of probation. Both men were ordered to pay $25,100.00 in restitution.
- A man identified by Postal Inspectors as responsible for two armed robberies of postal facilities, in Miami, Florida, was sentenced to 16 years and eight months in prison.
- Two men were sentenced in a Louisana court to hard labor for the armed robbery of the Ferriday Post Office in Louisana. One of the men was sentenced to 40 years for the postal robbery and for two non-postal robberies and forcible rape. The other man was sentenced to 25 years for the robbery and two non-postal robberies.

- A Georgia man was sentenced in a Fulton County Court to 20 years in prison for the armed robbery of a letter carrier.
- A man identified by Postal Inspectors as responsible for the 1996 burglary of the Little Rock California Post Office and four commercial burglaries was sentenced to 75 years in a California State Prison.
- An individual responsible for the July 1997 armed robbery of the Cashtown Pennslyviana Post Office and six additional armed robberies in the same area was sentenced to a mandatory minimum of 10 years and a maximum of 30 years in prison.
- The robber of a post office and a contract postal station in South Carolina was sentenced to over 52 years in prison.
- The mastermind behind at least 13 letter carrier robberies in Southern California was sentenced to nearly 11 years in Federal Prison and an additional two years in prison for committing armed robbery while on Federal probation.
- An individual was sentenced to 39 years and seven months in prison for armed robberies of post offices in West Virginia and New Jersey. He was also ordered to pay over $22,000.00 in restitution jointly with a co-conspirator who was sentenced to 11 years and six months in prison.
- Three individuals were sentenced for a series of armed robberies that included post officed in Virginia. The suspects were sentenced to 124 years and four months in prison and a total of over $216,000.00 in restitution, 26 years and 10 months in prison and over $103,000.00 in restitution, and five years in prison, three years probation and restitution of $3,790.00.
- An individual was convicted in Federal Court for the armed robbery of a New Jersey post office. The individual was sentenced to 32 years and four months in prison.
- Postal Inspectors arrested a professional burglar, who had 16 prior arrests, for burglarizing an Illinois post office. Several other businesses located in the same strip mall as the post office were also burglarized. The offender confessed burglarizing the post office and two Illinois contract stations and was sentenced to 25 years in prison.
- An investigation by Postal Inspectors in Massachusetts resulted in a sentenced of life imprisonment without parole for the man who

robbed a postal facility. The sentence was based on the Federal "three strikes" law that mandates life imprisonment for career criminals who commit a Federal crime of violence and have two or more other convictions for serious felonies. His sentence follows two previous convictions. He robbed a letter carrier in June 1995 and attempted to murder a witness to that robbery in July, 1995.

- A north Carolina man was sentenced for the May, 2000 armed robbery of the Biscoe, North Carolina Post Office. He was ordered to serve 85 months in prison and three years of supervised release, and must pay $3,250.00 in restitution to the Postal Service.

- The post office at Schodack Landing, New York, was robbed at gunpoint in July 2000. The robber tied the hands and feet of the postmaster before fleeing with $2,000.00 in postal money orders and $44.00 in cash. He was apprehended that same month while attempting a burglary in Albany, New York. The man pled guilty and was sentenced to 15 years and eight months in prison, and five years of supervised release, and was ordered to pay $2,000.00 in restitution.

- An Alabama man was sentenced to 70 months in prison and three years of supervised release for the December 2001 robbery of a letter carrier from the Brance Post Office.

- An Ohio man was sentenced to 96 months in prison, three years supervised release, and restitution to the Postal Service of $613.00. Postal Inspectors identified him as responsible for the May 2001 armed robbery of the Northridge Branch Post Office in Dayton, Ohio.

- A man and a woman pleaded guilty to the August 2001 robbery of the Tigerville, South Carolina Post Office. They were charged with robbing the post office and possessing property that was stolen during the robbery. The man was sentenced to 15 years and eight months in prison and five years of supervised release. The woman was sentenced to five years of probation.

- A man was sentenced to 92 months in prison, to be served concurrently with a 10-year sentence on unrelated charges, after pleading guilty to the April 27, 2001 burglary of the Alvordton, Ohio Post Office.

- A man was sentenced for the armed robbery of the Woodland Post Office in Wilson, North Carolina on January 14, 2004.

Postal Inspectors identified the defendant and two other suspects after they negotiated stolen money orders. The main defendant was sentenced to 120 months for the robbery and 84 months for using a firearm during the robbery.

- A federal judge sentenced a man to more than 25 years in prison and a women to 63 months for the armed robbery of the Fitzpatrick, Alabama Post Office. The pair took $176.00 in cash, 26 blank postal money orders, and a money order imprinter.
- A man was sentenced in September 2005 to 18 years and three months in prison for possessing a firearm and for the armed robbery of the Raywood, Texas Post Office on January 2, 2004.
- On January 24, 2005, an Amelia County Circuit Court Judge sentenced a juvenile to 60 years in the Virginia State Penitentiary, with 15 years suspended, after he was found guilty for the attempted capital murder, robbery, and abduction of a female rural letter carrier.

Mail theft

- A former clerk at the Nashville, Tennessee Airport Mail Facility had been stealing credit cards from the mail since 1994 and supplying them to an Atlanta based Nigerian credit card ring. He was sentenced to 33 months in prison, three years probation and immediate deportation upon his release from prison. He was also ordered to pay $492,805.00 in restitution.
- In May, 1997, an HCR driver in Connecticut was sentenced to six months in Federal Prison, three years probation and a $10,000.00 fine for stealing over $38,000.00 in postal remittances.
- In Hawaii, an airport fire and rescue captain was sentenced to 28 months in prison after an Postal Inspection investigation found him in possession of stolen registered mail totaling $43,255.00.
- An individual whom Postal Inspectors accused of stealing over 6,000 pieces of mail in volume attacks on postal jeeps was sentenced in a Maryland Federal Court to eight years and nine months in prison and $47,500.00 in restitution.
- A Southern California man was sentenced, after an Postal Inspection Service investigation, to 27 months in prison, five months probation and $57,233.00 restitution. Postal Inspectors

found that he used 10 bank accounts in seven different names at four banks to deposit $423,000.00 in "washed" checks. The checks were taken from the mail stolen from various collection boxes.

- An Iowa mailroom employee was sentenced to 10 years in prison and restitution of $33,659.00. Postal Inspectors discovered she stole over 135 state of Iowa warrants from the mailroom and successfully negotiated over 100 of the warrants.

- In a case investigated by Postal Inspectors, a 58-year old Florida woman was sentenced to six years in Federal Prison, five years probation and 240,000.00 in restitution for 45 counts related to interception of mail and identity takeover. The woman was the alleged caretaker of a neighbor. The case began with the 1995 discovery of the mummified skeletal remains of the neighbor on her living room floor. Investigation by Postal Inspectors disclosed she had been dead for at least five years. An air conditioning unit had been run continually to help dispense odors, and the caretaker used elaborate explanations over the years to explain the woman's absence. The caretaker cashed the dead woman's monthly social security checks and raided her financial assets.

- Two men were arrested by Postal Inspectors in Hartford, Connecticut, for using personal Ids of customers of a truck rental company to fraudulenty obtain credit cards. The men used the cards to order thousands of dollars worth of merchandise that was shipped via the U.S. mail. In July 2002, one man was sentenced to 38 months in prison and the other man was sentenced to 30 months in prison.

- On June 14, 2002, a former mail handler at the Tampa, Florida Processing and Distribution Center was sentenced to 18 months in prison, three years' supervised release and restitution of $21,295.00 to Netflix, an online DVD rental company. Postal Inspectors recovered thousands of the company's DVDs while searching the mail handlers vehicle and residence, with losses exceeding $100,000.00.

- A former registry clerk who was a 25-year employee was sentenced on March 4, 2002, to 41 months in prison, three years' supervised release and restitution of $497,014.00 after pleading guilty. Postal Inspectors arrested the former clerk in august 2001 for stealing

$3.2 million in registered remittances from the Phoenix, Arizona, Precessing and Distribution Center.

- Postal Inspectors arrested a clerk in Atlanta, Georgia, for stealing more than 100 U.S. treasury checks worth more than $100,000.00. The clerk was sentenced to more than four years in prison and three years' supervised release, and was ordered to pay restitution of $89,908.00 to his victims.

Narcotics

- A man was sentenced to 35 years in an Indiana prison for trafficking cocaine via express mail.
- A Mississippi man was sentenced to life in Federal Prison for using the mail to traffic in crack cocaine. It was his third felony conviction. Two of his accomplices were sentenced to prison terms of 105 months and 87 months respectively.
- In Charlotte, North Carolina, a man was sentenced to 12-and a half years in prison and five years probation, and his co-defendant was sentenced to 10 years in prison and five years probation for selling over one kilo of crack cocaine via the mail.
- A former postal clerk in Milwaukee, Wisconsin was sentenced in Federal Court in Hammond, Indiana to eight years and 10 months in prison and seven years probation for distributing over 500 pounds of marijuana via express mail from Texas to Indiana and Wisconsin.
- Two individuals were sentenced in U.S. District Court in Omaha, Nebraska to 30 years and 30 months respectively for trafficking crack cocaine via the mail.
- On July 17, 1998, a defendant was sentenced to life in prison without the possibility of parole in the Western District of Arkansas. The defendant had imported up to two pounds of methamphetamine every two weeks over an 11-month period from California to Arkansas via express mail and other parcel delivery services.

From October 1, 1996 through March 31, 1997 the Postal Inspectors working with other law enforcement agencies, arrested 911 individuals for trafficking drugs and laundering drug money via the U.S. mail.

Additionally Postal Inspectors seized over $20.1 million in drug proceeds, 64 weapons, 46 vehicles and 9,470 pounds of illicit narcotics.

From October 1, 1997 through March 31, 1998 Postal Inspectors working with other law enforcement agencies arrested 1,857 individuals for trafficking drugs and laundering drug money via the U.S. mail. Seizures during this time period include 16,503 pounds of marijuana, 268 pounds of cocaine, 131 pounds of methamphetamine, 68 pounds of heroin, 60 pounds of opium, 41 pounds of PCP/LSD/psychedelics. As part of these investigations Postal Inspectors seized $25.3 million in cash, bank accounts, 21 houses, 74 acres of land, 78 vehicles, five powerboats and 195 firearms.

From April 1, 2000 to September 30, 2000 Postal Inspectors working with other law enforcement agencies arrested 787 individuals for drug trafficking and money laundering. Seizures from the mail for this period of time include over 7,300 pounds of illegal narcotics and about 243,000 units of steroids. Investigations also resulted in the seizure of over $2.6 million in cash and monetary instruments, 21 vehicles, 67 firearms and two residences.

- Following a two-year investigation by Postal Inspectors, a former postal supervisor, who was an acting postmaster in Massachusetts, was sentenced in January 2002 to eight years and one month in prison and four years' supervised release. Postal Inspectors determined that between 1990 and 1998, the former employee opened post office boxes for the purpose of receiving marijuana through the mail. Each package weighed between 20 and 30 pounds.

- A California man was sentenced to life in prison on October 3, 2003 for running a multi-state drug conspiracy. His ring shipped at least 20 kilograms of cocaine a month to St. Louis, Missouri, from Los Angeles, California, and McAllen, Texas.

- An organized crime drug enforcement task force, headed by Postal Inspectors, identified a ring that transported 20 to 30 kilograms of cocaine a month, and mailed in excess of 240 express mail parcels of drug payments, from St. Louis, Missouri to Los Angeles, California, over a two-year span. The ringleader was sentenced to life in prison, and three of his top men received sentences of 17, 30, and 35 years in prison, respectively.

Child Pornography

- A husband and wife were sentenced in an Alabama Federal Court in March 1997, to 135 months and 51 months respectively, after Postal Inspectors charged them with using the U.S. mail in violation of child pornography statutes.

- In October, 1996 a man was sentenced in an Alabama State Court to four life sentences for rape, sexual abuse and possession of obscene material involving children under the age of 17. The sentence followed his federal conviction and sentence of 20 years in prison on children pornography charges brought by Postal Inspectors.

- In Raleigh, North Carolina, a man was sentenced to 78 months in federal prison, three years probation and $3,700.00 in fines and restitution. He admitted to molesting two boys, videotaping his sexual abuse of the boys and trading the tapes by mail.

- A man in Texas who is known to have sexually molested 16 children was sentenced to 20 years in a Texas prison. The offender was previously sentenced to 12 years and seven months in Federal Court for receiving and distributing child pornography through the mail.

- Postal Inspection Service participation on a task force of local and Federal law enforcement agencies in Indiana resulted in an individual being sentenced to 27 years in prison and fined $5,000. for offenses relating to ordering child pornography videos through the mail.

- Postal Inspectors identified a man from Whitfield County, Georgia, as part of a child pornography ring known as the "spanking club", a loose-knit group of individuals in the United States and Canada who derived sexual pleasure from the severe spankings of children. He was convicted of producing and mailing videotapes depicting the sexual abuse of his own children. The suspect was sentenced to 10 years in prison.

- Another member of the spanking club from Vanceburg, Kentucky, was sentenced to 20 years in federal prison with no possibility of parole for producing and mailing videotapes depicting the brutal and sadistic sexual abuse of his own children.

- A man in Merriam, Kansas, was sentenced to 24 years and six months in prison for repeatedly raping his six year-old daughter. The offender was identified during a Postal Inspection investigation of illegal child pornography mailings.
- A man in Hillsborough, North Carolina, was sentenced to 32 years in state prison for raping a three-year old girl. Postal Inspectors discovered the videotape, that was recorded of the man raping the girl, while serving a search warrant when the man received child pornography in the mail.
- In April 2004, a man in Tucson, Arizona, was sentenced to 450 years in prison after a jury found him guilty of 45 counts of sexual exploitation of a minor less than 15 years old. Postal Inspectors and FBI agents executed a search warrant on the mans' home after he mailed a tape of child pornography. For whatever reason, the man wasn't arrested at that time. Later that same month, April, 2004 the same man entered a Denny's restaurant and killed a patron, and seriously wounded another man. He was convicted of first-degree murder, but did not plead guilty to the child pornography charges, saying he wanted his day in court to speak out for oppressed pedophiles.
- A child pornographer, who is HIV positive, was sentenced to 100 years in prison after pleading guilty to recording his sex acts with at least 120 children, some as young as seven years old.
- A man in Brimfield, Ohio, was arrested by Postal Inspectors, Immigration and Customs Enforcement (ICE) & detectives from the Brimfield police department after identifying him as a suspected sexual predator. The man admitted during a polygraph exam to having sexual contact with three underage girls, two of the girls were less than 10 years old. The other girl, 14, was only eight years old at the time the molestation began. He was sentenced to life in prison.
- A man In Birmingham, Alabama was sentenced in June, 2006 to 100 years in federal prison for possessing and distributing child pornography, enticing a minor, and traveling to engage in illicit sexual contact with a minor.
- Postal Inspectors arrested a man in Vallejo, California, in December 2005 for attempting to receive child pornography in the mail. The man was a senior deacon and elder of his church.

The man admitted to Postal Inspectors that he had been sexually abusing two of his daughters since they were four years old. He persuaded the girls' mother to participate in the daily molestation. In April, 2006, he pled guilty to distribution and receiving child pornography and was sentenced to 22 years in federal prison.

- The U.S. Postal Service Office of Inspector General's Computer Crimes Unit detected a postal employee's detailed child pornography surfing activity on his Postal Service computer. The Kentucky postal employee was using the workroom floor computer almost one hour per day to visit websites containing pornography of pre-teenage girls. The former employee was sentenced to 78 months in federal detention, with seven years supervised release upon completion of his term.

- In October 2006, a former Huntsville, Alabama police officer was sentenced to 15 years in federal prison, followed by 15 years of supervised release, after he pled guilty to one count of producing child pornography.

Deliver Me Home is a joint program of the National Center for Missing and Exploited Children (NCMEC), the United States Postal Inspection Service, and the Postal Service. Postal Inspectors and other law enforcement officers use the program as a tool for investigating cases of abducted or missing children. Postal Inspectors work closely with the NCMEC. A Postal Inspector is assigned full time to NCMEC, serving as liaison between NCMEC and Postal Inspectors who investigate child exploitation cases throughout the country.

The 2 SMRT 4U Campaign was developed by the Postal Inspection Service in conjunction with NCMEC and teen Vogue magazine in support of the Attorney General's Project Safe Childhood initative. The campaign was launched in November 2006 and ran throughout fiscal year 2007. Its purpose was to encourage teens to practice safe, smart habits when posting information about themselves on social networking web sites and blogs.

Mail Bombs and anthrax

- On January, 22, 1998, the Unabomber suspect entered a guilty plea to federal charges returned against him in California and New Jersey.

May 4, 1998 marked the end of one of the longest and most extensive criminal manhunts of modern times. After an in-vestigation by the Federal Bureau of Investigation, the Postal Inspection Service, the Bureau of Alcohol, Tobacco and Firearms, and the Department of Justice, the infamous Unabomber was sentenced in U.S. District Court to four consecutive life terms, plus 30 years. The judge ordered victim restitution of over $15 million and the forfeiture of any proceeds the Unabomber may realize from books, movies, television or newspaper accounts related to his crimes. The Unabomber's spree began in 1978 and ended in 1995. He was responsible for killing three people and injuring 23 others.

- On march 26, 1998, a man already serving a life sentence for rape and murder was sentenced to 51 years and 10 months imprisonment for mailing a letter bomb in October 1995, from prison to a federal judge in Chicago who had denied his appeal.
- An Orlando, Florida man was sentenced to 40 years in federal prison and five years probation for mailing a bomb from New York, via express mail, to his father in Rockledge, Florida. The father was suspicious of the package and did not open it and the bomb was later rendered safe. The son's alleged motive was to gain an inheritance from his wealthy father.
- A man was sentenced in Waco, Texas to 38 years in federal maximum security prison after Postal Inspectors proved he tried to murder his ex-wife with a mail bomb.
- An Postal Inspection Service investigation resulted in an individual being sentenced to two life terms plus 10 years for mailing an explosive device, which caused the death of a person who was the roommate of the intended victim.
- A Chicago, Illinois women, with the help from her boyfriend used a mail bomb to murder her husband after fraudulently acquiring lines of credit in his name. She was found guilty in May, 2003 and was sentenced to 15 years in prison for conspiracy to commit identity theft, 10 years for access device fraud, five years for mail theft, and life in prison for conspiracy in the bombing murder of her husband. She was also ordered to pay more than $142,942.00 in restitution and a $400,000.00 special assessment.
- Following an investigation by Postal Inspectors, a West Virginia man was sentenced in November, 2002 to 16 years in prison and

three years' probation. Inspectors proved he had mailed letters containing threats and a white, powdered substance to President George Bush, West Virginia Governor Bob Wise, a U.S. District Judge, and other government officials.

- A 25-year-old woman was sentenced in June, 2003 to seven years and three months in prison for sending anthrax hoax letters to police and a hotel in Hawaii. The woman was the first person to be convicted and sentenced under a late 1990s federal law concerning threats of using a weapon of mass destruction.

Postal Inspectors were assisted in the case by the FBI's Joint Terrorism Task Force, and the Honolulu Police Department. The Inspection Service's national forensic laboratory provided evidence that led to the woman's prosecution.

- A man was convicted of mailing an anthrax hoax letter to the Connecticut State Attorney's office in Bridgeport and was sentenced to 35 years in federal prison. Working with other law enforcement officers, Postal Inspectors determined the man had mailed envelopes containing powder and written threats referencing anthrax and terrorism. The powder was found to be harmless, but the incident caused disruptions of government offices that required responses by several law enforcement agencies.
- An inmate at a Florida correctional facility in Pensacola was sentenced to 18 years in prison in August, 2005 for mailing a threatening communication and impending a federal officer. Postal Inspectors found the man had mailed a hoax anthrax letter to a federal court in 2004. His federal sentence will begin after he completes a 50-year state prison sentence for committing a robbery with a deadly weapon.

These are only a few of many investigations by the United States Postal Inspectors. There are so many more. I hope what has been written here was interesting to you, the reader. I found the investigations from the Postal Inspectors very interesting.

Chapter 24

LIFE AFTER THE UNION

AFTER BEING TAKEN OUT of my position as the Executive Vice-President of the APWU, Miami Area Local and the Secretary/Treasurer of the One Seven Two Holding Corporation on January 21, 2003 I went back into the post office working at the Country Lakes Post Office.

As the Executive Vice-President of the Miami Area Local I was on a leave without pay status with the post office getting paid by the union.

I had bid on a job At the Country Lakes Post Office, and was awarded the bid position on December 4, 2002. I started working at the station on February 1, 2003. I was a full time window clerk with Sunday-Tuesday as scheduled days off and the hours of 8:20 A.M. to 5:30 P.M.

I bid on this position because it wasn't too far from my home, 10 miles, and because of the management at the Country Lakes Post Office. The manager was Paulette Thomas and the main supervisor was Charles Smith. These are two people in management that throughout the years I was able to present grievances to and get along with. I knew I wouldn't have any problems with them. I could've bid somewhere else with a Saturday/ Sunday as scheduled days off but would've had to drive more each day, and not have the supervisors that I had. I felt as an former union officer I might have problems with some of the managers or supervisors. Also I worked almost every Tuesday on overtime so it didn't matter if I had split days off.

Paulette Thomas wasn't at Country Lakes Post Office too long after I started there since she was promoted to acting area manager of the West Area stations in Miami. Charles Smith covered as manager for awhile, but didn't want the position. While I was at the Country Lakes Post Office there were three or four different managers.

I thought I might have a problem with some of the clerks that worked at the Country Lakes Post Office since I was removed from my union position, even though the charges against me were bogus. I'm glad I didn't. I had represented some of these same people and I was trusted as a person and a union officer.

Approximately one year after I had started working at Country Lakes Post Office, Al Pereda, a former shop steward who had worked on tour 1, had started working at Country Lakes Post Office.

Al Pereda was fired as a shop steward after the elections of 2004. He was later brought back as a shop steward after he started working at the Country Lakes Post Office.

Because management didn't have the proper number of employees working at the station casual carriers and PTF (part-time flexible) carriers were being worked in the clerk craft spreading mail. Al Pereda and myself filed grievances and because of the lack of trust in the local union Al Pereda would settle the grievances at step 1. I was satisfied with what Al was doing in settling the grievances, mostly since I got paid for not working the hours, but because management violated the contract. In total Al Pereda got me approximately $20,000.00 up until the time I retired.

MEETING MY WIFE

On February 12, 2002, almost a year before I was taken out of my position with the union, I met Brenda Yeatts. We were married on June 19, 2004. I met Brenda through a friend from high school.

When I started my senior year at Miami High School I was voted into a fraternity called Titans. After I had graduated from high school in 1969 there was a 10 year reunion, a 20 year reunion and then a reunion every 5 years after.

At the 10 year reunion I met a guy who I had met when I was drafted into the Army. Wayne Keller. I saw him at the reunion and at first didn't know where I had first met this guy. I knew I didn't know him from high school. I was drafted on August 10, 1970 along with Wayne Keller. After basic training in the Army we both went different ways. Now nine years later I felt like I met him again. He was married to Billie weiss who I had graduated with at Miami High School.

When I worked for the American Postal Workers Union, Miami Area Local the union had bought land and had the union building constructed. The union building was big enough that offices were rented out. This was a two story building and on half of the first floor the union had a sports bar. It was here at the sports bar that I met Brenda Yeatts.

At my high school reunion in 1994, 25 years since high school, there was talk about getting together a reunion with the fraternity. The 25th Miami high School reunion was a three day affair. There was a meet and greet on Friday Night, the dinner and dance on Saturday night and a picnic on Sunday at Tropical Park in Miami. It was at the picnic on Sunday when serious talk about the reunion with Titans really started. Since I had keys to the sports bar that was inside the union building a few of us that were in Titans went to the sports bar to start planning out a reunion.

Most of the people that were contacted were from the graduating class of 1968, 1969 and 1970. We had the reunion in February 1995. Those invited were people that were in the fraternity of Titans and Saxons and a sorority named Angels. We called the reunion Titans, Saxons, Angels and friends. I believe the reunion was a success. We had another reunion in 2000. This time we invited another sorority called Lucians. The last time we had the reunion, still at the same sports bar that the APWU owned, was in 2002. Titans, Saxons, Angels, Lucians and friends.

My friend Billie Weiss, now Billie Keller, called me and asked if other friends, who didn't go to Miami High, could come to the reunion. I told her yes, the more people there the better. It was here I met Brenda Yeatts.

It took me over a month to finally get around to calling Brenda and for us to really start going out. I failed to tell Brenda, when I got her phone number, I would be busy traveling for the next month. I was going out of town teaching basic shop steward classes for the APWU of Florida in different locals. I had gone to Clearwater, Gainesville and Bradenton on the week end with each class being two days. I was lucky that Brenda still wanted to go on a date with me since she thought that I had stood her up for almost a month.

It had been almost 10 years since my first wife had passed away and it wasn't easy for me asking a women out. We started dating the end of March, 2002 and got married on June 19, 2004.

Brenda was divorced and has three children. Two beautiful daughters and a son. So I now have five children, same as my parents.

CHAPTER 25

LEAVING THE UNITED STATES POSTAL SERVICE TO RETIREMENT

I RETIRED FROM THE United States Postal Service (USPS) on June 2, 2007 after 37 years, 5 months and 17 days. I have to say the USPS was good to me. For someone with just a high school education, I just did get by in high school, this was a good paying job, with good benefits and a pretty decent retirement. Even with someone with a college degree the Postal Service is still a better choice. My bother could've been a teacher. He has a four year degree from college, but instead stayed with the Postal Service for over 40 years.

I had been thinking about retirement for some time and after checking out houses on the internet and looking at some houses we found the house we bought in August, 2005 in Lake County, just approximately one hour Northwest of Orlando, Florida.

I've still tried to see some people I met with the union. I have been to the last two state conventions that the APWU of Florida has held. I've also gone to some of the schools that the state has put on. I go to see my brother and other union officers and stewards that I've met throughout the years.

Overall the American Postal Workers Union was good for me. I worked over 10 years as the Executive Vice-President of the Miami Area Local of the APWU. I learn a lot going to the different state schools that the State APWU put on. I enjoyed teaching the basic shop steward classes for new shop stewards for the state and at the local level. Working as a full time union officer I was able to build social security. Whatever I get from social security is money I wouldn't have received without working for the union.

Then there's the politics. The politics in the union gets nasty, and not just in Miami. At every national convention of the American Postal

Workers Union there are charges brought up before the convention floor for a vote by union members, officers or former officers.

Of course the politics are everywhere and not just in the union. It's just upsetting as a former union officer that knows they did their job to the best of their ability only to be charged with bogus charges and then the National APWU, because of politics, failed to properly investigate.

I do wish the American Postal Workers Union and the United States Postal Service the best and can only hope that things improve for both.

During my time working for the United States Postal Service I met so many different people. There's a saying that I heard working in the post office, "you don't have to be crazy to work here, but it dam sure helps".

Now that I'm retired I go to a Miami retirement reunion that is held in Melbourne, Florida every year at the end of May. It's funny because I was a union steward and officer for over 20 years and most of the people that go to these reunions were supervisors, managers and even some postmasters. Most, if not all the people that go to this retirement reunion worked in the main post office in Miami, and I didn't have to deal with them with grievances. I think it's great to see people that I knew from working at the post office and to see them now in retirement.

I hope everyone has a great life. I hope everyone working for the United States Postal Service enjoys, or at lease makes the best of their time, working for the Postal Service. I also hope when the employees retire from the post office their retirement last a very long time.

Index